MEDILL ON MEDIA ENGAGEMENT

edited by

Abe Peck
Northwestern University

Edward C. Malthouse
Northwestern University

HAMPTON PRESS, INC.
CRESSKILL, NEW JERSEY

Copyright © 2011 by Hampton Press, Inc.

Printed in the United States of America

Library of Congress Cataloging-in-Publication-Data

Medill on media engagement / edited by Abe Peck, Edward C. Malthouse.
   p. cm.
 Includes bibliographical references and index.
 ISBN 978-1-57273-986-4 (hardbound) -- ISBN 978-1-57273-987-1 (paperbound)
 1. Mass media. 2. Journalism. 3. Communication. I. Peck, Abe. II.
Malthouse, Edward C.
 P90.M3737 2010
 302.23--dc22

             2010036881

Hampton Press, Inc.
23 Broadway
Cresskill, NJ 07626

CONTENTS

III EXPERIENCE CASE STUDIES

Join the engagement conversation at medillmediaexperiences.com

FOREWORD

Why Media Experiences and Engagement Matter

John Lavine

Today's advances in media technology create eye-catching, instant content—be it news, information, advertising, or marketing. The best of it bubbles with energy and animation, but if those who want to communicate cannot hold attention, if they do not know how to engage the audience they want to reach, all of the whiz-bang of technology is for naught.

This book provides that essential link—engagement. It lays out valuable insights for people in media and marketing who are vying for the scarce time and attention of consumers. It will enrich the efforts of professionals and nonprofessionals alike who, more and more, speak directly to consumers and must know how to engage them.

It is also important to point out that this book is based on a vast foundation of consumer research, which includes some of the largest audience studies ever done.

The work began in 2000. Northwestern University's Media Management Center, its Readership Institute, and a number of faculty members at the Medill School embarked on an ambitious research program to develop an audience-focused approach to media and journalism for the 21st century. (As Medill colleague David Nelson points out in his Chapter 16 review of some of Medill's Innovation Projects and their track record with clients, it is worth noting that this pioneering emphasis began in 1931, when a young social scientist named George Gallup—later to invent the Gallup Poll—taught a course at Medill on "Reader Interest.")

The Center's research initially examined *how* people used media and then quickly moved to understanding *why* they engage or disengage with newspapers, magazines, online, local broadcast news, and television. From the beginning, we developed measures of use and behavior that gauged not just whether someone had read, watched, or interacted with a medium, but also the extent and nature of the involvement. We paired that with our interest in news, information, and advertising content and the relationships among them.

Above all, we aimed for actionable results that individuals and enterprises could use to create more engaging news, information, and marketing—content with impact.

The insights were used by newspapers from Hamilton, Ontario, to Bucaramanga, Colombia, from Bakersfield, California, to Vorarlberg, Austria. The overall analysis of engagement and the particular demonstration that strong content "lifted" associated advertising dovetailed with a rising interest in the concept of engagement by major integrated marketing agencies such as Starcom.

Medill faculty and researchers also presented these findings to professional associations and media organizations in Europe, Asia, the Middle East, Africa, and North and South America. And the work is public—a complete archive can be found at www.readership.org.

The discovery and compilation of this substantial body of knowledge was supported at various times by the Newspaper Association of America, the American Society of Newspaper Editors, the Magazine Publishers of America, the Online Publishers Association, the McCormick Foundation, and the John S. and James L. Knight Foundation.

It is a product of the thought leadership that a great university with an interdisciplinary focus can provide. Northwestern professor Bobby Calder of the Kellogg School of Management and Medill professor Edward Malthouse, who teaches and researches in Integrated Marketing Communications, were the principal researchers; their work has won many prestigious peer-judged awards. Medill journalism professor Abe Peck brought deep knowledge of the magazine field to this endeavor. Thus, it is no accident that Ed and Abe emerged as co-editors of this book.

None of this would have been possible without the tireless efforts and leadership of Mary Nesbitt, who is now Medill's Associate Dean but who was the managing director of the Center's Readership Institute. Mary and her team wrote the grants, managed the studies, added key industry insights, and turned the research and scholarly endeavors into actionable results that industry leaders could use.

The professors and Institute staff also spent years traveling to industry meetings and working with media organizations that used the research to engage and grow their audiences. These researcher-practitioners included the Center's executive director, Michael Smith; Steve Duke (now a Medill associate professor); and online media authority Rich Gordon (now Medill's Director of Digital Innovation), all of whom worked with print and digital news organizations to help them understand and implement the findings of the experience studies. Past colleagues Stacy Lynch, Todd McCauley, Limor Peer, Sue Calder, and Vivian Vahlberg were also invaluable contributors.

This book continues Medill's tradition and mission of producing insights that media practitioners can use to better serve and lead their audiences in these challenging and exciting times. It also represents important insights that journalism and marketing communications education must not ignore.

John Lavine
Professor and Dean of Medill
Founding director of the Media Management Center 1989–2005

FOREWORD

The Importance of Media Engagement

Cathleen Black

It's no secret that the media industries are experiencing an unprecedented rate of change. When I first started at Hearst, as president of its magazine division, in late 1995, the introduction of company-wide email was resisted by some of our old-school veterans. Now my days are taken up with reviewing everything from iPhone "apps" to alliances with other major media and technology companies. Despite challenging times, there are the new titles, like *Food Network Magazine* or *Harper's Bazaar India* (its 31st international edition) and *Cosmopolitan Vietnam* (its 60th international edition) or Delish.com and Kaboodle, a social shopping site. And in the middle of all this, I'll steal a moment to answer a cell call from my twenty-two-year old son or a text from his eighteen-year-old sister.

Media today are about both precision use and long-term loyalty. As a recent advertising campaign from the magazine industry put it, media can be exhilarating or enveloping, can grab or embrace, can respond to an impulse or provide an immersive world.

But whatever the franchise or platform, one thing remains constant: providing rewarding media experiences is a key factor in creative and business success alike. Those of us in the field now operate brands rather than titles. And, since a brand is largely an experience in the reader/viewer/user's mind, knowing how an individual experiences and engages media across platforms empowers the creator-audience bond.

In partnership with leading media associations, the Media Management Center at Northwestern University conducted nearly a decade's worth of studies about how people experience media. This work went beyond traditional labels—"news," "entertainment," "shelter"—to amass a repository of deep knowledge about how the *consumer* defines her or his experiences with media. This research also discovered how leveraging experiences can allow media professionals to increase attachment to a particular brand.

Medill on Media Engagement is a valuable expansion on these insights. Faculty and administrators associated with the Media Management Center and Northwestern's Medill School of Journalism have worked closely with our professional associations and the Hearst Management Institute leadership program. Their expertise in audiences, experiences, and training the next generation of content experts has helped us move forward. Now a roster of Medill professors has drawn on decades of editing, writing, anchoring, or digital work, or on fresh theoretical wisdom, to explain what experiences are and do. *Medill on Media Engagement* explores how a dozen important experiences—from "Talk About and Share" to "Timeout"—can enhance and empower engagement and loyalty. Case studies provide keen perceptions and a valuable toolbox that will help professionals mobilize deeply felt needs and bind consumers to "their" magazine, newspaper, TV station, or Web site.

If it ever existed, the time has passed for simply offering information without profound understanding of what audiences truly desire (even as we exert leadership in giving them something they didn't know they wanted). When it comes to must-have ingredients for media success, understanding how experiences engage audiences ranks with formulating exciting ideas, apprehending deep needs, and nurturing talented people. *Medill on Media Engagement* will play a key role in linking creators with those they wish to serve and lead, and in helping us to innovate our way into a newer, leaner, and even more exciting era.

Cathleen Black is chairman of Hearst Magazines. *She has been president and CEO of the Newspaper Association of America, president and publisher of* USA Today *and* New York *magazine, and a board member of the Advertising Council, Gannett, IBM, and Coca-Cola. Her book,* Basic Black: The Essential Guide for Getting Ahead at Work (and In Life), *remains a best seller.*

ACKNOWLEDGMENTS

We express our sincere appreciation to all of the organizations that provided generous financial support for the experience studies underlying this book: the Newspaper Association of America (NAA), the Magazine Publishers of America (MPA), the Online Publishers Association (OPA), Windows on the World Communication (WTTW), the John S. and James L. Knight Foundation, the McCormick Foundation, Meredith Corporation, the RAM system, the Latin American Cable Association (LAMAC), and Starcom.

Many individuals contributed their time and expertise in executing the studies. It is impossible to mention everyone, but several stand out. Northwestern colleague Bobby Calder is the mastermind behind the experience concept and played a central role in all of the studies. Northwestern's Media Management Center (MMC) managed most the studies from start to finish, raising money, interfacing with the funding organizations, collaborating in the execution of the studies, interpreting the results, and presenting the findings to the world. We are indebted to all members of the center present and past, especially John Lavine, Mary Nesbitt, Todd McCauley, Limor Peer, Rich Gordon, Steve Duke, Stacy Lynch, Sue Calder, Vivian Vahlberg, and current executive director Mike Smith. Collectively, we have presented this research to numerous audiences and clients from around the world, and these interactions have helped us polish and refine our ideas.

We wish to thank those who gave us special permission to reprint material: Michael Cooke (*Toronto Star*), Doug Kelly (*National Post*), and Dr. Steven Merahn (modernmedicine.com/Advanstar Communications).

We are grateful to all our authors for writing excellent chapters that bring the individual experiences to life. We also thank our Medill colleague

David Abrahamson for his advice on producing this book, and Bob LeBailly for his technical acumen. Medill graduate students Natalie Bailey and Eleanor Goldberg—a.k.a. "The Wolverines"—proofread and fact checked the entire manuscript; Heather Jefferson studiously made our copy consistent; Thomas Malthouse and Suzanne Peck proofed it. Northwestern graduate Maria Delton-Kapp's cover design captured the engagement concept.

Above all, we thank our families, especially Suzanne and Elisabeth, for their encouragement and support.

A.P. and E.C.M.

I

ENGAGEMENT, EXPERIENCES, AND CONCEPTS

1

MEDILL ON MEDIA ENGAGEMENT

An Introduction

Edward C. Malthouse

Abe Peck

For centuries, journalists have been adept at conveying information in powerful ways, at forging and serving communities, at persuading audiences that an idea, a service, or a product is well worth their while. One type of great journalist has demonstrated the capability to see over the horizon and convince people to be interested in information they didn't even know they wanted or needed.

Now, seismic changes in media—and in our understanding of them—have significantly altered—even shaken—how journalists do their work even as they can now reach far more people than ever before.

Digital media erase geography or allow for hyper-local community interaction. Words with fixed meanings become fluid: "readership" and even "audience" are transformed when formerly passive recipients of information participate vigorously in social networking and citizen journalism. The bar for professional content rises even as the business and staffing models that have supported it quiver in the face of free and/or populist media, or as newer media offer instant accountability, cheaper ad rates and distribution costs, and the ability to outsource "commodity content." Although these shifts can represent tremendous opportunity to regain share of mind and share of pocketbook, their creative destruction is painful for those they roll over.

More than ever, journalists need to understand the mindset of the person with whom they seek to communicate—or co-create—and how the resulting journalistic content and media fit into that person's life. And this must happen even as journalists offer independent, unfettered information.

This book posits that one key tool for attracting, serving, leading, sharing, and gaining loyalty with empowered communities is to understand media engagement. This can be a difficult concept to pin down. Many different definitions have been proposed by different groups, so whenever someone mentions "engagement," we always have to ask, "What do you mean by that?" To some, it means that somebody is reading or watching a lot or often. According to this interpretation, engaged readers of a Web site are those who visit it often, spend a lot of time on it, and so on. To others, however, it means liking the journalistic product and perhaps "recommending it to a friend." The Advertising Research Foundation defines engagement as "turning on a prospect to a brand idea enhanced by the surrounding context."[1] If journalists cannot define the term, it will be defined for them.

We think of engagement differently. In our view, engagement is *the collection of experiences that readers, viewers, or visitors have with a media brand*.[2] Figure 1.1 illustrates this experience-based definition and shows how engagement is related to usage and other outcomes.[3] It is engagement that causes people to "use" the media brand by reading, viewing, or interacting with it. It is engagement that causes affective responses such as "liking" the brand, recommending it to a friend, or feeling loyal to it. Finally, engagement with the editorial content also affects reactions to ads and vice versa. If *you want people to like and read your publication, tune in your news program, etc., focus on engaging them.*

Again, our definition of engagement centers on the concept of an "experience," which is *a set of beliefs that people have about how a media brand fits into their lives.* Experiences are not about the media brand itself, but rather about the relationship between the audience member and the brand.

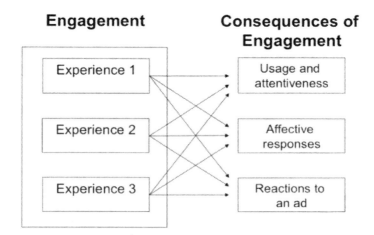

Figure 1.1. Engagement, Experiences, and Their Consequences

Experiences explain why someone uses media. This book argues that understanding this relationship is a significant key to engaging an audience.

We have worked with our Northwestern colleague Professor Bobby Calder for nearly a decade to understand the range of experiences people have with journalism. Collaborating with Northwestern University's Media Management Center, Calder, Malthouse, and other Northwestern colleagues conducted a series of experience studies funded by the Newspaper Association of America, the Magazine Publishers of America, the Online Publishers Association, and the Knight Foundation. Those studies explored how thousands of users perceived the media they used fitting into their lives. The Calder teams transcribed the interviews and identified verbatim comments (often referred to as "beliefs" or "sub-experiences") that captured different aspects of an experience with a specific title or news program. The beliefs/sub-experiences were placed on surveys (as questionnaire "items"), and respondents were asked to agree or disagree with them. These findings were aggregated across the numerous titles that respondents read, watched, or visited.

The studies unearthed more than 40 experiences that could motivate (or in some cases, discourage) media engagement and usage. These experiences are made up of descriptive statements that clustered by how they contributed to media usage. As we discussed the experiences with media professionals, we found they understood when we talked about them as "molecules" made up of "atoms" of audience statements (which we edited to remove slight anecdotal variety), as illustrated in Figures 1.2 to 1.5.

A few examples clarify the concept. Many people believe that journalists are adept at giving them things to talk about. By accessing a Web site,

Figure 1.2. The Talk About and Share Experience

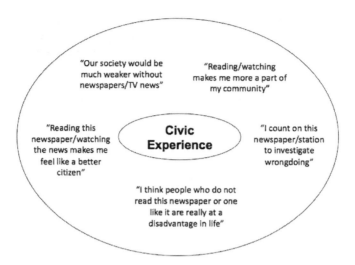

Figure 1.3. The Civic Experience

reading a newspaper or magazine, or watching on screens of multiple sizes, media consumers learn about things that they can bring up in conversations with friends and family. This is called the Talk About and Share experience (Figure 1.2 and Chapter 14), and, as with other experiences, the descriptors that comprise it may vary for different demographic groups.

People also believe that some Web sites, TV news programs, newspapers, and magazines look out for their interests and serve as a balance against the powerful, which is embodied in the Civic experience (Figure 1.3 and Chapter 4). People also believe that they get useful advice and tips from media, which we call a Utilitarian experience (Figure 1.4 and Chapter 5). And they perceive media enabling them to relax and escape from the pressures of daily life, which is the Timeout experience (Figure 1.5 and Chapter 11). Other key experiences are discussed throughout this book.

It is worth contrasting this "experience view" of media with a more traditional approach. When asked why people read, for example, a newspaper, the traditional journalist might answer that it covers local, national, and international news; has prominent columnists on the editorial page; and offers investigative reporting and great sections on sports, food, health, home, and entertainment. But this does not fully answer the question because that response is entirely about the newspaper itself and neglects the relationship between newspaper and reader. Although it gives reasons for why someone might want to read, it never says *why* the reader reads.

The experience view begins with this relationship. For example, readers need something in their lives to balance against the powerful and look out for their interests. Newspapers can play this role: One that wishes to do so

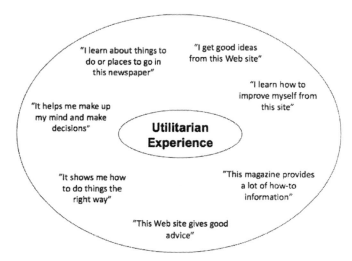

Figure 1.4. The Utilitarian Experience

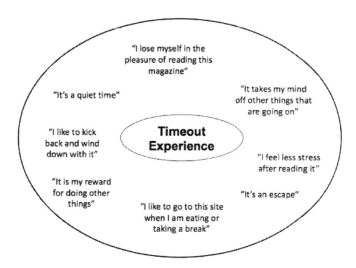

Figure 1.5. The Timeout Experience

should have strong investigative reporting and local news. The design of media brand follows from the experiences it intends to satisfy.

Understanding these experiences becomes especially crucial in a multimedia world in which information seems to be everywhere. Why? Because the intensity of the experiences causes audience members to be loyal and read (Figure 1.1).

Modernmedicine.com is a Web portal produced by Advanstar Communications, a major business-to-business publisher that is strategically bundling much of its content—and that of allied content providers—into several unified and deep Web portals (Abe Peck was the company's editorial co-reviewer from 1998 through 2009). "True loyalty only develops when there is a shared narrative, emotional connection, and respect for the cultural mores of the audience (in the case of healthcare professionals, this includes responsiveness, respect, simplicity, ease, and value)," wrote Steven Merahn, MD, vice president of modernmedicine.com, in an explanation of the site's continued development.

That connection—that engagement—is dependent on experience. "Irrespective of what we say we are, the audience will relate to us, and speak to us, based on their experience of us," the modernmedicine.com "road map" continued. "Brands are successfully managed when the brand experience aligns with the brand promise. Any disconnect becomes evidence of falsehood, and a pattern of falsehood [is] antithetical to loyalty. This is particularly true for healthcare professionals, for whom finding flaws is their primary mode of interaction with their environment...."[4]

A PROCESS FOR CREATING EXPERIENCES

We recommend a strategic approach (summarized in Figure 1.6, with each box discussed below) to develop an experiential media brand. In short, the media organization articulates a concept that will guide its creation of "contacts" for the media brand. The contacts create experiences for the audience and thereby communicate the concept. The audience's ideas about the concept create expectations, which can also affect their experiences with the brand, including the actions they take beyond it and any co-creation of content with it.

Again, the process begins with a concept, which is *the media organization's best idea of what the publication should mean to its readers and viewers*. This mission is, as the modernmedicine.com document puts it, "an aspiration and reflects the contribution the brand will make to the audience, not what we do, but our value or service to the audience." In the case of modernmedicine.com, that mission is: "To make healthcare professionals more effective, productive, and successful and assure their voice in the evolution of medical practice." Note how this statement is audience-focused.

"Once the mission is defined, the next step is to design the business to fulfill the promise of the mission."[5] The concept guides what should and should not be in, or associated with, any incarnation of the brand such as a Web site, newspaper, magazine, tweet, TV program, or other video. Without a clearly articulated concept, a media brand can lose focus and

Figure 1.6. A Process for Creating Experiences

never develop a distinct voice. (Chapter 2 discusses how to identify and articulate such concepts.)

ESPN has a strong experiential concept. Its cross-platform mission is, "To serve sports fans wherever sports are watched, listened to, discussed, debated, read about, or played."[6] This statement identifies the intended audience as "sports fans" and hints at the types of experiences it intends to create for its readers and viewers. For example, it explicitly mentions discussing and debating sports, which is a social experience (Figure 1.2). By doing this, ESPN acquires a distinct reputation. Many networks broadcast games and many news outlets report sports scores. ESPN goes beyond this by creating social experiences, which, coupled with a conversational voice and cross-platform execution, give it a distinctive presence.

After the media organization has articulated a concept, the next step is to create the various contacts that can deliver the intended experiences and communicate the concept to the audience. A contact is anything that affects the audience member's experience with the media brand. The editorial content, of course, is one important contact. If ESPN wants its readers, viewers, and Web site visitors to associate it with a social experience, then the way in which it tells stories must create that experience. For example, rather than having a single sports anchor giving scores and showing highlight clips, ESPN has multiple anchors and columnists discussing and debating the games. This contact enacts the Talk About and Share experience that the viewer or visitor will have the next day with his buddy.

Another media brand with a strong experiential concept is *USA TODAY*. Part of the concept involves helping readers avoid the negative Overload experience (Figure 1.7). Many consumers are frustrated because there is too much news and information to keep up with. One person we interviewed described this phenomenon as "drowning in the flood of information" that media organizations churn out every day. *USA TODAY* recognized this experience very early, and part of its concept has been to help its readers avoid it. An editorial contact that conveys this aspect of its concept is that its stories tend to be shorter, with fewer page turns.

Our point is that the editorial content of a media brand should be created so that it delivers the experiences that are central to its concept and of use to its audience. As then-editor of the Minneapolis *Star Tribune*, Anders Gyllenhaal, told our colleague from the Media Management Center, "Experiences are a way of converting traditional news judgment from edi-

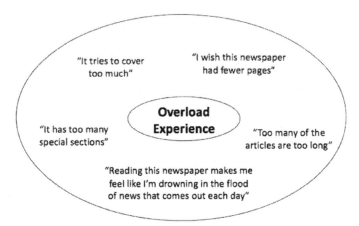

Figure 1.7. Overload Experience

tors' definitions (what's most interesting, what's important, what you just can't believe happened) to readers' definitions of how they react (what makes readers feel informed, what gives them something to talk about, what tells them the paper is looking out for their interests)."[7]

Editorial content is not the only type of contact that can associate the brand in the reader's, viewer's, or user's mind. There are many other ways to communicate a concept to the audience. Another type of contact is the advertising a publication does about itself. For example, ESPN has run TV ads that in essence tell its viewers that it creates social experiences.[8] One ad shows a guy playing cards with his buddies. He says something stupid about sports, and his buddies laugh at him. It then cuts to an interview with the guy, who says something like, "That was before I started watching ESPN.... Now when I talk about sports, I do it right." This ad clearly communicates the intended experience—the role that ESPN wants to play in the lives of its viewers.

The advertising for other products and services that appears in or on a media brand fashions another type of contact. Ads for products that are congruent with the concept of the brand can create the intended experience and reinforce the concept in the audience's mind. The association also goes the other way, with the readers' beliefs about the media brand transferring to the advertised product.

For example, suppose that a fashion title (print magazine and Web) intends to highlight the Inspiration experience (Chapter 6). The role this publication plays in its readers' lives is to inspire and/or help them aspire to live a beautiful and glamorous life—or to live vicariously in the world of those who do. Having ads with beautiful models wearing glamorous dresses and jewelry would be congruent with this concept. Ads for dowdy dresses would undermine it.

This is not an idle example. In the late 1970s, when Abe Peck became launch editor of *sidetracks*, an early youth tabloid within the *Chicago Daily News*, he debuted with a 48-page weekly section that included a cover interview with Stevie Wonder followed by similarly targeted editorial content. But the back-page ad was for a discount dress store, and the drab patterns and colors undermined the concept's credibility with young readers. Although we didn't have the data and language of experiences to draw on then, those younger readers wanted *sidetracks* to Make Me Smarter about popular culture (Chapter 3) and to give them "Something to Talk About." It didn't take long for a young ad salesman to be hired specifically for the section, to bring in advertisers compatible with reader expectations.

A more positive example of edit-ad synergy is how the Discovery Channel in Latin America partnered with Biobaby, a producer of biodegradable diapers. Discovery's association with covering environmental issues was reinforced by these ads, and vice versa.

Brand extensions are another type of contact that can create experiences and link the concept with the media brand. A strongly developed experiential concept creates opportunities for a brand to enter other product categories. *Better Homes and Gardens* has published up to 30 or so Special Interest Publications (SIPs), each targeted to the sub-interests of audiences who want to have a Utilitarian or Timeout experience. Martha Stewart sells everything from towels to paint to olive bruschetta. Even *The New York Times* has an online store.[9] When done right, such brand extensions can reinforce the concept and create additional revenue streams. The golden rule is that the extensions must create the experiences specified by the concept. Extensions that don't do this weaken the experiences and confuse the consumer about what the concept should mean.

Figure 1.6 shows a streamlined version of this process, but additional nuances are possible. In some cases, members of the audience create contacts, which create the brand experience for others as well as for the contributors. As discussed in Chapters 8 and 9, audiences participate in the Co-Producing and Community-Connection experiences via letters to the editor, discussion boards, and other user-generated content, Wikipedia, and Web sites that allow video sharing. Although issues of management and standards exist, the audience's ideas about the brand concept can also advance the organization's understanding of the concept.[10]

WHICH EXPERIENCES ARE RIGHT?

When we present this experience approach to practicing journalists, we are usually asked a question like, "OK, you have shown us a list of experiences that people have with publications, but which ones should I focus on?" Or, people ask, "What is the right set of experiences?" *The "right" set of experiences is those that are part of a particular media brand's concept* (and, of course, are meaningful and relevant to its target audience). The experiences that are right for ESPN are different from those that are right for The Discovery Channel, *USA TODAY*, *The New York Times*, Fox News, *Guideposts*, or modernmedicine.com, all of which have strong concepts that are highly differentiated. There is no one-size-fits-all formula for all of journalism.

Chapter 2 elaborates on how to identify and articulate experience-based concepts, but we make two general observations here. First, there is a tendency to copy what a successful direct competitor is doing, but this usually is not a good idea. Highly similar products often have no way of differentiating themselves except with price. In a world of ubiquitous user-generated content, professional media organizations cannot compete solely on price.

When a direct competitor zigs, a media brand should zag. An obvious example is *USA TODAY* versus *The New York Times*. *USA TODAY* struck a chord with (at least a segment of) the public by creating the non-Overload newspaper. It would be tempting for others to copy *USA TODAY*'s recipe for success, but this strategy likely would fail (at least as a national, head-to-head competitor) because *USA TODAY* already owns this positioning. *The New York Times*, in contrast, is committed to bolstering its reputation for being the paper of record and providing in-depth coverage and analysis even as it expands this position across platforms. In maximizing their core positions, both papers will attract—and delight—very different segments of readers by creating different experiences. Likewise, these organizations would be silly to try to create a vanilla blend, which would delight no one.

Although organizations should rarely copy direct competitors, they can successfully borrow ideas that are working for non-competing media organizations. For example, quite a few papers have adopted *USA TODAY*'s approach to infographics and shorter stories for their local products. And the success of *Cosmopolitan*—a magazine that clicked with women's rising sense of their own sexuality—led kitchen-and-bath women's titles to highlight "sex."

Our second general observation is that successful experiential media brands tend to focus on a handful of targeted experiences. It's becoming more difficult to find examples of successful media brands that focus on creating only one experience well, while organizations that attempt to create many different superlative experiences usually end up succeeding with none. Chapter 15 chronicles how Food Network, which originally focused primarily on utilitarian advice, found its distinctive stride when it mixed in elements of Anchor Camaraderie (Chapter 10), Makes Me Smarter, and Feel Good experiences (discussed below). *Glamour* magazine ostensibly is utilitarian, with its trademark "Dos & Don'ts," but the editors subtly combine Utilitarian, Feel Good, Inspiration, and Timeout experiences to endear *Glamour* to its readers.

THE EXPERIENCES SELECTED FOR THIS BOOK

We mentioned earlier that the Calder-Malthouse experience studies identified more than 40 experiences that people have had with various newspapers, magazines, Web sites, and TV stations (these are summarized in the appendix). Collectively, they constitute a rich and seemingly comprehensive description of how media fit into people's lives, but space constraints do not allow us to discuss them all in this book. The goals of this book are to discuss a concise set of experiences that can describe the multitude of relationships between a broad class of journalistic media and their consumers and to give media practitioners actionable opportunities to raise engagement with their brands. Just as a painter begins with a fairly small set of colors on the palette and then mixes them to produce any number of colors, we attempt to prepare a journalistic palette of experiences, which can be combined in creative ways.

The focus of this book is on journalistic media, which includes brands that cover news and information, as well as service, product-oriented, entertainment, and community journalism. With this focus, we omit experiences that explicitly concern advertising (Ad Receptivity and Ad Interference). We also do not discuss product-descriptive experiences such as Trust and Credibility, and High-Quality Content. Why? Because although these are crucial to the journalism we care about, they describe the media product more than experiences characterizing the relationship between consumers and brands, as with the Talk About and Share, Utilitarian, Civic, and Timeout experiences. And we do not deal with disengagement experiences such as Cynicism, Lack of Local Focus, Negativity, Overload, Political Bias, Poor or Annoying Design, Poor-Quality Content, Poor Service, Racial Bias, Sameness, Shallowness, or Skim and Scan. Of course media brands should avoid these experiences, but this book focuses on engagement rather than disengagement.

Some of the other original experiences can be derived from those included here, just as a certain shade of blue can be produced by mixing blue and white. For example, the It Helps Me Look Good; It's Sensual, Even Sexy experience is highly focused on a specific type of content that conveys elements of the Utilitarian, Inspirational, and Visual experiences. Likewise, the Political Bias experience is closely related to the Makes Me Smarter and Identity experiences (see Chapters 3 and 7). The It Reinforces My Faith, It Shows Diversity, and It Helps Me Keep Track of Celebrities are also derivative experiences. All of these experiences are important for certain media brands, but they are too focused on specific types of content to be included in our general palette.

Extensive factor analysis and careful judgment lead us to our "final cut" for our experience pallet. To confirm that our set spans a broad range of journalistic media, we turn to the uses and gratifications framework, which has been proposed by communications scholars to explain why people use media. This framework posits four broad categories of motivations, each of which is covered by our experiences:[11]

- **Information**—"Finding out about relevant events and conditions in one's immediate surroundings, society, and the world; seeking advice on practical matters or opinion and decision choices; satisfying curiosity and general interest; learning, self-education; gaining a sense of security through knowledge."

  Medill's Knight Professor, Owen Youngman, who oversaw much of the cross-platform expansion of the *Chicago Tribune*, examines the Makes Me Smarter experience. Professor Ellen Shearer gets inside the Civic experience. Professor Emeritus Abe Peck, who has worked with both service and business-to-business content, explores the Utilitarian experience. Assistant Professor Charles Whitaker uses his background as an *Ebony* editor to delve into the Inspirational experience.

- **Personal Identity**—"Finding reinforcement for personal values; finding models of behaviour [*sic*]; identifying with valued others (in the media); gaining insight into one's self."

  Dr. Rachel Mersey, a Medill alum who gained expertise at the University of North Carolina before bringing her audience knowledge back to her alma mater, provides insights into the Identity experience. Dr. Ashlee Humphreys, who has written extensively about Wikipedia, covers the Co-Producing experience.

- **Integration and Social Interaction**—"Gaining insight into the circumstances of others; social empathy; identifying with others, and gaining a sense of belonging; finding a basis for conversation and social interaction; having a substitute for real-life companionship; helping to carry out social roles; enabling one to connect with family, friends, and society."

  Associate professor and veteran experience researcher Steve Duke discusses the Talk About and Share experience. Medill's Director of Digital Innovation Rich Gordon (formerly with *The Miami Herald*) analyzes the Community-Connection experience. Medill senior lecturer Beth Bennett brings her broadcast background to an analysis of the Anchor Camaraderie experience.

- **Entertainment**—"Escaping, or being diverted, from problems; relaxing; getting intrinsic cultural or aesthetic enjoyment; filling time; emotional release; sexual arousal."

Assistant Professor and former *Self* editor Patti Wolter taps into the Timeout experience. Lecturer Josh Karp, who wrote a book about the *National Lampoon*, looks at Entertainment and Diversion experiences (Chapter 13). And Associate Professor Matt Mansfield, formerly with the *San Jose Mercury News*, collaborates with Assistant Professor Jeremy Gilbert, most recently the online design editor of the Poynter Institute's Web site, to bring what they've learned to bear on the Visual experience (Chapter 12).

Finally, we summarize two additional experiences from the entertainment category that did not make our final cut for this book but are worth noting in this Introduction.

The Feel Good Experience. The news can be depressing as it reports and even sensationalizes tragedies, disasters, poverty, corruption, political gridlock, and crash-and-burn celebrities. Some media counter this by consciously trying to show their audiences the silver lining to make them feel better about themselves and the world.[12] *Guideposts* magazine provides a regular dose of "positive thinking" to its devoted readers, and many women's magazines are successful in part because they help their readers to feel better about themselves and their bodies (even as other titles hold out images of impossible aspiration).

This experience is centered on some core beliefs:

- Reading this magazine makes me feel good about myself.
- Overall, it leaves me with a good feeling.
- When reading/watching this magazine/program, I am worry-free.

The Positive Emotional Experience. Some people feel touched emotionally by stories or programs they read or watch; media can create an emotional high. For example, seeing and hearing a children's choir during the holidays or learning about a neighbor who helped someone in need can create this experience.

This experience has these core beliefs:

- The magazine/show definitely affects me emotionally.
- Some articles/episodes touch me deep down.
- It helps me to see that there are good people in the world.
- It features people who make you proud.

Both of these experiences are close cousins to the Entertainment and Diversion, Timeout, and Visual experiences, in that all transport the reader/viewer to a different state of mind. We have not devoted entire chapters to these experiences because we feel the other three experiences convey the gist of the entertainment category.

CREATING AND MONITORING AN EXPERIENCE

We also want to show how engagement can be implemented in the newsroom. Rachel Davis Mersey's Identity experience chapter outlines how Phoenix fashionistas were engaged by targeted content when she worked at *The Arizona Republic*. Steve Duke's chapter on the Talk About and Share experience does double duty as he also describes the consulting on driving experiences in newsrooms he did for the Media Management Center. And in Chapter 16, Associate Professor David Nelson, another veteran of *The Miami Herald*, describes several engagement consultancies conducted by the Community Media Innovation Projects class he directs at Medill. The takeaway: Creating an experiential brand should be viewed as a process instead of as a one-time event; the organization should continually explore new contacts to build the concept,[13] and it should measure whether they are working.

Let's examine a specific experience to see how our process of creating experiential media brands works. Suppose a magazine decides to create a Timeout experience as part of its concept. The process delineated in Figure 1.2 suggests that the magazine's content creators should develop contacts that deliver this experience, but how can they do this? It helps to understand how people think about the experience and how it is part of their lives.

Remember the visual "molecule" of the Timeout beliefs and overall experience? The trick for our hypothetical magazine is for it to associate itself in the audience's mind with the very act of taking a break or reveling in having free time during a crowded day. An ideal Timeout reader would say, "The dishes are done, the kids are in bed, the laundry's put away, and now I finally have a few minutes to myself and I get to read my favorite magazine." The experience is one of having a break, rewarding oneself, forgetting about everything else, and being transported to a better mood or state of mind.

Chapter 11 describes techniques that journalists can use to create Timeout experiences. One way is to write beautiful narratives that lift readers out of their armchairs and take them somewhere else. Another is to provide luxuriant visuals of lovely and/or exotic locales: what magazine wags call "breathtaking vista" photos. A third ensures that the pacing of the pages flows as smoothly as possible and clearly flags specific content even as it wends its way around ad inserts; a euphonious reading experience contributes to the Timeout ambience. The best Timeout packagers will create a mini-world apart from the daily grind: *Real Simple*, for example, conveys the Timeout experience through an effective combination of white space, a pastel color palette, and, most of all, "relaxed" content that aids women in simplifying complex lives without dumbing them down (thus engaging the Make Me Smarter experience).

Other types of contacts discussed in this Introduction could also be employed. A house ad for the magazine might show an exhausted mother with her feet up, smiling as she unwinds with the magazine. And ads for products associated with taking a break or treating oneself, or ad executions that convey relaxation, should benefit from the surrounding editorial context even as they reinforce the magazine's concept. Our research validates the assumption that to get this "rub-off" effect, ads should be placed where they reinforce content without intruding on it.[14]

Overall, the reader should think, "The way to relax is to read _____."

Are these contacts successful in associating Timeout with the magazine? Focus groups and cover testing (and newsstand sales of those issues that maximize the experience) may suggest how well this is going. But periodic reader surveys should monitor what readers think about such a linchpin of the magazine's concept. These studies should ask readers to rate on a five-point scale whether they "agree or disagree" with several of the relevant beliefs from Figure 1.4. The average of these responses will provide a benchmark that the magazine can use to track its success in creating a brand image around this experience. The Engagement-Consequences of Engagement model in Figure 1.1 posits that higher experience levels will lead to more loyal readers who read more. It also says that certain ads will benefit from the more engaging context, which will further differentiate the magazine from other media and justify premium advertising rates (or at least minimize discounting in today's ad-depressed environment).

CONCLUSIONS

Medill on Media Engagement and the studies on which it draws attempt to make several contributions. On the theoretical side, we have essayed to systematically discuss (and show how to measure) all the various aspects of the four uses and gratifications groups. The studies verified relationships between experiences and outcomes concerning readership and advertising effectiveness; those organizations that improve experiences can see positive changes in these outcomes.

As for practitioners, caring journalists strive to implement craft excellence in service of their publication, TV program, Web site, or newer digital medium. Yet, in a world of folding titles and changing tastes, technical skill can prove insufficient. The strategic process shown in Figure 1.6, as well as the best practices and cautionary tales found throughout this book, can guide journalists in harnessing experiences to engage audiences.

Our team of authors is made up of media lovers. Nearly all of us are also professors at a school that has embraced audience understanding while continuing to foster standards of journalistic accomplishment, impact, and integrity. We have put our understanding of audience engagement and journalistic craft front and center so you can foster motivating experiences and minimize those that cause disengagement (or, if you are an interested nonpractitioner, can better understand the relationship between content creation and audience experiences). Our hope is that this book (and the accompanying Web site, medillmediaexperiences.com) will enrich your own experience as you move into a cross-media future rich in relationships between and among content creators and empowered audiences.

NOTES

1. Retrieved from http://www.thearf.org/assets/research-arf-initiatives-defining-engagement
2. We use *media brand* to refer to a wide class of journalistic enterprises, including but not restricted to Web sites, magazines, newspapers, and TV news programs.
3. This figure is adapted from Calder, B., & Malthouse, E. (2008). Engagement and advertising effectiveness. In B. Calder (Ed.), *Kellogg on media and advertising* (pp. 1–36). Hoboken, NJ: Wiley. That chapter provides further discussion and references on engagement and experiences and their effects on usage, affect, and reactions to ads. Also see Calder, B., & Malthouse, E. (2005). Managing media and advertising change with interactive marketing. *Journal of Advertising Research*, *43*(4), 356–361.
4. Merahn, S. (2009). *Modern Medicine 2009: product management road map*. Used by permission.
5. Merahn, S. (2009). *Modern Medicine 2009: product management road map*. Used by permission.
6. Retrieved from http://www.espncms.com/index.aspx?id=166
7. Nesbitt, M., & Lavine, J. (2005, April). Reinventing the newspaper for young adults: A joint project of the Readership Institute and *Star Tribune*. Retrieved from http://www.readership.org/experience/startrib_overview.pdf. Steve Duke first noted this study in Chapter 14.
8. For example, see http://www.youtube.com/watch?v=pAs6TDLuKgQ
9. Retrieved from http://www.nytstore.com/
10. For further discussion, see Hennig-Thurau, T., Malthouse, E., Friege, C., Gensler, S., Lobschat, L., Rangaswamy, A., & Skiera, B. (forthcoming). The impact of new media on customer relationships. *Journal of Service Research*.

Also see Deighton, J., & Kornfeld, L. (2009). Interactivity's unanticipated consequences for marketers and marketing. *Journal of Interactive Marketing, 23*(1), 4–10.

11. This summary of uses and gratifications is taken from McQuail, D. (1983). *Mass communication theory, an introduction.* London: Sage Publications, pp. 82–83.

12. Several "feel bad" experiences have negative correlations with usage and inhibit readership or viewership. See Peer, L., Malthouse, E., Nesbitt, M., & Calder, B. (2007). Negativity, hype, and all the same experiences in the local TV news experience: How to win viewers by focusing on engagement. Media Management Center technical report. Retrieved from http://www.mediamanagementcenter. org/localTV/localTV.pdf. See also the Wasting My Time and Unappealing Stories experiences in the Center's newspaper study (2004), and Malthouse, E., et al. (2007). Also see Malthouse, E., et al. (2007). This magazine irritates me and it disappoints me, from the Center's magazine study.

13. Although concepts must inevitably evolve over time, the organization should avoid changing its core because too many changes will confuse people about its intended meaning.

14. Malthouse, E., Calder, B, & Tamhane, A. (2007). The effects of media context experiences on advertising effectiveness. *Journal of Advertising, 36*(3), 7–18. Malthouse, E., & Calder, B. (2009). Leveraging media-advertisement experiential congruence. *Advertising Research,* 259–270. De Pelsmacker, P., & Dens, N. (Eds.). (2009). *Message, medium, and context.* Antwerpen: Garant Publishers. Calder, B., Malthouse, E., & Schaedel, U. (2009). Engagement with online media and advertising effectiveness. *Journal of Interactive Marketing, 23*(4), 321–331. Wang, J., & Calder. B. (2006). Media transportation and advertising. *Journal of Consumer Research, 33,* 151–162. Mersey, R., Malthouse, E., & Calder, B. (2010). Engagement with online media. *Journal of Media Business Studies, 7*(2), 37–56. Malthouse, E., & Calder, B. (2010). Media placement versus advertising execution. *International Journal of Market Research, 52*(2), 217-230. Calder, B., & Malthouse, E. (2004). Qualitative media measures: Newspaper experiences. *International Journal of Media Management, 6*(1&2), 124–131.

2

MEDIA CONCEPTS

Bobby J. Calder

Producing journalism or entertainment is a creative act. Nothing to be said here should be taken as denying this. Regardless what form the product takes—an article, program, film, blog, whatever—something is being created. It may be a routine, AP-style story about trends in local traffic problems, but a story still had to be conceived and produced. The aesthetics may be more on display with something like a long piece in *The New Yorker*, but it is always essential. Content will be as good or as bad as the creativity that goes into it. Therefore, the last thing one wants to do with any journalistic or entertainment product is to curtail creativity.

The primacy of creativity, of course, raises the question of "creative control." Should content producers be left alone to practice their art or should other factors, such as management objectives or consumer feedback, be considered? The question is the stuff of long-time debates and tensions in media organizations. Even the reporter with the local traffic story does not like to be edited, much less feel that a story was altered for "business reasons."

There is more here than just the usual control issues, however. The production of creative content is not just mysterious, but strange. As the philosopher John Dewey pointed out, the experience of someone engaged in the *production* of original content is fundamentally different from the experience of someone *consuming* that content.[1] It is not only different from the consumer's experience, it is essentially cut off from that experience. There is no way for the producer to have the experience of freshly consuming the product as a fully formed thing. Think of the difference between composing or even playing a piece of music and listening to it. The producer's experience is that of creating the piece and all that this entails. The consumer's experience is about being caught up in the piece and things like talking to others about it later.

What this means is that content producers are inherently limited in understanding the experience of consumers precisely because they are engaged in production. Does this have consequences? It does, and not just that consumers might not like the product, which is always a possibility. The real consequence is that the producer is limited in even being able to think about how the consumer will experience the product. Could some producers overcome this through empathetic understanding of the consumption experience? Yes, but it is more often the case that producers need help in being able to think about the experience of consumers and how to make that experience positive. (An alternative often found in the world of art is simply for producers to profess that they do not care what the experience of consumers is, but the assumption here is that we do care—we want the audience.)

The producers of creative products need help with understanding and affecting the experience of consumers. Helping should not be regarded as a form of creative control; it should be viewed as giving added direction to creative expression. This book is aimed at providing a process for helping content producers in this way. As described in the Introduction, the process revolves around understanding the experiences consumers will or could have. Based on this understanding, the goal is to create points of contact that deliver the intended experiences. These contacts can be part of the content or separate from it. The former is the focus of this book (the latter is more relevant to a broader discussion of marketing the content via things like promotional messages, events, etc.). Content contacts can be construed as any element of the creative product that could contribute to delivering the intended experiences.

In this formulation, the content producer does not lose control of these point-of-content elements, but is directed toward creating them in such a way that they have the intended effects on the consumer's experience. An editor for *The New Yorker* still has to come up with good titles. But if the intended experience is, say, one among the cluster of Personal Identity experiences noted in the previous chapter, the editor would be helped to focus on this experience and to write a title that speaks to it.

Again, the goal is to *engage* the consumer, where engagement arises out of experiences people have with the creative product. Take the audience for a television news program. It is easy to imagine that many, even most, viewers might not be engaged with a particular program. They may watch (although many could be multi-tasking), but they are not engaged. They know the lead story yesterday covered breaking news about an automobile accident. This might have been of interest, and they might be able to recall the story later. But they were not necessarily engaged. The program has not connected with anything going on in their lives. It is a little like eating a slice of toast for breakfast to keep hunger pangs away until lunch. It is not something that people experience beyond the mere act of consumption. Watching the news could be the same automatic, end-in-itself behavior.

Compare a light breakfast of toast with dinner at a famous restaurant where one begins the meal with caviar and a flight of different vodkas. This is something to tell others about (a Talk About and Share experience), feel important about (a personal identity experience), or learn which vodkas you like (an information experience). Now we have engagement. The person feels change; something is different. There is movement toward a larger goal.

It is possible for television news viewers to be engaged in the same way. This could of course happen merely by virtue of a news director and a reporter practicing their craft. The accident is reported in a way that viewers find engaging. The point of this book, however, is that this may or may not happen. It may be that the program could benefit from a process designed to facilitate viewer engagement.

THE IMPORTANCE OF CONCEPTS

To recapitulate, with our process content producers first need to understand which consumer experiences might produce greater engagement with their content. They need to decide on a set of specific experiences to focus on. Then they need to create specific contacts as part of the content creation process that affects the consumer's experiences in the intended way. (It is assumed that part of the content, or even most of it, will be produced traditionally. The goal with our process is to make sure that many of the content decisions specifically take into account the intended experiences.) The effect on consumer experiences results in a higher overall level of engagement.

There is an important intermediate step in moving from understanding consumer experiences to affecting them. In order to impact consumer experiences in the richest and deepest way, the content producer needs to identify and articulate a "concept." The purpose of the present chapter is to define more closely what we mean by a concept.

In the end, a concept is the idea that consumers are left with about the product based on their experiences with it. If the experiences are powerful enough to be highly engaging, this concept will be meaningful. It will represent what consumers believe that their experiences have meant to them. Moreover, the concept will be clear and specific, as opposed to vague and general. To produce such a concept in the mind of the consumer, it follows that we should anticipate it. Knowing in advance the concept we want consumers to be left with is what allows us to produce content contacts that help ensure consumers are left with it. Thus, a key step is to identify the concept that we want the consumer to have and to articulate it in a way that guides content creation.

So what would a concept, as something that could serve as the basis for designing content contacts, look like? The concept for Fox News might be as follows:

> To older individuals whose passionate conservative political views are an important part of who they are, Fox News is the news channel of choice because it provides a conservative perspective on news and events in a media landscape marked by an unfair liberal bias.

Clearly this concept is rooted in the various Identity experiences that Rachel Davis Mersey discusses more fully in Chapter 7. The understanding is that consumers of this type want news created in a way that reflects their own sense of passionate conservatism. This experience is heightened by the idea that this news is produced especially for them, thereby validating their identity, whereas other news networks do the opposite due to their liberal bias. When they encounter the slogan "Fair & Balanced," they understand it to imply "balancing the unfair bias of the liberal media."

Note that the concept above is a single-sentence statement. This is important in that a single, coherent idea should be capable of being expressed in a sentence. Elaboration might be useful, but not at the expense of clarity and focus. It is always wise to take the time to try to capture the concept as fully as possible in this elemental form. Using a single sentence imposes a discipline that ensures that the implications of the idea for impacting experiences through content creation are as clear as possible.

This single-sentence format can be referred to as the "concept statement." In the larger business world, the use of such concept statements is common, certainly in advertising as guides to promoting products but also in engineering as guides to designing products and services. Often in these contexts concept statements are referred to as "brand positioning statements." Indeed, the very notion of a brand is best thought of as a product for which there is a strong brand positioning statement that has guided both product and communication contacts.

In the case of the illustrative Fox News concept statement, notice the power it has to guide content creation contacts. What sort of on-air personalities and voice should the network have? All the usual rules of selecting television talent and production apply, of course. But the concept dictates that talent should reflect the them-against-us identity of the politically conservative target in order to heighten the Identity experience. If the tone is shrill or combative, this further impacts the sense of being heard and plays to the resentment of feeling socially unrecognized or even looked down on.

In contrast to the above concept statement for Fox News, suppose the network adopted the following concept:

> To 40-and-older individuals who are news junkies, Fox News is the channel that provides in-depth coverage of current news topics that you can count on as well to have the latest breaking events.

This concept is anchored in a more social experience of being able to talk about current events with others and to never be left out when something happens. The kind of content contacts called for by this concept would be quite different from the preceding one. The talent and voice here should be more serious and urgent. It is also the case with this concept, however, that it is weaker. Its ties to experiences are less clear; therefore, the implications for content contacts are weaker. The results would probably be lower consumer engagement.

COMPONENTS OF THE CONCEPT STATEMENT

There are three component parts to the concept statement. To anchor the concept truly in the consumer's experience, we first have to be clear about who *the target consumer* is. Only some consumers will be able to experience a product in certain ways, and never will all consumers experience the product in the same way. So in the case of the Fox News Network, it is important to describe to whom the concept is addressed: in our construct, "to older individuals whose passionate conservative political views are an important part of who they are." This usually works best if the target is not only characterized demographically but also is described with some psychological insight (such as "whose conservative political views are an important part of who they are"). This makes it easier to keep in mind the key identity experience on which the concept draws.

The core component of the concept has to do with how we *categorize the product*. This should imply a frame of reference that the consumer can use to locate the product in terms of to what it is similar or to whom it belongs. To understand anything, we have to be able to relate it to other things. If, for instance, I was describing an unfamiliar country, I might place it by saying that it is in Europe, near Germany. In the case of Fox News, our categorization is, "Fox News is the news channel of choice because it provides a conservative perspective on news and events." The network is placed in the category of a news channel and beyond this one that provides a conservative perspective.

The final component of the concept is the *point of difference*. If we really are to understand something, we must know what it is similar to, but we also must know how it is different from these things. Thus, to complete the constructed Fox News concept, a point of difference is required: In this case, "news and events in a media landscape marked by an unfair liberal bias." One way of looking at this is to ask how the consumer should know Fox News from any other news organization now or in the future that offers a conservative perspective. The difference would be the fighting quality of Fox News; it fights to be heard and respected in what its target audience perceives to be an unfair landscape of liberal opponents. Any concept can of course be copied, but having a strong point of difference not only makes a concept clearer and more complete (specifying what it is similar to but different from) but also makes it harder to copy. It makes it easier to recognize a copy as such as well.

A final point about the three components of a concept statement: Although the sentence format is necessarily linear, in crafting a strong concept statement it is important to go back and forth between the components. In thinking about the point-of-difference component, for instance, the target often becomes more sharply defined. For Fox News, we might have originally described the target as "having strong conservative views." But in anchoring the point of difference around fighting back in the face of perceived unfair bias, we could be led to develop a more insightful description of the target as people "whose passionate conservative political views are an important part of who they are."

DEVELOPING STRONGER CONCEPTS

The exercise of formally stating a concept anchored in consumer experiences and using it to direct content creation is, in itself, an important tool for creating media engagement. Even a loose concept can give important direction to content-creation contacts. But stronger concept statements can lead to even more impact on engagement.

Stronger concepts generally entail moving beyond a basic level of categorization at the core of the concept statement. A basic level of categorization most often involves stating the concept at the most obvious level of family membership. For example, suppose we have a woman's magazine devoted to decorating in a "country" style. The most basic concept statement might read as follows:

> To women 30 and older with a taste for traditional home décor, this is a country-style magazine that lets you take pleasure in unique, original, and natural things.

The categorization here is basic, in that it refers in a literal and product-oriented way to where the magazine belongs in the space of similar magazine products. The point of difference contributes more meaning by distinguishing this magazine from other similar magazines by pointing to a focus on the unique and original. It hints at a broader focus on a range of things other than just home furnishings.

A stronger concept would abstract the core concept of "country" as the key attribute of the product to a more consumer-oriented benefit. Why does "country style" appeal to this consumer? An insight would be that "country" signifies simplicity, a return to the cultural values of the past. The consumer appreciates the authentic and natural qualities characteristic of places, and with products associated with non-urban settings in the past. The concept statement below follows from this insight:

> To women 30 and older with a taste for traditional home décor, this is a country magazine devoted to surrounding yourself with simple things that are associated with unique, original, and natural ways of living from the past.

An even stronger concept would broaden this core abstraction to be even more inclusive of the underlying consumer experiences. The underlying experience is Utilitarian (see Chapter 5). The consumer is looking for information and advice, tips for how to decorate her home. But an even larger experience subsumes this. Consumers want to surround themselves with this style to achieve something in their lives. The experience they seek is one of greater tranquility. They want an environment that is free from the stress and complexity of modern urban living. They are literally seeking the experience of Timeout (vicariously from reading the magazine, as delineated in Chapter 11) or actual escape from their current situation (literally changing their home or even where they live).

The concept statement below follows from this fuller insight into the consumer experience:

> To women 30 and older who want to get to a simpler place in their lives, free from the stress of having to do it all, this is a country magazine devoted to helping them find simpler ways of living, to cutting complexity and noise out of their lives, and to letting them take pleasure in things that are unique, original, and natural.

It might seem that the last version of the concept statement is more confining. In one way it is; it is specific. But this is not as restrictive as it might seem. By being specific, the concept gives more direction. It rules out more things, but it makes clearer the kind of content called for. Should we include the sort of tips for organizing your life currently found in a magazine like *Real Simple*? No, this magazine is not about efficiency, getting it all done; it is about finding simple things that relieve the stresses of lives seemingly grown overly complex. Moreover, this concept statement actually opens the door to a wider range of content options. It should be clear that this magazine does not need to be restricted to home furnishings. The concept can be applied to a side range of content topics: food, travel, and almost anything else.

CONCEPTS AND CULTURE

Another property of stronger concepts is especially important for media products: namely, a really strong concept should also be at the front of cultural change. The reason is that the experiences people are more sensitive to most often stem from or are highly related to changes going on in the culture that surrounds them. Much as we think of ourselves, at least in Western cultures, as individually motivated, the experiences we seek as directions in our lives are influenced by cultural trends. So that if we experience our lives as overly busy and feel we need to seek simplicity, in large part this likely flows from a cultural trend that leads us to perceive ourselves in this way.

This link to cultural relevance is exceptionally important for media products because of the way consumers use the media as a way of staying in touch with their culture. As cultural trends emerge, consumers most often encounter them via media products. Consumers are in fact oriented to seek out media products that are on the leading edge of cultural change so that they can find the kind of experiences that the culture is pushing them toward.

What this means is that media products need to be a little ahead of consumers. Concepts must relate to the experiences that consumers are currently seeking in their lives, but these experiences should also be ones that will be even more culturally in vogue in the near future.

In our view, selecting experiences that are in the early stage of becoming culturally relevant is the key to creating "hits." Everyone knows the media business is all about "hits" that seemingly happen almost magically—the movie, the book that just takes off. In more cases than not, this can be related back to leading-edge sensitivity to experiences that are undergoing cultural change. In these cases, consumers are beginning to feel the need for a different kind of experience and are especially engaged with media products that feel part of this change.

Think back to the media hits of the past. Why was *I Love Lucy* such a successful television program in its day? Certainly it had a great comedic actor, consistent script writing, and the like. In our terms, it also had more than this—it had a strong concept. The original "pitch" description for the program went as follows.

> ...A radio and/or television program, incorporating the characters Lucy and Ricky Ricardo. He is a Latin American orchestra leader and singer. She is his wife. They are happily married and very much in love. The only bone of contention between them is her desire to get into show business, and his equally strong desire to keep her out of it.... But Ricky, who was raised in show business, sees none of its glamour...and yearns to be an ordinary citizen, keeping regular hours and living a normal life. As show business is the only way he knows to make a living, and he makes a very good one, the closest he can get to this dream is having a wife who's out of show business and devotes herself to keeping as nearly a normal life as possible for him.

Note that, although this does not rely on the single-sentence concept statement format, it is entirely consistent with this in that it makes the core concept very clear. Beyond the strength of the concept, however, what made this program such a hit was its cultural relevance. In each program, Lucy explored the possibilities of working outside the home in a more (at the time) male-oriented role. The program reached an even higher level of engagement by speaking to experiences that were just becoming culturally relevant.

Now consider a successful program of today: *American Idol.* Although just a talent contest (one initially turned down in the United States), the program has a strong concept, and this accounts for the high level of viewer engagement that it has attained. To account fully for the strength of this concept and the program's status as a mega-hit, one would have to understand how the experiences it taps into are undergoing cultural change. Is the experience of failure relevant to personal identity in a way that presently reflects cultural change? Identifying with the losers may be an even more important aspect of the concept than rooting for the winners.

MULTIPLE CONCEPTS

One final issue inevitably arises in using concepts. Often it is the case that products are nested within a hierarchy of products. So a television program is itself a part of a television network, which itself may be part of a multi-platform offering including other television networks, magazines, radio programs, Web sites, and the like (think ESPN). The question is, how should all of these products fit together?

The short answer is that concepts are even more crucial in this context. Each product should have a clear and specific concept that directs content creation regardless of the platform on which a particular show appears. In this way, the consumer's experiences are held together across platforms, maximizing total engagement. At the same time, the larger entities such as the television network, as opposed to individual programs, should also have a strong concept. This concept may or may not be subordinate to the lower-level concept. The television network may be the dominant concept, in which case it is important that the program concept be a reflection of that concept and the experiences it draws on. This has been the case for the USA Network, with its "characters" concept: No show has run without being centered on an appealing central character—from *Monk* to *The Closer*—and these characters contribute to a network-level promotion of the character concept.

In contrast, a signature program might help define a network's concept. The important principle is that each level should be defined by a concept that is consistent in the experiences that the content aims to impact to create engagement. It may be necessary to have filler content or content that inadvertently has an inconsistent concept, but this should be regarded as an exception to the ideal, and one that hopefully does not confuse or dilute the dominant concept.

* * *

In this chapter, we have focused on using experiences to create the engagement that is the theme of this book. We have seen that the process of starting with experiences and developing a concept that guides the creation of content contacts can be greatly assisted by the use of clear and specific concept statements. We reiterate that the use of concepts in this way does not deny the importance of creativity in content production. Concepts are a way of channeling that creativity toward the goal of heightened engagement with the final product.

NOTE

1. Dewey, J. (1934). *Art as experience*. New York: Perigee Books. [1980 edition].

II

CREATING LOYALTY
AND MAXIMIZING READERSHIP
THROUGH MEDIA EXPERIENCES

3

THE MAKES ME SMARTER EXPERIENCE

Owen Youngman

- It addresses issues or topics of special concern to me.
- It updates me on things I try to keep up with.
- It's important I remember later what I have read/looked at.
- Even if I disagree with information in this magazine/newspaper/television programming/site, I feel I have learned something valuable.
- I look at it as educational. I am gaining knowledge.

"Mr. Rockefeller, how much money is enough?"

"Just a little bit more."

This oft-quoted exchange between a reporter and Standard Oil baron John D. Rockefeller is almost certainly apocryphal. Like many widely circulated but imaginary quotations, it neatly summarizes something that people believe: Even those who possess something in abundance—beauty, power, Facebook friends—are just like those who perceive a personal shortage. They would be only too happy to get some more.

And so it is with intelligence. Consciously or unconsciously, most people say they would like to be smarter regardless of how "smart" they might already be; one widely publicized study in 2007 found that 69% of respondents ages 16 to 29 would rather be smarter than better looking.[1] Although it may not be universally possible to become prettier or more powerful through one's own efforts, a person can acquire the trappings of "smartness" by setting out with intentionality to acquire information—be it from textbooks, TV, Twitter, or the *Times*.

Trouble is, most people have their hands full just acquiring the news and information they need to get by in a complicated 21st-century world, let alone any extra knowledge they'd like to layer on in subjects they care about—technology, sports, bird watching, pop culture, the environment, to list just a few. They may once have been motivated by what the Stanford professor Carol S. Dweck[2] has called a "growth mindset," in which a commitment to learning is a primary determinant of people's activities and of their success in feeling smarter. But now they need help, and they are unlikely to add anything to their already busy days.

So although much opportunity to make people feel smarter still falls to media brands, more than ever brands *themselves* need to be smarter. By creating engaging experiences—and, importantly, by doing so in convenient ways that encourage repeated use and lead to viral marketing by audience members—they can improve their own business prospects while they improve their customers' knowledge and self-image. Of these experiences, the Makes Me Smarter experience is among the most effective, as we discuss here.

SMARTER ABOUT WHAT?

Consider just one topic that a news consumer was confronting (or, worse, being overwhelmed by) in mid-2009: the state of the U.S. economy. "Overwhelmed," as a matter of fact, has been shown to be an inhibitor of news consumption by the foundational research we cite later in this chapter, and so this particular topic presented an educational challenge for any media concern: Even though people might benefit from "getting smarter" about it, few would sit down with their papers or at their keyboards with that as a goal for their next few precious minutes.

The Makes Me Smarter experience is one in which, having decided to use Information Source M, I feel current and well informed because Source M served me with the valuable interactions that concern, educate, or are worth my keeping up with noted at the start of this chapter. In fact, when I put down the paper, change the channel, or head for a different Web site, I might well ask myself, "How would I ever keep up with [Topic T] if I didn't check with M?"

In this example, fresh ideas about the causes of the economic downturn; illuminating anecdotes about other people's situations and reactions; clear explanations for changes in one's own life or experience; enhanced understanding of what might be next, leading to a better ability to cope; or memorable images that make arcane topics easier to grasp—any of these would reinforce the value of continued and repeated engagement with a Source M.

The New York Times' response on one weekend of 2009 included:

- How the downturn had blown a hole in the number of pro tournaments in women's golf;
- How the oldest family-run Dodge dealer in the country, which had transformed itself into the leading repair shop for Dodge Vipers on the Eastern seaboard, was being cut loose as Chrysler shrank;
- How at least one economist and federal judge saw the recession as a failure of capitalism itself, not a manifestation of greed and evil;
- How credit-card companies used psychological tools to get consumers to pay their bills; and
- How some laid-off workers were recapturing the lost camaraderie of their offices by "co-working"—sharing space with people pursuing unrelated endeavors, or just looking for work.

Interestingly, only one of these stories—the last—was in the business section. As a result, a reader or online user could wind up knowing something entirely new—feeling smarter—no matter where she began. She wasn't just smarter, of course; she had something to talk about (Chapter 14), and she felt better about herself for knowing something important (Chapter 7). But the other experiences began with, and were tightly linked to, feeling smarter.

It's perhaps a cliché to use *The New York Times* for this example, so perhaps we should go to a different part of the daily newspaper spectrum, that occupied by the *Chicago Tribune*'s free tabloid for young, urban commuters, *RedEye*. When it was launched in October 2002, *RedEye* was widely derided for "dumbing down" the news[3]—a criticism that also had been leveled at the Internet extensions of most newspapers when they arrived on the scene beginning in the mid-1990s.

But the *Tribune*'s research, informed by research at the Media Management Center on younger readers as well as by proprietary studies, told the *Tribune*'s editors and managers that the target audience still valued news. In fact, they expected hard news, in particular, to be played "straight"—early prototypes that made light of serious subjects were viewed with suspicion ("Are these real stories, or is this like *The Onion*?"). Just because these people felt they had less time to consume a newspaper didn't mean they wanted their stories both short and silly. Straight news played straight would be a component of *RedEye* from Day One so that its readers could trust their new newspaper to keep them up to date and feeling smart.

And so, while *RedEye*'s sports section had a Stuart Scott-like attitude, and while the tone of its entertainment coverage bordered on the snarky, its audience could and can end a 20-minute commute feeling smarter about

Chicago, the world, and celebrities great and small. In fact, the first change made to *RedEye*—within its first week of publication—was to add more Chicago news because overnight reader surveys found a majority of respondents feeling the balance was out of whack in favor of "fluff."

They wanted to know more, to feel smarter about news as well as sports and celebrities; *RedEye* pursued all three. One year, it shone a light on police response to sexual assault by writing about every rape within the City of Chicago. Another year, it took on Chicago's substandard record on recycling; in another, it campaigned for safer building structures in its readers' neighborhoods. Within three years, *RedEye* was profitable, had established a clear voice and role in its readers' lives, and had more than 700,000 engaged readers every week, with a median age of 34.[4]

And yes, we are talking about the dead-trees edition. In assigning blame for the difficult economic straits of the news industry in the first decade of the century, one widely repeated canard is that so-called "younger readers" aren't interested in news. An even better refutation of this idea than *RedEye* is *nrc.next*, a Monday-through-Friday morning newspaper launched in the Netherlands in 2006 and that, by 2009, was reaching 351,000 readers each day with its 83,369 copies. And, by the way, not only is it a printed newspaper; it's paid, not free.

Nrc.next, a spinoff of the storied daily *NRC Handelsblad*, explicitly targets "the new generation of news consumers (20- to 39-year-olds with at least an undergraduate degree," according to its online marketing kit).[5] Its editors assume that its readers already know what happened yesterday, and most of the space in the paper goes to analysis, commentary, background, information graphics, and photography.

Further, readers know each day what they're going to feel smarter about when they finish reading because each day of the week has a different theme: sports on Monday, for instance, jobs and careers on Wednesday, movies and entertainment on Thursday. And, recognizing that some in the audience will want even more information on a topic of particular interest, *Nrc.next* has created a particularly interesting implementation: A subscriber can request additional information via text message, and the supplementary data will be posted to a personalized Web page.

None of these primarily print-oriented examples is intended to ignore how the Internet, and related means of communication, has affected media brands. It is possible to argue that the first 15 years of the Internet era have shown that much of the job of communicating information can be done "automagically," through the creation and deployment of technology-based tools that improve access to knowledge (e.g., search engines, collaborative filtering algorithms, RSS feeds). The best of these tools have become brands in their own rights, generally by helping people to learn more about specific topics or events in which they have a predetermined interest; these tools are utilitarian at their heart (see Utilitarian—Chapter 5).

Indeed, given how well many of these tools accomplish their tasks, it has become hard for either traditional or emerging media brands to compete on utility alone. By evaluating, filtering, organizing, and curating information on personally relevant topics—sorting through mounds of data and thousands of Web sites for the time-pressed but curious reader—a brand such as *The New York Times*, *ESPN*, or *Wired* magazine acquires, earns, and sustains a reputation for making people smarter. *Nrc.next* doesn't just use its newspaper and Web site in this pursuit, for example; not surprisingly given its audience, by early 2009, it was also using Facebook and Twitter to make sure it was almost perpetually keeping its audience up to date.

"Curating" may seem to be an unusual word in this context, but it combines intentionality, audience knowledge, filtering, and quality control. For example, it can be extrapolated from the World Health Organization's mortality tables that more than 50 million people die in the world each year. Only a portion is reported in the press—in the United States, about 60% make it to Legacy.com, the news industry's online aggregator. But *The Economist*, Great Britain's 166-year-old news weekly (in early 2010), generally publishes one obituary per issue, at most. Its readers know that reading it will educate them about one particularly interesting, if not always particularly famous, individual—and make them smarter about the world in which they have been living. It is curation in every sense and one of the experiences *The Economist* brand repeatedly delivers.

As we have seen, experiences are not about a brand itself, but about the relationship between a person and a brand. I might stipulate, for instance, that my relationship with ESPN is built around its ability to winnow down a day's worth of competitive athletics into just the results and highlights I need to know and see. Therefore, as ESPN has expanded beyond cable TV— into radio, the Internet, magazines, mobile services, telephony—it is out to make me smarter in consistent, related ways. And, interestingly, as my interest in sports began to wane in the years after I ceased being a sports editor, ESPN's ability to keep me up to date meant that I watched *SportsCenter* even when I didn't look at an actual event for months.

But how can a brand, a company, a service, a product set out to occupy the "makes me smarter" space? Are there methods that work, road maps to follow? It turns out that there are.

FOUNDATIONAL RESEARCH

In the body of research that has emerged to identify and codify the areas of greatest opportunity for relationship building by media enterprises, the Makes Me Smarter experience repeatedly bubbles to the top. Most pertinently, it is repeatedly cited in the series of Media Management Center studies that between 2000 and 2005 examined audience experiences of print, broadcast, and online media.

The Institute conducted its "Newspaper Experience Study" and "Magazine Experience Study" in 2003, identifying about 40 experiences for each medium. Most were motivators associated with higher readership, and some were inhibitors linked with lower readership. The Makes Me Smarter experience was the second strongest descriptor of newspaper readers' experience, just behind A Regular Part of My Day, a fact that not incidentally reinforces the value of habit. The correlation between the Makes Me Smarter experience and actual readership behavior was fifth among the 26 motivators studied.[6]

In 2003–2004, the Readership Institute conducted a follow-up "New Readers" study among 10,800 younger adults, in part focusing on which experiences might motivate younger adults to read newspapers more and which might inhibit them from reading more at all.[7] Of 34 experiences studied, 8 were identified as "key": judged by the Institute as being applicable to service, news, and advertising content; of special relevance to young adults; and actionable for newspapers. The Makes Me Smarter experience was the second most powerful motivator.

Across the studies, the Makes Me Smarter experience expanded to include the following components:

- I look at the newspaper as educational. I gain something [such as knowledge].
- Even if I disagree with things in this newspaper, I feel like I have learned something valuable.
- This newspaper has columns that give good advice.*
- This newspaper is good at telling stories about things that happen and how they turn out.
- It is a way to learn about new products.*
- It shows me how other people live their lives.
- I learn about things to do or places to go.*
- It's important I remember later what I have read/looked at.
- It addresses issues or topics of special concern to me.
- It updates me on things I try to keep up with.

These aspects are covered in Chapter 5 of this book, which focuses on the Utilitarian experience.

Which is not to overlook what can happen online. In 2005, the Media Management Center followed up five years of print work by the Readership Institute with an experience study of 2,215 online users, done in conjunction with the Online Publishers Association.[8] Once again, the Makes Me Smarter experience was found to be among the most important, ranking third of 22 dimensions of engagement. In the online context, it is summarized as follows:

- The site makes me smarter and up to date on things I care about. It has depth and seems very professional.
- It is time well spent.
- Even if I disagree with information on this site, I feel I have learned something valuable.
- I look at this site as educational. I am gaining something.
- They do a good job covering important topics. They don't miss things.
- It addresses issues or topics of special concern to me.
- This site goes really in depth.
- It has a very professional image.
- It updates me on the things I try to keep up with.

In both the offline and online studies, one of the Readership Institute's core points was that news organizations needed to become intentional about creating experience. In many media companies at that time—and, frankly, for hundreds of years before—decisions about what to cover, and how to cover it, were partly driven by how it made the reporters, editors, producers, and managers feel. The Institute proposed a new starting point: thinking directly about the audience in creating "experience-oriented" content, "including new criteria for content selection, different story treatment, additional tools, or features, etc."[9]

MAKING THE EXPERIENCE REAL

Having defined a Make Me Smarter experience appropriate for the medium and the audience, then, how best can a news organization or individual settle on criteria, deliver the experience through its content, and then reliably do so again and again? Although the approach will vary based on the particular content and a given individual's "use case"—where, when, and how the information in question will most effectively be accessed, and then learned—in every case, the starting point is the same: understanding what a target reader wants to be smarter about.

For the selected examples of consumer benefits that follow, I have drawn from several different analyses of the Makes Me Smarter experience gathered over the years by the Center and the Readership Institute. (Emphases are mine. I use the word "consumer" in its sense of one who encounters content, not of one who purchases goods or services.)

- When telling me about things that happen, be sure to explain *how things turn out.*

"How things turn out" is different than "what things happened." Essentially, this is about tying up loose ends, as if the reporter were Miss Marple or Inspector Poirot. To do this, make sure the narrative *feels* complete—that a consumer can summarize what occurred; can learn its impact on key individuals; and can understand how the event and its aftermath will affect other people, other stories, or even her own family.

So-called "night meeting" stories—coverage of city councils, school boards, zoning, or sewer commissions—have long had a reputation of being unsatisfying for both reporter and reader, yet they have filled the inside pages of local dailies and weeklies for generations. (I once had a reporter who stored the stock sentences for these stories in keyboard macros, only half in jest.) But a simple Make Me Smarter idea, implemented by Gregory Mellis at the *Sun* newspapers outside Chicago in the 1990s, changed both the content and the impact of this coverage.

Gone were the narratives that recounted each meeting in careful detail, including the background of any issue that seemed worth including. Instead, readers found something that today we might call "Web-like": short boxed items that listed important agenda items, what had changed since each item had last made the news, what action was or wasn't taken, and what would happen next. If an issue actually was resolved, readers learned what would be disappearing from this "blotter" of municipal governance.

In a single glance, residents of places such as Naperville, Illinois, were smarter about what city government might soon be doing for them or to them—not least because it is just plain difficult to extract this same kind of information from a "traditional" night meeting story. In the current era of shrinking news holes and shrinking staffs, the format has been so widely copied that the boldness of its approach is no longer obvious. Nevertheless, the principle of focusing on the outcome instead of the process is applied just as easily to trials, road construction updates, and economic development debates.

Habitual application of an approach such as this one lives up to an aspect of the Makes Me Smarter experience that has cumulative benefit for both the consumer and the brand—namely, *"this publication/site/station is educational."* How would someone keep up without it? If the journalists are doing this day in and day out, update after update, the consumer will realize she couldn't.

- When something is really important, *make sure I can remember it later.*

Often in an effort to squeeze in every last drop of information, reporters forget to fully emphasize what's most important (and editors forget to help them). The journalist's job is to resolve the inherent tension between completeness and simplicity and to make sure a consumer can retain the essence not only of an event but also of a policy or personality.

One of the best sports columns I can recall was written by Bernie Lincicome[10] after Chris Evert Lloyd won the French Open tennis title in 1985. I never met Chris Evert, but because Lincicome's column laid out what made her special and then powerfully restated his point at least 10 times within 28 paragraphs, nearly 25 years later I still think I understand her better than many people whom I actually know.

"I can count the athletes who never disappointed me on one thumb," he wrote. "Chris Evert Lloyd never disappointed me…. She lost tennis matches only slightly more often than she lost her grace, and that was never."

> Why? Ask her competition because:
>
> …as they imitated the Evert game, they imitated the Evert style, which was, for the most part, good manners as well as good tennis… "I never preached being a good sport. What they were copying was my attitude. It was important to have good ground strokes but good behavior, too."
>
> Why? Because
>
> She weathered her reign at the top and more recently her position behind [Martina] Navratilova without taking on that hard edge that many athletes get. She never became petulant or arrogant.
>
> Why?
>
> She gave a style to winning that has not been duplicated often. In the age of the athlete as horse's rump, she seemed out of place, like a flower in a patch of thorns. When everything else is musty memory, that will be her legacy.

From an experience standpoint, here is the moral of this story: Instead of adding one more tangential detail, repeat yourself.

MORE THAN MEETS THE EYE

Sometimes an important idea may not be memorable because a full description needs to be wordy and complex. In such a case, repetition doesn't help; what's needed is to look elsewhere in the Makes Me Smarter toolbox and use an image or a graphic to tell the story with clarity, grace, precision, and impact.

Online, few if any applications are more successful in educating users in such topics than are interactive graphics and maps. Obviously, they also can contribute to other experiences, particularly utilitarian ones, as sites such as everyblock.com (formerly chicagocrime.org) and many other "Google mash-ups" have shown. But as the integration of databases, programming, and interactive technologies expands, media has remarkable educational possibilities.

Many news sites excel in this area, but NYTimes.com is successful in educating its large and engaged audience in a wide variety of areas. Here are three particularly successful examples:[11]

- http://www.nytimes.com/interactive/2008/08/04/sports/ olympics/20080804_MEDALCOUNT_MAP.html

This map of the world, a cartogram that distorts the size of the countries in relation to the number of medals won in a given Olympiad, is consistent with many of the principles set forth by Edward Tufte in his four books, beginning with *The Visual Display of Quantitative Information*.[12] Beyond the medal counts and lists that are a daily staple of live coverage, the inter- activity in this map lets a user explore changes in the relative strength of each country over time. As a bonus, it integrates a database of individual medal winners throughout history.

- http://www.nytimes.com/2007/04/19/arts/20070419_MET_ GRAPHIC.html

The New York Times' print coverage of the opening of the Metropolitan Museum of Art's new Greek and Roman galleries in 2007 was of course extensive, containing maps and photographs as well as expert commentary from critics. This NYTimes.com implementation allows a user to manipu- late individual objects, viewing them from all sides as a critic explains their significance. It's not unlike a personal docent-led tour of the Met.

- http://www.nytimes.com/interactive/2009/05/15/nyregion/ 0515-foreclose.html?ref=new-jersey

In *Envisioning Information*, Tufte shows examples of chloropleth maps — "blot maps...that paint over areas formed by *given* geographic or political boundaries." This NYTimes.com map by Matthew Bloch and Janet Roberts communicates complete data about mortgage foreclosures in the New York metropolitan area by census tract. It vivified the understanding that foreclosure rates were highest in areas with a high percentage of minor- ity residents and allowed users to track changes in rates over a four-year period.

The consistent execution of "infographics" at this level of sophistication brings users back not because they are pretty or because they "can't be done in the newspaper" but because they make me smarter for spending time with them. It's a far cry from putting "extra" photos or longer stories online "because there's room."

THE PERSISTENCE OF MEMORY

Deep involvement with a particular piece of content often leads to the feeling of being smarter for a reader or online user. The challenge can be different for a television viewer, more accustomed to having entertainment or information wash over him than actively exploring it (an inhibitor to the adoption of "interactive TV"; "It seems clear," *The Economist* wrote in 2002, in one in a series of skeptical articles on the topic that dates at least to 1997, "that TV viewers slumped in front of their box do not want to take decisions"[13]).

Which is not to say that they don't want to feel smarter. A six-month Media Management Center study of news on five local TV stations in Chicago[14] found that viewers feel smarter when they "feel that the local night-time news program keeps them up to speed and stimulates their thinking," and have "confidence that stories the viewer thinks are important are covered." This helps build viewership.

One component of the Makes Me Smarter experience can accomplish the latter while overcoming the problem of the former: "I can remember this important information later."

Traditional pedagogical tools such as repetition, simplification (the "minimum information principle"), the inclusion of relevant examples, and particularly the use of imagery obviously can all be seen in any newscast.

Repetition obviously has proven just as successful in television as in one of my favorite media, Sunday morning sermons, where two sets of three dicta almost always lead to success: (1) "Make 'em laugh, make 'em cry, make 'em feel religious"; (2) "Tell 'em what you're gonna tell 'em; tell 'em; tell 'em what you told 'em." Heavy promotion of upcoming stories, both inside and outside a newscast—a staple of any local TV news outlet—thus can be effective not only in keeping someone watching but in ensuring that she will recall a story later...and feel smarter.

Similarly, health coverage has become a broadcast staple over the last 10 years as repeated research has demonstrated both particularly strong interest in the topic and a reliance on local TV news as a primary source of health information.[15] Almost without exception, local TV health reporters simplify stories from the major medical journals, illustrate them with local examples, and include images, all of which make a story easy to recall. Although the acquisition of medical knowledge can also be a Utilitarian experience— 76% of adults have said they act on health information they get from TV[16]— it is primarily Makes Me Smarter because not every piece of health information will be directly relevant to a given viewer or her family.

Similar sets of questions and filters can be constructed for every element of the experience in every medium of communication. Not all will apply to every piece of content, and not every piece of content will have the Makes Me Smarter experience as its raison d'être. But this approach, which starts by forming a picture of the audience and how it can benefit from a particular piece of content, can easily inform the tools and media that can best be used to publish it.

A LITTLE HELP FROM MY FRIENDS

Taking advantage of different tools and technologies to educate users, viewers, and readers is not effective, of course, if consumers don't know of their opportunity to keep up with a topic of importance. The so-called "serendipity" of the printed newspaper used to take care of this for its readers, but that behavioral model has no real analog online. Despite search engines, RSS feeds, and automated alerts, audiences rarely find stories they're not looking for; the stories have to find them, and they need a little help. Recently, the wide adoption of social media networks, and more important the tools that users employ to derive benefit from these sites, has given news brands a way to work across platforms to establish and reinforce their Makes Me Smarter credentials.

Of course, it has been possible from the first days of the Internet for people to share something of interest electronically with a handful of acquaintances (or, through tools such as listservs and newsgroups, with many people with whom they share a previously identified interest). But MySpace, Facebook, Twitter, Digg, and scores if not hundreds of other sites have changed the game because an individual can:

- Recommend an item to hundreds or thousands of people based on their affinity with her, as well as with the topic or content;
- Target a single friend with an item of interest and, without any effort on the friend's part, reach people unknown to her but who may share interest in the item;
- Improve her reputation outside her own network of direct acquaintances through reliable and consistent recommendations to the community whose value is openly trackable over time; and

- Pass on others' recommendations as easily as her own and some-times even more easily if she chooses to rely on a friend's repu-tation rather than pass judgment herself.

The potential benefit for a news brand is considerable. The opportuni-ty exists within these networks to establish a Makes Me Smarter reputation with people who never have used it before or who may have misconceptions about it, merely by getting relevant content in front of the right users in the right places.

The *Chicago Tribune* established the efficacy of this strategy in 2008 by hiring three interns to learn about the audiences who frequented a number of leading social media sites, and then, while establishing credibility within those sites, begin promoting and linking to relevant content. The *Tribune* needed to expand its audience beyond people who had joined its online audience in the previous 15 years, and it was interested in proving the proposition that stories in particular categories, such as travel and business, could become as readily forwarded as disaster or celebrity stories.

Thanks to the measurability of the Web, it didn't take long to see the impact. Within weeks, there were days when the top referrer to chicagotri-bune.com was no longer Google but the recommendation site Digg. Within three months, traffic and unique visitors to the site had grown by 10%, cre-ating a reliable amount of additional advertising inventory that could be sold in advance not just filled with remainders. And the reputation of "Colonel Tribune," an online persona that had been introduced to multiple social net-works, had been established as a guide to valuable, timely content.

The Colonel was making people smarter—more up to date, more cur-rent with important topics. The life and impact of stories that for all practi-cal purposes had been read only in print, in Chicago, was extended in both time and geography. And soon reporters and editors were joining the interns in the effort: thinking quite specifically about their stories' audience, lever-aging their own networks and joining new ones, and using the feedback from their networks to report new stories and pursue new avenues of inquiry that would create further motivating experiences the next time those users came back.

That last part is particularly important because habitual, repeated behavior has been at the core of nearly every successful media business for centuries. It goes almost without saying that if no one in today's audience comes back tomorrow, the practice of journalism and the successful commu-nication of knowledge will be damaged beyond its current practitioners' recognition.

But if you leave feeling smarter—well, Mr. Rockefeller, would you like some more of that tomorrow?

NOTES

1. Net generation, global survey conducted from April 5, 2007, to May 3, 2007, among 7,692 respondents in 12 countries. New Paradigm of Toronto, www.NewParadigm.com.
2. Dweck, C. S. (2006). *Mindset: The new psychology of success.* New York: Random House. Dweck, C. S. (1999). *Self theories: Their role in motivation, personality, and development.* Philadelphia: Psychology Press. Numerous other publications.
3. To cite just three of dozens of critiques that appeared during *RedEye's* first six months of publication: Unsigned editorial (2002, November 4). Youth must be served, but is this the best way? *Crain's Chicago Business*, p. 10; Shaw, D. (2002, November 17). Chicago newspapers have young readers seeing red. *Los Angeles Times*, p. E14; Whitaker, C. (2002, December 4). Still wanted, hip daily for young readers. *Newsday*, p. A34.
4. Gallup poll of media usage and consumer behavior. Chicago market, 2005.
5. Retrieved from http://www.pcmmedia.nl/english-information/nrc-next/nrc-next.html
6. The newspaper experience study. © 2003 Readership Institute.
7. Key newspaper experiences. © 2004 Readership Institute.
8. The user engagement study. © 2005 Media Management Center.
9. The user engagement study. © 2005 Media Management Center.
10. Linicome, B. (1985, June 10). For Chris, it's a matter of style. *Chicago Tribune*, p. D1.
11. I am grateful to my 1990's chicagotribune.com colleagues, Steve Duenes and Drew DeVigal, for helping to guide me to some of the best examples at NYTimes.com, their most recent employer. pp. D1.
12. Tufte, E. (1983). *The visual display of quantitative information.* Cheshire, CT: Graphics Press. Tufte, E. (1990). *Envisioning information.* Cheshire, CT: Graphics Press. Tufte, E. (1997). *Visual explanations.* Cheshire, CT: Graphics Press. Tufte, E. *Beautiful evidence* (2006). Cheshire, CT: Graphics Press.
13. Unbylined. (2002, April 13). Entertain me: Television viewers just want to have fun. *The Economist*. Survey on television, section 4.
14. The local TV news experience: How to win viewers by focusing on engagement. © 2007 Media Management Center.
15. Cooper, C. P., and Roter, D. L. (2000, July–August). If it bleeds it leads? Attributes of TV health news stories that drive viewer attention. *Public Health Reports*. See also multiple studies cited in: Medical news for the public to use? (2006, March). *The American Journal of Managed Care*. Page not known.
16. Americans talk about science and medical news. (1997, December). Washington, DC: National Health Council.

4

THE CIVIC EXPERIENCE

Ellen Shearer

- Reading this newspaper/watching the news makes me feel like a better citizen.
- I count on this newspaper/station to investigate wrongdoing.
- Reading/watching makes me more a part of my community.
- Our society would be much weaker without newspapers/TV news.
- I think people who do not read this newspaper or one like it are really at a disadvantage in life.

The role of watchdog is among the most central to people's concept of a news organization—a powerful driver that can instill and enhance loyalty or, if tarnished, cause serious damage to a news brand.

The importance of guarding that role was brought home recently to a newspaper long known as one that "comforts the afflicted, afflicts the comfortable"[1]—*The Washington Post*.

Readers expect *The Washington Post* "to look out for their interests. Investigative reporting in this community is important," according to Executive Editor Marcus Brauchli.[2]

"...The *Post* takes very seriously our watchdog role, particularly in local news. Other media derive their news from ours; we set the agenda. It carries a responsibility."

On the day Brauchli made those comments, *Politico*[3] reported that the *Post* was planning a series of so-called salons—off-the-record meetings among newsmakers, *Post* journalists—and private sponsors who would pay

$25,000 to underwrite the events. The first meeting was to be held at the home of Publisher Katharine Weymouth in late July 2009. But by having outside underwriters, the *Post* was effectively charging for access to newsroom personnel. After the disclosure and a resulting furor, the *Post* canceled the salons.

"One of the things that stuck me about the reaction was that it was very swift and came in two broad categories," said *Post* Ombudsman Andy Alexander. "First, those who hate the *Post* and mainstream media generally. Second, I got a large number of emails and calls from local and longtime readers of *The Washington Post* who were terribly hurt by this. They just couldn't believe their newspaper would contemplate something like this."[4]

In a way, readers were paying the *Post* a backhanded compliment. "It was damaging to the *Post*," Alexander said, "but in a way it was heartening to know that historically people have regarded the *Post* as their protector in terms of watchdog journalism."

Brauchli, several days later, offered a similar analysis. "It's a legitimate interpretation to say the people view the *Post* as a civic watchdog and it's certainly true in the comments we received that people were concerned that this episode could be interpreted to suggest the *Post* was slipping" in this role, he said. "We immediately retreated and concluded that it was inconsistent with our values."

The incident demonstrated forcefully the overriding importance to readers of the "looks after my civic interests" experience and the need to preserve it—not only in the newsroom but also in all parts of a news organization. "We have to be expressly attentive in a fast-changing world to the values that underpin this organization. They matter as much to our audience as they matter to our journalists. [Our watchdog role] is a central part of the *Post*'s brand and identity," Brauchli said.[5]

BEING ESSENTIAL

It's not only central to the *Post*; it's central to the experiences that drive people to newspapers and other news media. With the proliferation of vehicles for instant information, reliable or not, news organizations—particularly print newspapers—no longer can use breaking news as the key differentiator. But they can provide a value-added experience by monitoring public officials' actions, by investigating and exposing wrongdoing, and by offering solutions—all aimed to keep people coming back. In other words, to remain essential.

In fact, the "looks out for my civic interests" experience ranked second only to "A Regular Part of my Day" ("Habitual") for readership in the

Readership Institute's "Newspaper Experience Study." The study found that people consider the news media to be vital to the health of a community because they serve as a balance against the powerful. People believe in the roles of news organizations to investigate government corruption and illegal business practices—and to be a watchdog or even advocate for the community's civic interests. News organizations that can increase the Civic experience have a good chance of increasing readers and viewers.

After the *Chicago Tribune* revealed that the village of Crestwood sent drinking water contaminated with cancer-causing chemicals to residents,[6] a reader wrote: "Why do we need newspapers? Here's one reason: 'Crestwood officials cut corners and supplied residents with tainted water for two decades.' Unknowing residents drank the tainted water with toxic chemicals linked to cancer and other health problems for more than two decades. There would have been no story without the *Tribune* investigative reporting" (*Tribune* reader Eileen Hansen, Tinley Park, IL).[7]

Clearly, this reader valued the watchdog role of the news media—and believed her community would suffer without it. Her letter shows the benefit of the newspaper's decision to make watchdog journalism about its community a core mission and to explain that mission to readers.

But investigative or watchdog reporting alone isn't enough anymore. News consumers now want to participate in that experience and, in fact, to contribute to it. Smart news organizations use the strengths of their traditional platforms in combination with the latest online tools to give consumers a role in defining and creating the "looks after my civic interests" newspaper experience.

"The advent of interactive is a game-changer," said *Chicago Tribune* Editor Gerould Kern.[8]

When *Newsday* released its 2007 investigation of accidents caused by gaps between platforms and trains on the Long Island Railroad (LIRR),[9] it used its Web site to create a powerful interactive presentation—to, in effect, create a community conversation around this important issue. The site provided a forum for LIRR riders to share their stories, a map of stations so riders could check gap incidents at their stops, an interactive look at how a gap is created, and PDFs of accident reports so readers could go as deep as they wanted. The online package continues to be updated with ongoing coverage and reader comments.

In December 2008, *USA TODAY* printed a front-page investigative report outlining the impact of industrial pollution on the air outside schools across the nation, finding more than 400 schools with serious toxic chemical problems. Reporters worked with scientists at three universities to create a computer simulation to determine what sort of toxic chemicals children breathe when they go to school.

The paper ran a two-part series with extensive graphics and directions for going deeper on its Web site. Online, readers could use an interactive database to check out specific schools or areas around the country and then browse through different parts of an interactive map to learn more about the chemicals in the air at a school, including their composition and danger to humans, and to see the number of schools in areas of high chemical concentrations. Videos with stories of those affected were part of the online package. Those who wanted to get more involved could offer comments, give tips to reporters, or ask questions.[10]

Giving people more control over how and what information they read or watch resonates in research on news consumption preferences. However, they still want an authoritative voice leading the way.

"People don't want full-time crooks to be chased by part-time cops," said Tom Rosenstiel, director of the Project for Excellence in Journalism.[11] "We [citizens] have a vested interest in an independent press with traditional journalism values."

Despite the popularity of such cable shows as *Hardball with Chris Matthews*, *The O'Reilly Factor*, and *The Daily Show*, Americans prefer their news from a nonpartisan source. Two-thirds of Americans say they want news with no political point of view, according to the Pew Research Center's Biennial News Consumption Survey.

Young people in particular, who overwhelmingly prefer to go online for news, also prefer to get political and government news from Web sites that are known for their news.[12] They trust sites that are dominant in their field, that are known for something specific and stick to it.

Young or old, citizens don't trust government to look out for their best interests. According to a Pew Research Center for the People and The Press 10-year study on Americans' political values released in 2009, the U.S. public is cynical toward politics and elected officials, believing that Washington lawmakers "lose touch with the people pretty quickly."[13]

But citizens are watching. The same survey found that almost 90 percent of Americans are interested in keeping up with national affairs, about 80 percent are pretty interested in local politics, and, despite their skepticism of elected officials, most believe the issues debated in Washington affect them personally.

WHAT IS "CIVIC EXPERIENCE" JOURNALISM TODAY?

Trusted news organizations generally also are associated with strong Civic experiences. But while those news organizations can continue to play to their traditional strengths in creating Civic experiences, interactivity is a key part of the Civic experience today—the ability to be part of the experience, to contribute to it. Consumers used to TiVo, Facebook, YouTube, and Twitter expect news organizations to offer their Civic experiences using online tools and multiple platforms as well as traditional forms to allow for individualized Civic experiences.

So, creating a 21st-century Civic experience must provide outstanding public interest journalism in new ways:

- Using multiple platforms to offer audiences many entry points into the reporting and storytelling forms appropriate to the different platforms;
- Providing interactive opportunities to ask questions, offer information, help report the stories, start a dialogue, tailor information, use tools to gather data, and employ other means of participation;
- Pointing to other information sources, providing a conduit to other watchdogs, or partnering with nonpartisan organizations such as the non-profit ProPublica (founded by veteran journalists to do investigative reporting) or The Huffington Post Investigative Fund can add value and authority and enhance the civic experience. Quality collaborations don't dilute the brand.

Creating Civic experiences also is much more solution-oriented and activist than in the past. "We can't just be observers and reporters," Kern said. "We've got to be advocates for improving the life of the community.... This is up close and personal."

Finally, although producing journalism that offers the Civic experience is the goal, it is important to explicitly explain and reinforce the commitment to an audience's civic interests as part of an overall strategic plan.

The *Chicago Tribune* published a spadia—an outer wrap that covers about one-third of the front and back pages of a newspaper—titled "On Guard for Chicago" to overlay its June 14, 2009 edition. In it, Kern explained that the paper's watchdog role is part of its core mission and will be a focus of the entire newsroom; the paper has identified five key missions, with watchdog second on the list behind reporting on "the Chicago experience"—what it means to "work, play, and live in this region."

The spadia outlined recent investigations, offered online tools to help readers get information themselves, and noted an online help desk where callers can ask *Tribune* experts for aid in getting public records. The help desk is part of the paper's "Your Government in Secret" effort to push for more open records. In addition to helping readers find government records, it uses the *Tribune*'s Web site to offer a tutorial on finding documents, including a how-to on filing a Freedom of Information Act request. It also runs a database of complaints about the difficulty of getting public records.

Kern also told readers that they are part of the reporting team: "We want you to help us find stories of wrongdoing and injustice. Send your tips and ideas to watchdog@tribune.com." He introduced the three watchdog teams of reporters—government, consumer, and editorial board—with accompanying photos and emails.

In addition, whenever a *Tribune* story touches on open records issues or watchdog reporting, it now carries the label "Tribune Watchdog" to reinforce to readers that this is central to the paper every day.

"Watchdog journalism isn't just projects or investigative stories, it's a mentality, a way of thinking and a way of acting," Kern said. The spadia and the "Tribune Watchdog" icon tell readers that "this is why we are here, what we do for you, why we're valuable…. We have to stand out and make the value proposition clear."

AFFLICTING THE COMFORTABLE

Of the many investigations that news organizations have conducted over the years, most have a strong public service component. They are honored and archived in places such as The Pulitzer Prizes Web site, http://www. pulitzer.org.

The 2009 Pulitzer winner for public service was the *Las Vegas Sun* "for the exposure of the high death rate among construction workers on the Las Vegas Strip amid lax enforcement of regulations, leading to changes in policy and improved safety conditions."[14] The 2009 Pulitzer Prize for investigative reporting honored David Barstow and *The New York Times* for stories that revealed how some retired generals-cum-media analysts were deliberately used by the Pentagon to push its Iraq strategy and how many of them had undisclosed ties to defense companies that benefited from the resulting Pentagon policies.

Stories that make readers or viewers *feel* the Civic experience often have a component suggesting potential solutions to problems raised in the investigation, resulting in changes to laws or government procedures. They also routinely provide means for readers or viewers to enter into the story—through searchable databases, innovative uses of interactive techniques such as games or timelines, or even direct involvement through links to methods of activism.

In June 2009, *The News-Press* in Fort Meyers, Florida, began investigating how the hungry are fed in that community. But what the reporters uncovered was that the number of hungry had grown by tens of thousands in a year, and that, during summer, a lot of them were children who no longer were getting school lunches. The paper brought together 20 civic leaders to ask them for solutions, which resulted in a drive that raised $400,000 to feed the hungry, especially the kids.[15] The reporters had found that city agencies didn't have a means to feed the kids, but the civic leaders, including school officials, found a way to open some schools to offer meals.[16]

"Because of our leadership, kids are getting fed," Executive Editor Terry Eberle said.

KTRK-TV in Houston not only uncovered evidence of racism, secret spying on citizens, and help for donors to the sheriff's election campaign, it sued the county to stop the sheriff's policy of deleting emails after two weeks. As a result, the county revised its email policy—and the sheriff was defeated in his re-election bid.

Another TV station, WWL in New Orleans, withstood heavy political pressure as it aired more than four dozen stories on corruption in the New Orleans Affordable Homeownership program. The station found that the program paid contractors to repair homes that never received any improvements—or didn't even exist. Many of the contractors had ties to agency managers and city officials. As a result of the reporting, a federal grand jury launched an investigation, and the program was suspended.

Watching out for your audience's interests extended beyond general-interest media. Niche publications have a long history of watchdog reporting.

Aquatics International, a Hanley Wood business-to-business publication for the commercial and public swimming pool industries, used database analysis several years ago to report that "minorities make up a disproportionately large number of drownings in the United States" and explained how the aquatics industry had failed to address the problem.[17] After the stories ran, the Red Cross launched inner-city swim training efforts, and USA Swimming, a national governing body for competitive swimming, began a program to promote swimming among minority communities. The series scored the second highest number of reader emails and calls of any the magazine had run.

In addition to long-term investigations, watching out for news consumers' civic interests means just being there—bearing witness at city council meetings, zoning board hearings, school board meetings, and myriad other government doings. *The Sun* newspapers in suburban Chicago, mentioned elsewhere in this book, provided short boxes listing agendas, what actions were taken, and what would happen next.

In cash-strapped newsrooms, finding creative new ways to continue this important function—one that demonstrates a continuing commitment to looking out for civic interests—is essential. Readers and viewers have been enlisted by some organizations to help in the monitoring. *The Washington Post*, through its Loudoun County, VA, online site, LoudounExtra.com, is among those news outlets that have used citizen journalists to cover routine events. WPIX-TV in New York City enlisted journalism students as citizen reporters, providing flip video cameras to students at Stony Brook University.

This type of civic monitoring tells readers: *We're* going to cover this no matter what.

PARTICIPATING IN THE EXPERIENCE

From *The Des Moines Register's* house-by-house map chronicling the path of a tornado through Parkersburg, Iowa, and the stories of people in its path[18] to National Public Radio's covering a health care hearing by posting a photo panorama of the audience that lists all the lobbyists among the crowd,[19] media organizations are using their Web sites to augment traditional storytelling by providing information in a way that lets the audience participate in the experience.

Bicycling magazine was watching out for its readers' interests when it investigated car vs. bicycle traffic accidents and found that legal protections had failed cyclists. But it went further, offering readers a list of actions they could take—creating an effective advocacy campaign to change laws or making their communities more bike-friendly (http://www.bicycling.com/article/0,6610,s1-3-12-16637-1,00.html). Then, on its Web site, it offered forums for cyclists to share accident experiences and insights into the problem generally.

More and more, news organizations are helping readers navigate government by letting readers do the searching themselves, reinforcing the idea that the news is not just a product but also a service. One of the more exciting developments in this area is DocumentCloud (http://www.documentcloud.org), the brainchild of journalists at *ProPublica* and *The New York Times*. It will offer software and a set of open standards to make original source documents easy to find and collaboratively use anywhere on the Web. "Think of it as a card catalog for primary source documents," the Web site suggested.

However, even without this new application, news organizations have found exciting ways to show their dedication to citizens' civic interests by giving them ways to access and investigate government information. *The New York Times* created "Represent" (http://prototype.nytimes.com/represent/), an interactive feature that determines a reader's elected officials at all levels of government and gives detailed information on each one. It is similar to "Your Government" (http://gov.oregonlive.com), created by *The Oregonian* in Portland, which lets readers find their representatives in the state legislature and Congress, as well as track bills. And the site http://fili-busted.us allows users to keep track of senators in Congress who block leg-islation. It also describes the type of legislation being blocked.

The 2008 presidential campaign spawned many ways for news con-sumers to dig into the election in whatever way they wanted. PolitiFact (http://www.politifact.com) is a Pulitzer Prize-winning project of the *St. Petersburg Times* and *Congressional Quarterly* that rated candidates' state-ments on an "Obameter" and continues post-election by tracking how Barack Obama is meeting his campaign promises in the White House. It fea-tures "Promise Kept," "Compromise," "Promise Broken," "Stalled," "In the Works," and "No Action." CNN offered one of the best primers on how the various election processes worked—giving easy-to-digest information explaining campaign processes from the Iowa caucuses to the Electoral College and everything in between, demystifying an often-confusing system.

The Wichita Eagle is among the many news organizations that have taken advantage of mapping software to provide readers with more oppor-tunities to participate in their community's life. At http://www.kansas.co006D/potholes, readers can find out what shape their roads are in. They also can get information on how to get a road fixed, determine the cost of fixing it, vote on how to pay for improving roads, and see detailed informa-tion on the worst roads in the area.

The San Diego Union-Tribune began a stand-alone column in its paper encouraging readers to write in with their complaints about local infrastruc-ture and expanded it to the Web (http://www.signonsandiego.com/news/justfixit). The "Just Fix It" column promises to check out any problems for which a local or state government agency is responsible. On the Web site, it also provides a guide for "getting things done" and lists various city infra-structure projects underway, particularly related to road repairs.

One of the most innovative efforts to watch out for citizens' civic inter-ests is EveryBlock (noted in Chapter 3), which is not a site created by a news organization, although it has partnered with newspapers in some cities. It evolved from http://www.chicagocrime.org; both were created by Adrian Holovaty, a former Web leader at washingtonpost.com and co-creator of Django, an open-source framework to help build Web sites. It filters local news by location to give users information on their neighborhoods and cities, including such civic information as crimes, building permits, and restaurant inspections, news articles and blogs, and photos. Much of the information comes from public databases; the rest is generated by users.

Crime databases similar to EveryBlock have spawned operations such as New Haven Crime Log (http://www.newhavencrimelog.org/), created by local journalist Paul Bass under the auspices of a nonprofit journalism organ-ization he runs. Its audience can sort crimes by type, description, count, and date and then view incidents on a map, with even more details provided.

Interactive sites such as Rethink College Park (http://www.rethinkcol-legepark.net/blog/), which focuses on suburban development news in and around the University of Maryland community, have been copied by news organizations as a way to engage audiences in growth issues. It provides a forum for discussions about the area's growth and attendant problems, information from news stories, and a rollover map that gives background on many of the neighborhoods around the university.

CO-CREATING THE EXPERIENCE

As my colleague Ashlee Humphreys will point out in Chapter 8's explo-ration of media production, "Audience participation in the production of news has exploded in the last decade." And as colleague Rich Gordon will point out in his chapter on the Community-Connection experience (Chapter 9), "Although technologies change, what doesn't change is the value that people derive from interacting with others."

The Bakersfield Californian uses print as well as online to partner with and demonstrate its commitment to readers' civic interests. The Bakersfield Voice, an independent subsidiary, is a 70,000-circulation print publication and Web site whose content comes from community members. Its content ranges from news and opinions about city council decisions to children's sports. The Californian also created Bakotopia (http://www.bakotopia.com) to give area residents a local social networking site. Its vice president for interactive called it "a MySpace for Bakersfield."[20]

The Washington Post created a Web site separate from its main site, http://www.washingtonpost.com, called WhoRunsGov (http://www.who-runsgov.com), to enhance the Civic experience it already provides in its newspaper and on its Web site. "Our goal is to become the Web destination for business, opinion, and political leaders—as well as students, educators, and engaged citizens—looking for crucial, real-time information on the individuals who shape the policymaking process in the nation's capital," the site says. It debuted in the traditional journalistic form of reporters provid-ing information on the key figures in Washington policymaking. But it intends to become a collaboration with readers—a moderated wiki, inviting registered users to edit or add profiles and other information.

This use of the wiki form already is familiar to Post readers at reach-forthewall.com, a separate Web site operated by the Post. Its content is large-ly based on user input about youth swim teams and other swim news in the area, including stories, photos, and statistics.

Launched during the 2008 election campaign, CNN's iReport.com, a user-generated news Web site (http://www.ireport.com/), invites participants to submit a story and share it as well as rate and discuss others' stories. Software automatically puts stories with the most community activity at the top. Then, CNN takes it a step further—CNN reporters verify and expand on the best of the bunch and put them on CNN.com.

These examples of crowd-sourcing, the use of audience members or experts to create content, show the increasingly common collaboration between media operations and community members. But this is only one form of co-creation of content.

Wired magazine combined crowd-sourcing with a new technology innovation to create a unique Civic experience—and an important project in public service journalism. Through its blog (http://blog.wired.com/27 bstroke6/2007/08/vote-on-the-top.html), called "Threat Level," it asked readers to be reporters investigating Wikipedia to look for whitewashing of entries by companies or others seeking to improve their online images. The magazine used a new technology called Wikipedia Scanner to help uncover "spinning" or outright lies.

KCPT, Kansas City's public TV station, partnered with the Mid-America Regional Council and others to create the real-world equivalent of a wiki called "Imagine KC" (http://www.apts.org/stories/Imagine_KC. cfm). In October 2008, it launched a series of 45 public forums with the goal of building a more sustainable future for Kansas City. "Imagine KC" offered citizens several ways to participate—attend the forums and offer comments, watch them on KCPT or online, take political action or answer surveys. Its One KC Voice Web site (http://www.onekcvoice.org/Issues/Environ ment/ImagineKC/index.asp) provided ways to comment as well as numerous ways to take action, from planting a tree to taking the "Five Green Things" challenge.

The News-Press in Fort Myers, Florida, includes readers in content creation by asking area experts for help on stories. As part of a database-driven project analyzing differing salaries for school superintendents, the experts helped gather documents and provide context in understanding the components of a superintendent's responsibilities compared with pay.

In addition to bringing volunteer experts into the news process, news organizations can co-create content by capitalizing on outside expertise such as foundations and think tanks to maximize the Civic experience.

The Henry J. Kaiser Family Foundation has a long tradition of providing nonpartisan health policy news. During the 2008 election, its Health08.org site (http://health08.org) provided a clearinghouse for resources and information about health policy issues in the campaign. The Pulitzer Center on Crisis Reporting commissioned a site named http://www.livehopelove.com/, which uses poetry by Jamaicans as an entry-way into documentary-style coverage of HIV/AIDS on that island.

Partnering with or linking to independent online news operations is yet another way to increase a brand's own Civic experience quotient. The previously mentioned ProPublica and Talking Points Memo, a muckraking for-profit Web site focusing on government and politics, are examples of potential partners.

Partnerships also should be fostered with the growing number of entities that can help media organizations provide a hyperlocal Civic experience. West Seattle Blog (http://westseattleblog.com/), a for-profit neighborhood news service started by journalists, has covered a proposal to stimulate job growth by repealing a business tax, the filming of a movie in the neighborhood, and local city council races. It also provides lists of local government meetings. In addition to using their Web sites as portals to such hyperlocal news, news organizations then could partner with the "hyperlocals" to showcase the information on the air or in print.

Dan Gillmor, director of The Knight Center for Digital Media Entrepreneurship at Arizona State University, said he has seen a number of such local sites that have broken news of interest to a neighborhood "in ways that fit anyone's definition of journalism…. That happens all over the world in communities of geography and interest. It goes on at the granular level and is almost invisible at the wider sense. What traditional media need to do is to help people know they are there and to be a portal. [They are] covering communities that are too small for newspapers, much less TV, to pay attention to. The traditional media should see it and point to it rather than co-opt it" as another way of offering a Civic experience for readers or viewers.[21]

AUDIENCE ADVOCACY

The Post's Brauchli told newly minted columnist Bob McCartney to be "partisan in favor of Washington and the people who work here."[22]

In Florida, Eberle of *The News-Press* said: "Our first amendment watchdog role is what we tout every day. We do it through billboards, online and by example…. As a community newspaper, our role is to say we're part of this community…. Sure, we report the bad numbers on [home] foreclosures, but I'm hearing from people, 'You've got to be part of the solution because otherwise when things get good again, I may not need you.'"[23]

Using the newspaper for in-depth information to augment its Web site offerings, *The News-Press* branding effort aims to "show we're part of the community and to know what they care about." It's not enough to care about the community—whether geographic or interest-based: News outlets must state to their audience clearly and repeatedly—and loudly, via billboards, Twitter, in-house ads, and any other means possible—that this is a core mission. *The News-Press* ran a 31-part series on how to survive the economic downturn—the area has one of the highest home foreclosure rates in the country. It included numerous lists and narratives of how to save money; it was so successful that the company printed 15,000 booklets with the series' information and distributed them for free. In addition, it ran a 15-part series on 15 success stories of businesses that had survived the bad economy and what their strategies were.[24]

"People said, 'You're trying to help us,'" Eberle noted.

"It's being more responsible to the community. We're still accurate and objective, but when the community is suffering, we can't look the other way."[25]

NOTES

1. From Dunne, Finley Peter. *Observations by Mr. Dooley, Newspaper Publicity.* Quoted in Bartlett, John. (2002). *Bartlett's Familiar Quotations,* 17th ed. Boston: Little Brown, p. 646.
2. Interview with Brauchli, M. (2009, July 20).
3. Allen, M., & Calderone, M. (2009, July 2). Washington Post *cancels lobbyist event amid uproar.* Politico.com
4. Interview with Alexander, A. (2009, July 30).
5. Interview with Brauchli, M. (2009, July 30).
6. Hawthorne, M. (2009, April 19). Crestwood officials cut corners and supplied residents with tainted water for 2 decades. *Chicago Tribune.*
7. Staff. (2009, June 14). Investigations with impact. *Chicago Tribune.*
8. Interview with Kern, G. (2009, June 30).
9. Maloney, J., & Shuster, K. (2007, January 19). Thirty years of neglect. *Newsday.* Updated package available at http://www.newsday.com/long-island/transportation/lirr/investigating-the-gap-1.1269849
10. Morrison, B., Heath, B., & Reed, D. (2008, December 30). Retrieved from http://www.smokestack.usatoday.com/
11. Interview with Rosenstiel, T. (2009, June 29).
12. From too much to "just right": Engaging millennials in election news on the web. (2008). Media Management Center.
13. Independents take center stage in Obama era. (2009, May 21). Retrieved from http://people-press.org/report/?pageid=1523
14. Retrieved from http://www.pulitzer.org/citation/2009-Public-Service
15. Interview with Eberle, T. (2009, July 30).
16. Breitenstein, D. (2009, June 21). Turnout for hungry in Fort Myers astounds charities. *The News-Press* (Fort Myers, FL). Retrieved from http://pqasb.pq archiver.com/news_press/access/1754354681.html?FMT=ABS&date=Jun+21,+2009
17. Retrieved from http://www.aquaticsintl.com/2005/oct/0510_minority.html, http://www.aquaticsintl.com/2005/nov/0511_reaching.html
18. Retrieved from http://data.desmoinesregister.com/parkersburg/parkersburg.php

19. Retrieved from http://www.npr.org/news/specials/2009/hearing-pano/

20. Fulton, M. L., in Williams, L., with Gillmor, D., & MacKay, J. (2007, March 5). *Frontiers of innovation in community engagement: News organizations forge new relationships with communities.* Center for Citizen Media.

21. Interview with Gillmor, D. (2009, July 13).

22. Interview with Brauchli, M. (2009, July 30).

23. Interview with Eberle, T. (2009, July 30).

24. Staff. (2009, May 1–31). The road to recovery. *News-Press.*

25. Interview with Eberle, T. (2009, July 30).

5

THE UTILITARIAN EXPERIENCE

Abe Peck

- I learn about things to do or places to go in this newspaper.
- This Web site gives good tips and advice.
- It shows me how to do things the right way.
- I get good ideas from this magazine.
- I learn how to improve myself from this TV program.
- It helps me make up my mind and make decisions.
- This magazine provides a lot of how-to information.

Utility is the Ed Asner of experiences. No Redford looks a la *All the President's Men*. No brooding Al Pacino as with *The Insider*. No Albert Brooks yoks like those found in *Broadcast News*.

But as Asner ran newsrooms as crusty Lou Grant, often as the boss of the more comely Mary Tyler Moore, utility can be the backbone of experiences, either as a standalone or in concert with other motivators. And now, search, lead generation, relational databases, applications, and the like are maximizing the power of utility.

Think about it: The typical Sunday paper provides the news, analysis, and opinion needed to inform (if too rarely challenge) citizens. But it also notes where that hit movie is playing, how to maximize the weekend, how to cook that special meal. In fact, an alternative theory of newspaper history might say that dailies missed the boat by not offering more utility information. In Chicago, for example, would the *Sun-Times* be in at least slightly better shape if it had concentrated on personal finance instead of chasing the *Tribune*'s big-business approach or *Crain's Chicago Business*' targeted coverage, with too few people manning too few pages? Would the *Reader*, the main alternative paper, have been able to block the service-oriented *Time Out Chicago* from launching in town if it had provided more where-to-go editorial beyond its indisputably valuable listings (which in turn were cannibalized by Craigslist)? It might be déclassé, but what if some of today's troubled papers justified their price by noting that they offer hundreds of dollars in utilitarian coupon savings?

Many consumer periodicals have long understood the value of "This magazine provides a lot of how-to information." DIYers can learn how to build everything up to a nuclear sub, while auto club titles provide the nuts and bolts needed for no-fuss travel. Even in these down times, titles from *Every Day with Rachael Ray* to the venerable *Better Homes and Gardens* succeed by offering readers solutions amid a sense of community. *Better Homes* also has produced numerous Special Interest Publications (SIPs) that provide information for upgrading every cranny in a home this side of a crawl space or an outhouse—by now, there may be one for *The People Under the Stairs*.

The Utilitarian experience provides a floor for audience members and creators to meet over other experiences. Aficionados seemingly come to *Martha Stewart Living* predisposed to turn two napkins and a chopstick into service for sixteen even as the package is embossed with the Timeout (Chapter 11), Entertainment and Diversion (Chapter 12), and Talk About and Share (Chapter 14) experiences. Similarly, the brand circle that is Food Network can be found on TV and in print. As Ben Sylvan points out in Chapter 15, that network began by maximizing its utilitarian aspect, and then took off when it added feel-good, camaraderie, and social connections to its own recipe for success.

Utility-seekers share the remote in the broadcast spectrum, especially in the proliferating world of vertical-market cable and dish content. On the typical mid-afternoon that I write these words, utilitarian shows include: *Lose Weight with Hypnosis, Rock Hard Abs!, Slim in 6 Weeks, Best Indoor Grill, Scrapbooking Made Easy, Relieve Back Pain, Designer and Vintage Jewelry*, and the house/garden rehab show with my favorite name: *King of Dirt*—you get the idea even though I'm quitting one-third of the way through the scroll. Some of this array may be infomercial, but the landscape is rife with tips and techniques, tape measures, and tablespoons—as well as the more outré measurements of *Shop Erotic*. Entire networks and a Google's worth of online sites allow viewers and visitors to purchase just about anything under the economic sun.

Although valuable thought-leadership editorial is found in business-to-business (B2B) titles from *Aviation Week & Space Technology* to *Pharmaceutical Technology*, B2B information is rooted in utility. Product listings or product searches, diagrams for highway reconstruction, and online calculators join more traditional journalism in service of an industry or profession. In 2009, when *Heavy Duty Trucking* won American Business Media's Grand Neal for best-of-the-best execution in B2B journalism, the package included both overview material about dealing with the gas-price crisis and specific tips on how even experienced drivers could maximize their mileage.

What follows explores time-tested and new notions of the Utilitarian experience, and how "It helps me [and thee] make up my mind and make decisions." Because utilitarianism is so pragmatic, I differ from some of my colleagues and prescribe various ways to bring utility to the fore rather than waiting for the end of the chapter to do so. I touch on the concepts of: targeted content and editorial level; life cycles and business cycles; search, lead generation, and comparability for buying decisions; the realm of social networking; and the apertures when audience members most want information.

UTILITY IN TRADITIONAL AND EVOLVING MEDIA

Even with shrunken editorial wells, it's not too late for mainstream media to ramp up utility and thus brand loyalty.

At the baseline, multiple events listings and calendars across platforms can fulfill the "I learn about things to do or places to go in this newspaper" sub-value. But understanding the sophistication (or lack of same) of a particular audience should suggest the editorial level at which particular information can be best provided. Utilitarian material with local angles—perhaps in print on Sunday, with interactive and video elements online—can allow outdoor types, basement boys, and cross-stitchers alike to learn "...how to do things the right way" and leave those users feeling that "...it gives good tips and advice."

For example, enough gustatory happenings occur in my foodie town for the *Santa Barbara News-Press* to offer a "Culinary Calendar." And residents in a literate city may look for its "Reading 101," a syndicated pickup about children's literature, as well as a list of more erudite "Literary Events." As the audience's financial dilemmas continued, one Sunday edition addressed reader concerns with a budget-birthday story from the McClatchy News Service and with "Dave Says," a syndicated Q&A on high car payments.[1]

A few blocks away, the *Santa Barbara Independent*, a weekly print alternative with an ungated Web site, punctuates its "Living" section with listings and "4-1-1" recommendations, "The Week Spot," and an online weekly sports "highlight schedule" and arts exclusives (disclosure—I write occasionally for the *Independent*).

Meanwhile, *Santa Barbara Magazine*, *Edible Santa Barbara* ("Celebrating the Food Culture of Santa Barbara County"), and *Destination Wine Country* provide local utilitarian information in attractive, nichier packages.

Other media also can bond with audiences over utilitarian concerns. Branded, non-schlock cable shows demonstrate how "You learn how to improve yourself from this TV program," while Station on Your Side-type solutions and Web links/alliances to useful material can earn brand credibility.

Consumer magazines beyond traditional service and shelter titles customize how they incorporate Utilitarian experiences to satisfy the audience sub-experience "I get good ideas from this magazine." Magazine editors use both their gut and extensive audience research to determine what their audiences feel is the "lot" in "This magazine provides a lot of how-to information." *Real Simple* initially was criticized by some (not me) for dumbing down the interactions of busy, smart women; more recently, executive women in India, Hong Kong, and China have snatched copies away from me, sensing a glossy ally in managing their complex lives.

Utilisima.com, a South American Web site and cable channel, is structured around key audience interests. It carries video coverage of handicrafts, cooking, pictures, decorative cakes, and the like. Closer to home, *Condé Nast Traveler* is tony and up-market while aware of recessionary times, and its mission to provide "Truth in Travel" involves a utilitarian component alongside its timeout and status lushness. A visit to concierge.com/cntraveler.com found a roster of use-oriented stories, among them "Deal of the Day," "The Insider" city guide, "The Ombudsman" consumer advocate, "Tipping Guide Worldwide," and "Islands on Sale."

The *Nast* site also exemplifies an increasingly powerful aspect of utilitarianism: audience members sharing tips and advice in near-real time. They trade information and opinions on pages, sections, or entire sites that resonate with the topic. The myconcierge.com "travel community," for example, provides space for tips, reviews, photo sharing, and the visitor's own Trip Plan.

As educator, welcome mat, or advisor, utility can draw in new readers, viewers, or visitors. Medill colleague (and my former student) Ibrahim Abusharif grew up on the South Side of Chicago of Palestinian parentage. Abe, who now teaches at Medill's campus in Qatar, recently recalled the "special place in my early life" that *Reader's Digest* occupied. "It was the sole magazine subscription my father ordered. He learned so much English from reading it, along with broadcast news. I have very early…recollections thumbing through it to read those short quips, gag lines, and quotes. That's when I first learned to read. Those memories are important to me, especially of my father reading *RD*, moving his lips in the process."[2]

That was years ago. But today, metro areas marked by growing immigration can offer advice on acclimatization (school registration, driver's licenses, health, etc.) without backlash-provoking advocacy. More up-market venues can provide similar material to transfers and retirees.

On the "Living Here" section of its Web site, the *Pocono Record* of Stroudsburg, Pennsylvania, maintains a "Pocono FAQs" section with categorized answers to nitty-gritty questions that newcomers (and maybe even longtime residents) have. It grew out of the realization that, despite its distance from New York City, the Poconos area was becoming a bedroom community for Manhattanites looking for cheaper housing and quieter living. It offers all kinds of detail, from, "Why doesn't my street address match my mailing address?" to "Can I burn leaves in my yard?" to "Who picks up my garbage?" as well as material about local government.[3] In Lawrence, Kansas, parents can chart their kids' participation in youth sports via the *Journal-World's* "game" site, which includes interactive maps of team contests.[4]

PRODUCTS AND PRODUCT SEARCH

Those of a certain age remember when nearly all business-to-business magazines carried "bingo cards," hard-paper-stock mailers on which potential buyers circled numbers and received product/supplier information in the mail after a while. Now searchability links buyers and sellers in near-instantaneous communications.

The goals of these transactions are lead generation and, as a result of delivering that effectively, audience loyalty. "The digital subsection, lead generation," Bob Carrigan, CEO of major B2B company International Data Group USA, told *Magazine World*, "accounts for 40% of all digital revenue in the U.S."[5] Talk about the value of "It helps me make up my mind and make decisions!" The material found, as the mantra goes, needs to be compelling, relevant, deep, and hard to duplicate. But audiences also want seamless access. A site that doesn't load quickly is a site abandoned, and a Harley dealer who finds parts only for Yamaha products may not try again. He will be far happier if he encounters a deep roster of desirable products, products with like attributes, most popular products, and products from a favored manufacturer. These days, he also may look for peer feedback.

My reviews of client sites have unearthed all sorts of issues, from content management glitches to such "doh" stuff as search boxes being really hard to find on the home page. Sites must align market segments and data/product availability with the keyword language favored by relevant users, yet some staffers haven't ascertained and tested the audience's vocabulary and thought processes. This needs to become part of media literacy.

"Pushing" rather than engaging audience experiences can be counter-productive in gaining leads that convert to orders. Marketers and salespersons can obsess over quarterly goals instead of achieving them by ascertaining where buyers are in their purchasing decision cycle, by "qualifying" key prospects, thus making the process cost-effective. Sales and marketing staff that truly know customer thinking can create a lead-scoring system and ramp up "the propensity to buy."[6]

By now you may be saying, "Well, this is important, but it sure sounds dutiful." But utility can be fun. Judging an editorial contest for the Lebhar-Friedman portfolio of retail and medical titles, I came across an entry in the "Best Video/Photography" category. Produced for *Home Channel News TV* (FYI, a "home channel," is a DIY store, not a television station), it was called "New Product Juggling" and featured editor Ken Clark noting the attributes of an LED light, a hand moistener, and a small sander—and then literally juggling the products. Sounds silly, but it was informative, it kept my interest, I laughed out loud, and I'd watch the next one even though I'm not even in that business.[7]

DATA AND COMPARABILITY

I don't spend a fortune on cars, but I do buy them new. And while I've never purchased a vehicle online, edmunds.com has served me well in choosing the last four I've bought. For me, edmunds.com embodies the sub-experience "This Web site gives good tips and advice." It can display up to five models simultaneously, pricing information provides benchmarks, and dealer search within a user-defined radius has allowed me to learn what's in stock and how much it should cost before going through the root canal of negotiation. Out-linking to traditional media that rate and review autos provides trusted evaluation. For me, edmunds.com has outflanked the newspapers.

The ability to digitally aggregate data has been truly revolutionary, and one consequence of the rise of data has been the opportunity for small niches to make smart choices. Cosmetic surgeons, for example, can access the "Laser Hook-Up" tool on the modernmedicine.com portal and then plug in the variables of "maximum cost," "time," "number of treatments," "ROI," "treatable skin types," and other parameters. Suggestions quickly appear.

Even financial data can provide a fun experience. Take mint.com, "the best free way to manage your money." This Webby Award-winning site draws in your financial credits and debits and provides weekly summaries. Newbies and the financially averse will especially appreciate such features as advisories on personal credit spikes and cash flow spurts, all rendered in reassuring pastel charts and "mint-y" phrasing. As *The New York Times*

Magazine sub-headed: "Mint.com transforms personal finance from an onerous task into a fun diversion."[8]

Still, for publishers, comparability raises issues of protection versus openness. Truthful and/or cantankerous information sources (no longer just journalists) may provide valuable input—that sends advertisers rushing to the exits. Yet sites need traffic—and a sense that the users are partners in something valuable to them—to support a cost-per-click business model. User-generated evaluations can provide plausible deniability (ignoring for the moment rowdy raters and interested parties gaming the system). Issues surrounding the level of management to put against such content are discussed further in the chapters on Co-Producing (8) and Community-Connection (9) experiences.

UTILITARIAN APERTURES

Every editor—and advertising department—tries to match up to basic reader experiences: vacations, back to school, holidays. But empowered audiences that now can engage 24/7 require deep understanding of their "interactive-niche lifestyles."

Meet Dr. Jones. Actually, this dentist can't really fix a filling; he's a prototypical DDS that Advanstar Dental Media—a division of the large cross-platform B2B publisher—created to show when practitioners are most likely to want versions of the company's information and when they are most ready to receive it. The evolution of this story-telling device matches up well with the argument of this book. Initially, Dr. Jones' Day in the Life was a sales tool. Then, two editorial retreats shifted the balance to center on what I call the practitioners' "professional biorhythms," matching cross-platform story ideas and formats to them. The key development was that the presentation moved from the company's convenience to when dentists themselves were most likely to want particular content and sales solutions.

Other health care media have isolated particular needs. Uptodate.com provides physicians with abstracts of the latest research across specialties, allowing doctors to save time by having their staff order only those full peer reviews that they find of key interest. Prescription services also can save doctors' time and allow them to enter the coming world of electronic medical records (perhaps with growing pains around some providers' demands for exclusivity, smoothness of delivery, and the time it takes to enter data).

Digital media allow for an "ever-presence" that, while costly, can bond audience and content providers. Knowing recipients' work schedules can place e-newsletters into inboxes at times that maximize usefulness and lift open rates. Similarly, virtual trade shows may lack on-site schmoozing but can allow for targeted, anytime exposure to products and information; companies with sufficient resources and/or partners may well move toward a "360-degree, 365-day" strategy of touch-point engagement.

Consequently, calendar-driven stories that have been editorial staples now can take on three-dimensional life. Runnersworld.com offers a useful "SmartCoach" calculator that can "Create a personalized training plan." The more general-interest but local *New York Times* honed in on the "life cycle" aperture of the 2009 New York Marathon with "Run Well," a Web application that *The New York Observer* reported "allows users to compare marathon training programs, customize their running regime, track their mileage, and access other relevant content from the Well blog and NYTimes.com. It's kind of [a] home page for *Times* readers in marathon training."[9]

MESSAGE BOARDS, SOCIAL NETWORKING, APPLICATIONS, AND UTILITY

Craigslist and Angie's List, China's Baidu and AutoPro Workshop at workshop.search-autoparts.com—a world of social networking is dedicated to matching people with boxes with people who are moving, people who want to remodel and tradespersons who won't rip them off, and people with specialties who can share tips and techniques (or just blow off steam).

Some message boards are fairly pure-play, others are moderated, and some offer utility tied to exclusivity. Veterinary Information Network (VIN) is a paid, password-protected site that allows veterinarians to speak freely away from clients, hear from experts, and share, learn from, and contribute to numerous threads. The result is worth hundreds of dollars a year to them.

Social networking offers many experiences, and the Utilitarian one is among them. Sites that were solely sales tools—think Amazon.com—added people-who-like-this-like-that recommendations to create loyalty and community, and thus increase sales. As with other media, the iPhone combines Utilitarian and other experiences. Apple now hypes the chance to "discover tens of thousands of apps that let you do even more with your iPhone." Some are found under vertical categories and "staff picks," but the explosion of iPhone applications is equally a viral, long-tail phenomenon. That's why Apple has a "Developing Apps for iPhone" spot on its site, with a video, and a second button in which the normally proprietary company proclaims "Get everything you need to create the next great iPhone app."[10]

The advent and success of the iPad only has enlarged the world of apps and allowed for the introduction of "tablet magazines," such as that from *Wired*. As of June 2010, thousands of apps had been specifically designed for the iPad, which also could run "almost all" of the 150,000 iPhone and iPod touch apps available as of that date.

What does this have to do with experiences? Well, one of my 20-something sons has an iPhone, but in his household it is known as "Doug's I'm-right machine." As fast as thumbs can fly, Doug becomes, for example, 1 of 26 million to visit yelp.com within the past 30 days (as of December 2009), locates and assesses a restaurant using 1 or more of the 7 million reviews that have populated the site since it started in 2004, and forwards the choice to friends, fully loaded with address, map, menu, and reviews. Now he can use a new Yelp trick: an "augmented reality" that overlays links to Yelp reviews on the iPhone screen when the phone's camera lens is aimed at a streetscape.[11] All this is utilitarian—but it also fits fluidly into Doug's on-the-fly social circle, making him both smarter and a maven-like hub of community connection, to name just two of the experiences discussed in this book.

Evidently, we ain't seen nothin' yet: Nokia is developing a mobile app that, as *The Economist* put it, "lets you point your phone at a film poster in order to call up local viewing times and book tickets...." And Nokia is working on an app that will "let people hold up their handsets to see the locations and statuses of their friends."[12]

THE CONTINUING POWER OF UTILITY

As my friend Abe's father, Naseem Abusharif, knew, *Reader's Digest* provided a classic example of the value of utility for both readers and publishers. Launched in 1922, it became a multimillion-circulation title by capturing the core values of a certain America—but also because readers rallied to an article-a-day formula that condensed stories to fit into busy lives and keep readers informed about a rapidly changing world. It also provided such self-improvement elements as "Word Power."

Now, nearly 90 years after its founding, the title seeks to overcome financial uncertainty by updating prescriptive approaches into "Travel Deals," "Grill Healthy," "Cut Your Home Costs," and, for the numerically fearful homeowner, both "10 Things Your Home Remodeler Won't Tell You" and "9 More Things Your Contractor Won't Tell You."[13]

As with other audience experiences, utility is not a panacea. Whether stock tables that are now obsolete in newspapers or obsolescent online apps, utility material needs to be re-evaluated over time. Again, is the information differentiated, compelling, relevant, and/or hard to duplicate, either because of content, format, accessibility, or degree of difficulty and cost? Just how much innovation can be carried and afforded?

But push back from the table (perhaps one you built using DIY utility media). Understand and engage the DNA of your audience even as you seek to provide it with information it didn't even know it wanted and needed. Walk the proverbial mile in the audience's shoes so you know how, why, and when it accesses information. Customize utility for the specific circumstances of your region, niche, or market. Provide the proper editorial level, slightly ahead of the core audience, so it is neither baffled nor bored. Partner with said audience's creative abilities.

Whether you offer it as a standalone or skillfully mesh it with other experiences, utility can be a powerful arrow in your experiential quiver.

NOTES

1. *Santa Barbara News-Press.* (2009, August 2).
2. Abusharif, I. Email. (2009, August 18).
3. Retrieved from http://www.poconorecord.com/apps/pbcs.dll/section?category=LIVING01
4. Retrieved from http://www.ljworld.com/news/sports/game/
5. Carrigan, B. (2008, Q4). Lead generation is the key focus. *Magazine World*, p. 12.
6. The statements about goals, lead scoring, and the decision cycle were informed by Improving B2B marketing and sales alliance: Lessons from the field. (2009, September 10). A webinar featuring Adam Needles of Silverpop, Jay Hidalgo of the Annuitas Group, and Ellis Booker of *B2B Magazine.*
7. Retrieved from http://homechannelnews.com/hcntv/NewProductJuggling.html
8. Heffernan, V. (2009, May 24). The medium. *The New York Times Magazine*, p. 18.
9. Reagan, G. (2009, July 13). Running on appy! *Times* connects with marathoners thanks to interactive crew. *The New York Observer*, p. 10.
10. Retrieved from http://www.apple.com/search/?q=apps&sec=global
11. Usage statistics retrieved from http://www.yelp.com/about
12. Unbylined. (2009, September 5). Information from social networks can be overlaid on the real world. *The Economist*, Technology quarterly, p. 21.
13. Retrieved from http://www.rd.com (2009, September 10).

6

THE INSPIRATION EXPERIENCE

Charles Whitaker

- It makes me feel like I can do important things in my life.
- Reading it makes me want to match what others have done.
- It inspires me in my own life.
- Reading this magazine makes me feel good about myself.

> "I'm watchin' sis go pitterpat. Said, 'I can do that! I can do that!'"
> —Edward Kleban, lyricist, *A Chorus Line*

Just as the young man in *A Chorus Line* was stirred by his sister's early, albeit clumsy, effort at tap dancing, so, too, are the audiences for many magazines, Web sites, and television shows moved to take on—if only in their minds—the ideas and activities they encounter on their favorites' pages and screens.

Inspiration—it is the essence of many successful media ventures. It was encoded in their editorial DNA at conception and remains the force that hooks readers and keeps viewers coming back. For some media brands—*Real Simple*, for example—inspiration is about captivating an audience with content that compels them to act and think in life-changing ways. Other properties, like the stable within Martha Stewart Living Omnimedia, take a more aspirational approach. For them, inspiration is as much about being part of a "community that celebrates the art of creative living"[1] than actually being creative.

Whether it's *Better Homes and Gardens'* "I Did It!" column, with its soft-sell approach to domestic enhancement, or *Men's Health*'s "Belly Off! Club," with its monthly challenge to chisel rock-hard abs, "inspirational media" engage and convince those who fall under their spell that they can accomplish all the feats the editors and producers lay before them. That many of those readers, viewers, and Web site visitors may never actually play out those editorial fantasies is beside the point. Inspiration is all about presenting ideas that *seem* possible—getting that reader to say:

"Hey, I can do that!"

"O" SO OPRAH

No media properties embody inspiration quite like those marked with megastar Oprah Winfrey's brand. From the debut of her nationally syndicated television show in 1986 to the launch of her eponymous magazine, *O, The Oprah Magazine*, in 2000, and with the Web site that bridges the two, Winfrey has tapped into the hopes and dreams of her largely female audience.

In every medium, the raison d'être of the Winfrey properties is to inspire Oprah devotees to seize control of their lives so, as one of the Inspiration sub-experiences puts it, "It makes me feel like I can do important things in my life." The tag line of the Winfrey brand—"Live Your Best Life"—is a clarion call for them to emulate their heroine, whose well-chronicled triumphs over a number of adversities (including poverty, sexual abuse, and weight) are an inspiration to all who worship at her multi-media altar.

Winfrey, with her personal commitment to helping her followers find inner strength, urges her audience to plumb the reservoir of resilience that she has mined to become an international icon. Declarations such as "You're stronger than you know" and "Find the diet that fits your life" practically scream from the magazine's cover, inviting readers to sample self-help Oprah style. The not-so-subtle message of each story is: "Oprah did it, so can you!" Undergirding that message is the fact that Winfrey—stylish, coiffed, but ever the accessible superstar—appears on every cover, alone except for when she invites other first name-sufficient women—Michelle or Ellen—to share the winner's circle. In print, online, and during her daily chatfest, Winfrey shares intimate details about her life laced with hefty doses of advice.

Yet the success of the Oprah brand rests on more than the cult of personality. Each story in *O*—whether it is a short front-of-the-book blurb or a feature on the celebrated women who've made the *O* "Power List"—and every segment on her television show offers a blueprint for a life-changing transformation. "Forget the idea that being powerful is about how rich or 'important' you are," Oprah declares in one of the columns that opens every issue of *O*. "What I find powerful is a person with grace, with courage, with the confidence to be her own self and to make things happen."[2]

The advice is always simple and rendered in plain-speak:

"Ignorance is not bliss where money is concerned," warns Winfrey pal and financial guru Suze Orman in her advice column.[3]

"You should love somebody not because you 'should,' but because he 'deserves it,'" cautions Dr. Phil McGraw, another of Winfrey's confederates.[4]

Product pages splattered with some of Winfrey's "favorite things" (shoes, purses, belts, jewelry) and television segments devoted to makeovers (in one, Winfrey and Adam Glassman, *O* magazine's creative director, announce that "every woman needs a pretty sneaker!")[5] contribute to the notion that, with a few key purchases and actions, you too can be like Oprah. So what if it's just an illusion. For the readers of *O*, anything endorsed by their idol nudges them that much closer to greatness.

And that's an inspiration.

THE INSPIRING WORLD
OF HEALTH AND FITNESS

Inspiration (along with the Utilitarian experience) is the hallmark of the health and fitness category of media properties. Although tentative newcomers may approach these magazines, books, and sites cautiously, once they get up close they are often sucked in by the editorial entreaties to hike, bike, run, and shed pounds. That's particularly true of the properties produced by Rodale, the Emmaus, Pennsylvania-based publishing empire that is home to titles such as *Runner's World*, *Men's Health*, *Women's Health*, *Running Times*, *Bicycling*, and *Mountain Bike*. Rodale properties exist to inspire their audiences of health enthusiasts to stay committed to their workout goals and thus to help them explore "the relationship between how we grow our food, what we eat, and our personal health" that has been the company's brand promise since its founding in 1930."[6] Replete with "metoo" stories about former fatties—both celebrities and common Joes and Janes—who changed their binging ways and climbed aboard the health bandwagon, the Rodale vehicles help couch potatoes see their way to becoming fit, fleet, and healthy.

> Our entire focus is on inspiring the readers of our magazine and the visitors to our Web site to get the most out of their running experience, whether they're beginners or seasoned marathoners. We're not about guilt or obligation. We're about the joy of running—and yeah, inspiration.[7]

***Runner's World*'s merry marathoners.** Although the cover of *Runner's World*'s print magazine always features an impressively toned (usually shirt-less) runner of some repute, the cover lines invite novices to peek inside with suggestions such as "Run (And Enjoy) Your First Race."[8] Once inside, the reader is encouraged to join a community where runners of all stripes congregate. No matter what your fitness level or experience, *Runner's World* welcomes you with a tone that suggests you belong and inspires you to join its band of merry marathoners.

It accomplishes this with a raft of tips on everything from correct running form to proper nutrition, as well as comprehensive shoe reviews that are must-reads and speak to the authority this book commands. But the inspiration also comes from *Runner's World*'s overarching ethos, a contention that running is more than a diversion: It's a way of life. Sections such as "Desk Inspiration" provide readers with motivational tips and words of encouragement to help them find balance on and off the track. ("Post a picture of yourself from a race where you PRed to remind yourself what you're capable of.") Departments such as "The Newbie Chronicles" offer funny first-person accounts to show readers they're not the only maladroit would-be marathoners on the road. ("I bent my face up like Clint Eastwood in order to mask the pain. A Clint Eastwood face makes you look fierce, but you really can't see much. As the car passed, I ran into an overhanging branch that tore across both eyelids."[9])

At its core, *Runner's World* has one aim: to motivate runners at every level to push for more endurance, better times, and longer distances. Although level-specific recommendations engage both beginners and veteran runners, it is not just the utilitarian features that have made this book the bible of running. It's the fact that *Runner's World* conveys a "You can do it" spirit that makes running a marathon seem like an accessible goal for anyone with the desire to train.

"The thing about running is it's a club you think everyone should join," Editor-in-Chief David Willey said. "Runners are like the ultimate proselytes."[10]

Online, *Runner's World* ramps up the inspiration with personal stories and video diaries from runners of various fitness levels as they prepare for marathon season (these include some member-participants from the editorial staff). Whether online or in print, one comes away from the *Runner's World* experience with a sense that: "We're all in this together, so let's train for the next big race!"

***Men's Health*: Abs-solutely fabulous.** The brand that convinced skeptics in the publishing world that guys really will read a "lifestyle" magazine, *Men's Health*, another Rodale property, was created to inspire 20-something Average Joes to put down the six-packs in their refrigerators and work on the ones in their abs. Although its mounds of recipes, workout spreads, and sex tips are essentially utilitarian, its "Tons of Useful Stuff"—as its tagline brags—includes heaps of anecdotes from readers who have shed pounds and shaped up. The "Belly Off! Club," as one of *Men's Health's* most popular online and print features, is the perfect example. Online, Menshealth.com allows visitors to tailor a weight-loss plan using the success stories of members of the "club" as examples. This exemplifies the "Reading it makes me want to match what others have done" sub-experience.

Videos show the correct exercise form. A searchable database of restaurants points the way to low-cal options in your favorite fast-food joints. And a downloadable calendar enables new club members to record their progress. In print, reformed foodaholics chart their paths to flatter midsections in short, confessional pieces that illustrate how their full-body transformations were accomplished. The rehabilitated heavyweights never sugarcoat the difficulty of changing their chubby ways. ("Even knowing the health risks of obesity, I couldn't motivate myself to change," writes a former 300-pound, 23-year-old professional circus clown.[11]) Still, their stories of struggle and streamlining are a huge source of inspiration to others looking for the stimulus to start their own fitness campaigns.

Seeing the success of "someone who looks like me" is a key to the inspirational appeal of many media properties, and *Men's Health* taps into this wonderfully with the "Belly Off!" brand, which the company has spun into successful books and videos.

Backpacker: **Exhilarating expeditions.** With postcard-pretty photography and personal stories of hikers ambling through breathtakingly beautiful and often remote locales, *Backpacker* magazine—once a Rodale property, now a part of Active Interest Media—inspires its audience of outdoorsmen and women to hit the trails with gusto.

Yes, there's gear galore in this very practical magazine and loads of trip planners to help would-be hikers plot their journeys, but inspiration comes in the form of its colorful spreads of bucolic paths and the stirring accounts of exhilarating expeditions undertaken by the backpackers solicited to compose its narrative features.

> Fritz and I kept climbing. Flakes of schist, weakened by the freeze-thaw cycle, peeled off in our hands. We followed what we thought was a deer path. Then I took a closer look at the poop.
>
> "Um, Fritz, I think this is bighorn sheep territory," I said. I glanced at my altimeter. We were 400 feet above the river.[12]

Like the best travel magazines, *Backpacker* inspires readers by taking them on vivid treks through the most scenic parks and paths on the planet. It captures the thrill, tranquility, and splendor of being outdoors. It literally, as its tagline states, puts "The Outdoors at Your Doorstep" and encourages backpackers and would-be backpackers to take in the beauty of traipsing the trails.

MARTHA STEWART LIVING:
INSPIRATION THROUGH ASPIRATION

Martha Stewart makes being the perfect homemaker and hostess seem to be within the reach of every woman. Even if it's not very likely that her followers will ever attempt to re-cane an antique bentwood rocker or stuff their own kielbasa, Stewart convinces aspiring domestic goddesses that, with a little effort and inspiration, they most certainly could.

The success of the Stewart properties—the magazine, books, and television shows—lies in the steely authority that Stewart wields. Let's face it: Personalities such as Stewart, cooking everywoman Rachael Ray, and hunky handyman Ty Pennington are sources of inspiration. We admire them and want to be like them, even if we're a klutz in the kitchen or a menace with a nail gun. So, while the women in Martha Stewart's audience may never have given a thought to sewing their own duvet covers or weaving their own placemats, watching the patrician Stewart adroitly tackle these projects is motivation enough to at least consider the possibilities.

There's also the novelty and exquisite styling of the ideas that Stewart and her staff come up with. Of course few people really have the time, energy, or inclination to decoupage their light switch plates with the candy wrappers culled from their kids' leftover Halloween haul,[13] but discovering this cute, kitschy craft on Martha Stewart.com makes a visitor to the site say, "Yeah, one of these days I'm going to try that." Videos of Stewart in full craft or baking mode as well as searchable databases of recipes, decorating tips, and the dos and don'ts of wedding planning make MSL Omnimedia the ultimate "laboratory of ideas"[14] for aspiring Marthas.

Stewart's endorsement of these sometimes over-the-top "good things" and the pluck she displays when demonstrating how to pull them off inspire her audience to want to be like Martha, even if they know they really can't.

"I DID IT!" THE CAN-DO SPIRIT
OF WOMEN'S SERVICE MAGAZINES

In many ways, traditional women's service magazines are the anti-Martha vehicles. While Stewart promotes the notion that, with a bit of effort, expert woodworking and nouvelle cuisine are well within her followers' talents, properties such as *Ladies' Home Journal, Better Homes and Gardens, Good Housekeeping*, and *Real Simple* espouse a philosophy designed to calm the frazzled nerves of these busy women.

Within their pages and on their Web sites, wives, mothers, and professional women share their secrets to conquering the vicissitudes of everyday life. They inspire through tales and triumphs harvested from their own experiences:

> Perhaps the greatest lesson of our experiment was realizing that the act of buying things, exciting as it can be at times, is rarely as nice as the alternatives. Having time free of shopping is empowering."[15]

> It may be that a truly disciplined person gets up and goes directly to work, but I've accepted that I'm not that kind of person. So after the kids go to school, I give myself an hour each morning to head down to the coffee shop and gossip.[16]

It is the confessional tone that gives these magazines and companion sites their everywoman appeal. Who among us hasn't shopped or gossiped too much? Yet the authors and editors allow us in on their secrets, inspiring us to take life—whether in the form of our credit cards or our penchant for prying into others' affairs—into our own hands. It is the antidote to the Martha Stewart aspirational model. Here, inspiration is accessible, taking the form of everyday accomplishments that are well within reach.

EBONY MAGAZINE: ONCE BLACK AMERICA'S INSPIRATIONAL BLUEPRINT

When he launched *Ebony* magazine in 1945, then 27-year-old entrepreneur John H. Johnson envisioned a picture book—modeled on Henry Luce's *Life* magazine—that would chronicle the under-reported accomplishments of black Americans and serve as a blueprint to inspire youngsters to emulate those successes.

"At that time, you didn't read anything about black doctors or lawyers or artists," Johnson wrote in his 1989 autobiography, *Succeeding Against the Odds*. "They were there, but the white press ignored them. I wanted to show that these people were out there, while also showing black boys and girls how they could be like them."[17]

For the close to 60 years that Johnson was at the helm of the magazine, it did just that. Practically every story faithfully adhered to a classic *Ebony* narrative formula, charting the rise of a celebrated African American from poverty, his or her encounters with individual and institutional acts of racism, and the resilience and resolve that resulted in his or her ultimate triumph.

The message was this: Success is possible even in the face of seemingly insurmountable odds. Although by the time of John Johnson's death in 2005 the magazine's formula seemed stale and many had come to pejoratively refer to *Ebony* as "the chronicle of African-American firsts"—a swipe at the magazine's breathless coverage of any breakthrough by a black person— those tales of black trailblazers were a definite source of inspiration for many African-American baby boomers. I found that was still true well into the 1990s. As a senior editor at *Ebony* in the mid-1980s, I traveled to the Baltimore home of noted neurosurgeon Benjamin Carson, who despite having just performed a historic separation of twins who were joined at the head, greeted me breathlessly with, "I've wanted all my life to be one of those people who had a story written about him in *Ebony*. I guess now I really have made it."[18] More than twenty years later, Carson's comment proves that inspirational media offer more than a fleeting, feel-good moment. It can be the fuel that ignites the dreams of a lifetime.

NOTES

1. Martha Stewart Living Omnimedia online media kit. Retrieved from http://mslomediakit.com/index.php?/martha_stewart_living_omnimedia/our_philosophy/
2. Winfrey, O. (2009, September). Here we go! *O*, p. 37.
3. Orman, S. (2009. September). What money has taught me about personal power. *O*, p. 62.
4. McGraw, P. (2009, August). You love somebody not because he "deserves it" but because you connect at a level that lights you up. *O*, p. 68.
5. Oprah's shoe, handbag, and accessory intervention with bra updates. (2009, October 29). *The Oprah Winfrey Show*.
6. Retrieved from www.rodale.com/rodale-story.
7. Interview with Willey, D. (2009, July 23). [Editor-in-chief of *Runner's World*]
8. *Runner's World*. (2009, September).
9. Parent, M. (2009, September). Watch your step. *Runner's World*, pp. 44, 51.
10. Interview with Willey, D. (2009, July 23). [Editor-in-chief of *Runner's World*]
11. Portillo, D. (2009 November). Belly Off! Club. *Men's Health*, p. 56.
12. Barcott, B. (2009, September). Footprints needed: Colorado's undiscovered Black Canyon. *Backpacker*, p. 72.
13. Retrieved from http://www.marthastewart.com/article/candy-wrapper-decoupage
14. Retrieved from http://mslomediakit.com/index.php?/martha_stewart_living_omnimedia/our_philosophy/

15. Miller, K. C. (2009, September). Could you survive a year without shopping? *Good Housekeeping*, p. 83.
16. Barry, R. (2009, November). Post-school drop-off. From The most meaningful moment of my day. *Real Simple*, p. 242.
17. Johnson, J., with Bennett, L. (1989). *Succeeding against the odds*. New York: Warner Books, p. 78.
18. Interview with Carson, B. (1987, April).

7

THE IDENTITY EXPERIENCE

Rachel Davis Mersey

- I like to have it around so that others might read it.
- I show some things in this magazine to others so that they will understand.
- Reading/watching is a little like belonging to a group.
- I like for other people to know that I read/watch it.[1]

Alex, Bethenny, Jill, Kelly, LuAnn (aka the Countess), and Ramona...they are stars of *The Real Housewives of New York City*, a world-of-privilege docu-drama on the Bravo television network. In each of the New York ladies' second-season episodes, they popped into more than 1.5 million homes, including mine (unbeknownst—until now—to just about everyone). What revealed my interest in such things as the Skinnygirl Margarita (Bethenny's recipe for staying thin and having fun) was an off-handed comment to a mentor of mine referencing a plastic surgery the youngest housewife discussed in the 2009 reunion episode.

Her immediate response: "Sad to know that you watch something called *Real Housewives of NYC*. Reunion special or not, you really should not watch something that trashy. Or at least not admit it."

The show simply did not reconcile with the professional, or professorial, image she had of me. It would have been better suited in her mind for me to reference the latest issue of *The New Yorker*, readership of which confirms one's membership among a certain intellectual community.

We could spend time in another venue discussing how the "Housewives" have no plans to take up residence in an intellectual community. For now, let us settle on this concept: the media that we consume are a part of who we are and how others perceive us. The best media create what we can call an Identity experience. We have been able to isolate some behaviors and feelings, highlighted at the beginning of this chapter, associated with the Identity experience. But identity is complicated. For help in fully understanding and implementing the identity experience, instruction comes from the field of psychology and specifically social identity theory (SIT).

THEORETICAL BACKGROUND

SIT is based on the idea that people have both personal and social identities. European scholar Henri Tajfel, the seminal author in this area, stated: "We shall understand social identity as that part of an individual's self-concept, which derives from his knowledge of his membership of a social group (or groups) together with the emotional significance attached to that membership."[2] Tajfel's point: That part of who we are as individuals comes from the groups to which we belong.

Let's consider a prominent example: Barack Obama. Although we cannot ultimately know the "emotional significance" President Obama attaches to his social position in certain groups, we can be sure that he is a part of many small and large groups: U.S. presidents, husbands, biracial children, fathers, Harvard Law School graduates, community organizers, Democrats, recreational basketball players—the list continues. Now think about the groups to which you have emotional attachment. Are there several? More than you expected?

Social identities may be based on age, gender, race, or other cultural monikers, and they can rise and fall in prominence based on the social setting.[3] Interestingly, what we know from SIT is that the number of group memberships is really not the important factor. Rather, it's the idea that we are constantly striving to achieve positive social identities and that social identities are obtained primarily through these group memberships.[4] That is, we use those groups—belong to them, manipulate them, and even leave them—to feel as good as we can about ourselves.

This means that we really need to understand the concept of groups to fully understand the Identity experience. According to Tajfel, "A group becomes a group in the sense of being perceived as having common characteristics or a common fate only because other groups are present in the environment."[5] That is, we know we are members of one group in part because we are not members of other groups. To our Obama example: He is a Democrat, not a Republican.

However, sometimes the distinction is not as clear as the primary two-party system. Consider a more "complicated" aspect of Obama's identity, his race. Being biracial can result in a variety of group memberships. In their research, *Beyond Black: Biracial in America*, sociologists Kerry Ann Rockquemore and David L. Brunsma established four potential identities: the border identity, when the individual identifies as black, white, *and* biracial; the singular identity, when the individual identifies as black, *not* white, or vice versa; the protean identity, when the individual uses different racial identities—black, white, biracial—in different settings and for different needs; and the transcendent identity, when the individual does not use race as a defining element of his or her identity.[6]

See, identity can get complicated quickly, especially when you start to consider that individuals' characteristics—in this case, race—may have no emotional meaning to them whatsoever. Consider the mental list of groups you made earlier. Are there groups people might assume you belong to that didn't even make your list?

What is most important is the behavior that drives that membership and, ultimately, their choice of the media outlets with which they relate. Individuals have a biological drive to order their environment based on group membership. As psychology professor Marilynn Brewer explained, "The human species is highly adapted to group living and not well-equipped to survive outside a group context."[7]

Also, individuals not only identify themselves with different groups but identify others with groups as well. That means you know where you "belong" and where others "belong" as well. Remember how we categorized Obama? Think about how you do this with your own friends and family.

From this classification, individuals then assume norms and attitudes associated with these groups. Then they adopt these behaviors, securing their social identity as part of that group. And media play an important, albeit more subtle, role related to learning and adopting elements of the Identity experience.

The umbrella that covers this body of work is a merging of SIT and what is known as a uses and gratification framework, which suggests that individuals seek out media for the purpose of satisfying specific tangible and intangible needs. Relying on this intersection, Professor Jake Harwood, now at the University of Arizona, posited that "social identity gratifications are one determinant of media choices."[8] Remember however, from SIT, that individuals use groups to feel as good as they can about themselves. For the Identity experience to be "gratifying," individuals must leave the experience—or media content—with a positive sense of self. For this reason, identity is closely related to a concept all teenagers and their parents understand as "self-esteem."

In fact, a high school gives us an approachable setting to explore aspects of identity development. Remember the crowds or, it might be better to say, the cliques of high school? There were the jocks, the cheerleaders, the nerds, the theatre kids, the prepsters, and the Goths. Your high school might have had all or none of these, but it definitely had groups. The idea is so ever-present that even the 2009 season of *Big Brother*—the CBS reality show that puts strangers in a house and then forces them to compete and vote each other out, and chronicles every minute of it—was based on four high-school cliques: the popular, the athletes, the off-beats, and the brains. The point is that the cliques then and now are defined by their looks and actions—and, of course, by what they read, watch, listen to, and use. That means media play a part in constructing and maintaining identity.

Think about some easily understood examples:

- Watching CNN means something different than watching Fox News. We'll discuss Fox later, but the initial distinction is clear: Democrat versus Republican. However, watching Jon Stewart, another example we review in this chapter, means you are the cool kid regardless of party affiliation.
- A subscription to *Reader's Digest* confirms one's commitment to a traditional sense of community. To its readers, faith and patriotism matter. *Reader's Digest* knows that and cares about it.
- A *New York Times* commercial drove the point home. A couple expressed their relationship by announcing which Sunday sections constituted their first reads. Picking the front page, rife with international news, says something very different than selecting the "Styles" section, pictures of brides and bridegrooms included.

Now consider how these examples tie into the four components of the Identity experience identified at the beginning of this chapter.

- Watching Fox News is mostly about belonging to a group (of Republicans).
- Ask a room full of young adults whether they read *Reader's Digest* and just a handful will say yes, and they may tell you it's because their grandmothers bought them a subscription. Those grandmothers are sharing their identity; they want their grandchildren to understand a community-based, family-loving culture.
- Sharing *The New York Times* allows others to know that you read it regardless of what section you favor.

These are all elements of identity construction and maintenance. But before we discuss the means for creating and maximizing Identity experiences, let us consider some entertainment and news media entities that have been particularly successful at creating them.

THE BEAUTY OF THE IDENTITY EXPERIENCE

Photography and the identity experience. *Coastal Living*, the Birmingham-based magazine, launched in 1997 with a unique mission: to bring together disparate geographies—the east coast, the west coast, and all other lakes and rivers in between—through a unifying love of waterside living, whether it be full or part time. It is not an identity that initially sounds compelling. What does a Nantucket homeowner have in common with someone from the tiny, master-planned, pastel-painted community of Seaside on the Florida Panhandle? In fact, a regional magazine, *On the Sound*, failed in part because Long Islanders and those on the Connecticut and New York sides of the Long Island Sound lacked sufficient community ties; they didn't have a shared identity.

Let's examine the elements of *Coastal Living* to understand the identity of its readership base. *Coastal Living* says, "Our subject matter reflects not only a lifestyle but a state of mind."[9] It is a state of casualness and comfort, of spending time with family and friends, of cooking and caring for the environment. It is a state—an identity—that bridges geography. And it is an identity that is particularly well communicated via lifestyle photography: nautical-striped directors' chairs set around a table piled with seafood, light blue-painted floors in a kitchen filled with family, a cocktail party on a screened-in porch decorated with sailing paraphernalia. Through photos and associated narratives, the magazine becomes a platform for visualizing, for transporting yourself to another time and place. Readers see the joy of others taking pleasure in their waterside homes and vacations, which reinforces their own love of or desire for similar experiences. (For more on this "transporting" concept, see Chapter 11 on the Timeout experience and Chapter 13 on the Visual experience.)

Coastal Living capitalizes on the depth of these connections with editorial content and added-value propositions such as the magazine's annual, inspirational "Idea Houses" and a photo contest for which readers submit photos of kids and pets on the beach. Through readers' submissions, the magazine encourages sharing real-life moments. Remember, one of the elements detected in the earlier MMC/Medill experience was that reading felt like belonging to a group—here, a group of "water babies." And in sharing, readers feel good about their experiences. In viewing others' photos, readers see their lifestyle and values reflected. It is all part of a rich identity experience.

Cultural references and the identity experience. The fare of *Vanity Fair* is culture, politics, and fashion. But those three categories could leave the magazine within an array of pop culture products. *Vanity Fair*, instead, stands ahead of its class. This magazine is about a sophistication, an air, a breeding—and most certainly, it's about money.

An August 2009 article by regular writer James Wolcott, "What's a Culture Snob to Do?" began:

> Pity the culture snob, as Kindles, iPods, and flash drives swallow up the visible markers of superior taste and intelligence. With the digitization of books, music, and movies, how will the highbrow distinguish him- or herself from the masses?
>
> We've all had that moment. That dial tone that hums in your head after you glance across the train aisle or spot someone perched upon a park bench or peer into the window at Starbucks and, based on the cover of the book a stranger is reading, zings the hope that he or she must be a kindred spirit, a literary soul mate, because you too dig Mary Gaitskill down to the nasty bone. Or perhaps it's *Netherland* being held like a hymnal, the acclaimed novel by Joseph O'Neill that you keep meaning to read and never will, and here it is, being read with such care by someone so cute. If only you could strike up a chat, the two of you might stroll off like French lovers thrown together by capricious fate, scampering to take cover from the christening rain. Romantic fantasy isn't the only driver of curiosity—our inner snob is always clicking away, doing little status checks.[10]

Note the embedded cultural references: Mary Gaitskill, who has written novels but is most well known for her essays in the likes of *The New Yorker*, *Harper's Magazine*, and *Esquire*. And the strong, intelligent language (e.g., "capricious fate") establishing a magazine for those with real cultural chops.

In the same issue, frank, well-researched articles on three tony topics appeared: "the meltdown" of Sarah Palin as a vice presidential candidate;[11] the collapse of AIG, suggesting an ultimate villain, former executive Joseph Cassano;[12] and the huge hit to Harvard's endowment, which had topped out in excess of $35 billion and sent jealousy whipping through the academy.[13] There were some fashion and celebrity tidbits, but even these were high tone. Consider an ode to seven movies set in the Depression, including *Paper Moon* and *The Grapes of Wrath*, but offered up in the *Vanity Fair* way, wearing Givenchy and Galliano. Oh, the irony of it all.

The real message of *Vanity Fair*? You're hipper than a *New Yorker* reader; you're smarter than a *People* reader; you're more well rounded than a *Vogue* reader. And a *Vanity Fair* reader dies for that kind of elitism, whether or not she or he always admits it. They like for other people to know they read the magazine (one of the behavior elements that is part of the Identity experience), that they belong. Remember, part of the Identity experience can be establishing who you are by who you are not.

Tone and the identity experience. The opening of an average *Daily Show* lets you know this is no ordinary news program:

Narrator: "From Comedy Central's world news headquarters in New York this is '*The Daily Show* with Jon Stewart.'"

Jon Stewart: "Yes, yes, welcome to *The Daily Show*. Thank you so much. I'm Jon Stewart. Our guest tonight, Kathleen Sebelius, the Secretary of Health and Human Services. They love, they love their human services. If there is a public option for health care, she will be the bureaucrat standing between you and your doctor. Be nice to her, or she will let you die."[14]

Stewart came onto *The Daily Show* scene in 1999. He brought a satirical look at national politics and offered an interesting new venue for vibrancy around the news. The audience laughing at home: young adults. According to a report from the Pew Research Center for the People & the Press, more than 40% of the show's regular viewers are less than 30 years old.[15] This compares to figures from 10% to 20% for other major talk shows and newspapers. But youth isn't the key to this audience's identity—youth, as an identity, would lead viewers to choose cartoons.

These viewers know about the world's events from Twitter or CNN or the Web *before* they watch the show, and, more important, are skeptical enough about mass media to enjoy a clever, humorous dissection of the mainstream nightly news. Their identity: smart; don't buy "machine-produced," general-circulation news; too busy to be bogged down in long interviews; entertained by nuances that provide next-day office chatter. In fact, recounting Stewart's jokes around the water cooler proudly confirms this identity to others ("I like for other people to know that I watch"). An identity you may have thought was driven by youth really has many more intricacies.

Topics and the identity experience. Mostly black and white, *The Wall Street Journal* (*WSJ*) may be a bit staid for the average news consumer, but it is exactly what businessmen and women want with their coffee every weekday morning. It is as much of who they are as Brooks Brothers and wingtips are what the men among them wear; that is why you will often see the *WSJ* on their desks—people in this audience want others to know that they are *WSJ*ers.

There is an old but applicable joke with unknown roots: *The Washington Post* is read by people who think they run the country; *The New York Times* is read by people who think they should run the country; *The Wall Street Journal* is read by the people who actually run the country.

WSJ readers like this identity. It is about power, and power is about money. Consider the above-the-fold headlines on an average day:[16]

- "Obama Ups Ante on Health: President Prepares to 'Wade In' Amid Growing Questions About *Costly* Initiative"

- "*Credit* Card Disputes Tossed Into Disarray"
- "Fed's Bernanke Testifies *Economy* is Mending"

The emphases are mine and are meant to drive home that this newspaper is for people redeeming stock certificates not supermarket coupons.

The *WSJ* style of using briefs as the key component on the front page reinforces an "I'm an important, busy person" identity, and the topical coverage remains consistent. On the same day, the top briefs are (abbreviated without loss of impact):

- "Two arbitration firms will stop resolving consumer-debt disputes..."
- "CIT Group described its restructuring plan..."
- "Temasek CEO-designate Charles 'Chip' Goodyear won't be taking the job..."

Note the business and finance through and through.

What is most important is how this on-topic coverage drives conversations on the financial news networks and across cubicles (for more on this, see the Talk About and Share experience, Chapter 14). In fact, the *WSJ* is people's ticket into the "club." Many a business school class requires reading the paper, and, at least before the economic downturn, many businesses bought subscriptions for employees.

Even now, the *WSJ* is one of the few newspapers able to charge for online subscriptions. Understanding why is not complicated. Businesspeople need this content, and no one else provides it with the accuracy, context, brevity (when it is needed), depth (also on a need-to-know basis), and focus that the *WSJ* does with such skill. And let us not forget the key to *WSJ* readers' identity: money. It is not surprising that they are willing to spend it.

The key question, however, is: Will the *WSJ* be able to maintain its essential keen, green focus of its audience's identity under Rupert Murdoch's push to make it a broader-than-a-business paper? It is a challenge. To do so, the *WSJ* will have to keep its readers thinking they are inside a club to which not everyone is invited. That means retaining its connection to its readers' finance-first identity even when covering family, fashion, culture, and foreign affairs.

Language and the identity experience. Another inside-business example is the *Harvard Business Review* (*HBR*), but this magazine takes an important step that differentiates its audience from that of the *WSJ*. The *HBR* is not just for a mass of business people; it is specifically for business leaders. The lead-in to a 2009 special issue, "Managing in the New World," announced: "In times of crisis, people's behavior and perspectives change irrevocably. As we begin to emerge from a worldwide economic collapse, it will be critical that business leaders understand what the new norms are and—most important—how to adapt. Here are some articles that can help."[17]

Throughout the articles, the same embedded language and perspectives are found:

- "The task of leading during a sustained crisis—whether you are the CEO of a major corporation or a manager heading up an impromptu company initiative—is treacherous."[18]
- "Your company has been operating on the premise that people— customers, employees, and managers—make logical decisions. It's time to abandon that assumption."[19]
- "If you feel as if government officials are breathing down your neck, get used to it. For the foreseeable future, governments are going to take an especially keen interest in how you're managing your business."[20]

The language oozes "you: person in charge." The *HBR* provides its readers with the intellectual underpinning that allows them to make informed business decisions; it makes them feel part of an elite group that actually gets to make those decisions.

Slant and the identity experience. Per Bobby Calder's discussion of concepts in Chapter 2, Fox News can barely be said without its tagline, "Fair & Balanced," and you can barely say "Fair & Balanced" without hearing jests against the right-leaning reporting of the popular cable news network. You may remember the 2003 book by Al Franken, *Lies and the Lying Liars Who Tell Them: A Fair and Balanced Look at the Right*. Franken, now a senator from Minnesota, targeted Fox News specifically, and conservative media in general, with claims of dishonesty. Yet critiques such as these play right into the identity of Fox News, cementing it as different from the other cable and national news networks.

More important to us is that its audience is different too. About 40% of regular Fox News viewers are Republicans, more than any other cable news outlets. But the real identity-driven detail is that the viewers see the rest of the mainstream media as being too liberal. It is an "I am not one of them" mindset. This is a powerful, unifying element.

CREATING IDENTITY EXPERIENCES

As you may have noticed, not surprisingly, the more focused the media operation, the better it is at creating a successful Identity experience. This is exactly why general-circulation media such as newspapers have struggled with creating these experiences. Newspapers are "for-everyone" products; journalists writing "for everyone" have a limited number of opportunities to use the intricacies of writing and presentation we've established because they can be seen as isolating or elitist. Notably, we train new journalists writing for local, general-circulation newspapers to write at the eighth-grade level. There are no Mary Gaitskills or auteurs in the eighth grade.

Now, focused products for non-elites can be successful. Consider, for example, the *Taste of Home* line of magazines, which as of this writing includes four regular titles and more than 40 special editions. These share inexpensive recipes that remind readers of home—think Cracker Barrel cuisine. But more than a recipe swap, the brand involves the sharing of a mindset—joyous appreciation for a simpler life and time focused around family and food.

Another example, *Real Hunting Magazine*, finds its niche complaining that the other hunting magazines have become too polished and professional. It asks for readers' submissions with a down-to-earth, swap-stories tone: "Whether it is a kid's first deer or elk, a trophy of a lifetime, or a memorable family hunt, we need your pictures and stories. We are looking for any fair chase stories that you would tell around a campfire at hunting camp. We challenge you to make this magazine the best in the industry, after all it's yours!"[21] This is a magazine for real hunters; they know who they are.

Newspapers, however, have not enjoyed the "luxury" of focus. But rather than discarding newspapers as a lost cause—there is enough of that chatter in the industry already—let's consider opportunities for newspapers to create Identity experiences based on what we know of SIT and the examples of success we've already discussed.

The question is, "Who still needs a newspaper?" Clearly, newspapers do not have the joy of general circulation they once did. This is about a new audience. Its members identify with their local community, prefer local vendors to ordering online, and like to see their neighbors and friends in print. Therefore, the identity of any city or town newspaper (not the national sisters such as the *WSJ* and the *NYT*) should be local, ruthlessly local. Showing you exactly how to create relevant identity-based experiences is the goal of the next segment.

RESEARCH REQUIRED

To create Identity experiences, you have to understand your audience. In some cases, media enterprises already know exactly who their audience is; in the best circumstances, those media are already serving up thoughtful Identity experiences. In other cases, media entities may know their audiences but aren't willing to go after them aggressively. This is most certainly the case with newspapers still trying to attract a general-circulation audience. In the worst situations, they do not even know at heart who their audiences are. There is no chance of being able to create meaningful Identity experience without that answer.

So the outstanding opportunity for media is to determine the identity of their audiences and serve them with focused identity-based products. At Medill, we believe that understanding audience is key to being a journalist today, and we require our master's students to define an audience for each of their stories. But we have found there is a weak audience-content effect if it only goes so far as for the journalist to simply say, "I'm writing this for single moms" or "business commuters," or whomever else. Meaningful content comes from real insights into the audience's psychology and behavior, which is gained through studying your audience quantitatively and qualitatively.

When I worked at *The Arizona Republic*, we launched a new style section, "*YES*," with real attention to understanding our audience's identity in this manner. We looked at strong national magazines such as *Lucky* and *InStyle* as our content competitors. But to establish "*YES*" as a product that connected with our readers' local identity, we focused on local content, used local models, and shot local venues for photography.

Our insight was that we soon realized there was an identity that was underserved by other products—let's call it being a desert fashionista. Anyone who has spent time in the Valley knows there is a look to the Phoenix-area women we are talking about here. We knew their environment (warm, OK, hot), their style (casual; this is the desert), their shopping venues (area malls and boutiques), and their hangouts (very popular to show women-on-the-street style). These are all marks of their identity that the competitors missed on the regional and local levels. And publication continues today, though in 2010, *The Arizona Republic* wisely rebranded the section as "Fashion & Beauty" to solidify its identity to audience and advertisers.

How can you mobilize *your* audience's chemistry? Find a focus relevant to your audience by studying them, their interests, and their media use. Use quantitative and qualitative techniques and primary and secondary research that can lead to the fullest understanding of your audience. You may begin with your intuition, but you should not end up there; this is about evidence-based research. Of course, your audience should be desirable and sizable enough to constitute a business opportunity; at this point, however, the key is to identify a constituency that shares experiences strongly enough to be loyal to a product you might generate to serve and lead them. Your aim is to develop a product that satisfies your audience's needs with regard to editorial content and tone, design, delivery, timeliness, usability, interactivity, and related services because you truly understand them, and in doing so you fill a gap in the marketplace.

But it is only an interim step to figure out a product that is uniquely relevant to your audience. The real challenge is to ruthlessly maintain your focus. One of the caveats of drawing and maintaining an audience through Identity experiences is that your audience must feel the identity-based connection with every story, every angle, every tool, every reporter. As soon as you—and therefore your product—waffle, audience members will start to think you don't understand them and therefore aren't a part of who they are.

If you go into the process of understanding your audience with eyes wide open, as curious journalists should, it can yield potentially surprising and valuable results. Consider this: My adoration for *The Real Housewives of New York City* has nothing to do with the program's identity being associated with that city, its lifestyle, or the women who live there. But I do have an identity tied up in pop culture knowledge and with references that I can use in the classroom with first-year students. Reality television, celebrity news, fashion magazines, interesting Web sites, blogs, tweets—whatever it takes to engage an 18-year-old. See, identity can be complicated and ultimately unexpected. What an opportunity for media.

NOTES

1. These measures of the identity experience were culled from the original research done at Medill and the Media Management Center using factor analysis. In the earlier work, the identity experience was conceptualized differently. It has been refined based on the theoretical context provided in this chapter.
2. Tajfel, H. (1974, April). Social identity and intergroup behavior. *Social Science Information, 13*(2), 69.
3. See, for example: Fortman, J. (2003, March). Adolescent language and communication from an intergroup perspective. *Journal of Language and Social Psychology, 22*(1), 105.
4. See also: Tajfel, H., Billig, M. G., Bundy, R. P., & Flament, C. (1971). Social categorization and intergroup behaviour. *European Journal of Social Psychology, 1*(2), 149–178. Tajfel, H. (Ed.). (1978). *Differentiation between social groups: Studies in the social psychology of intergroup relations.* London, England: Academic Press. Tajfel, H., & Turner, J. (1979). An integrative theory of intergroup conflict. In W. G. Austin & S. Worchel (Eds.), *The social psychology of intergroup relations* (pp. 33–48). Monterey, CA: Brooks/Cole Publishing. Tajfel, H. (1981). Social stereotypes and social groups. In J. C. Turner & H. Giles (Eds.), *Intergroup behavior* (pp. 144–167). Chicago: The University of Chicago Press. Tajfel, H. (1984). Intergroup relations, social myths, and social justice. In H. Tajfel (Ed.), *Social psychology, the social dimension* (Vol. 2, pp. 695–715). Cambridge, England: Cambridge University Press. Tajfel, H., & Turner, J. (1986). The social identity theory of intergroup behavior. In W. G. Austin & S. Worchel (Eds.), *The social psychology of intergroup relations* (pp. 7–24). Chicago: Nelson Hall.

5. Tajfel, H. (1974, April). Social identity and intergroup behavior. *Social Science Information*, *13*(2), 72.

6. Rockquemore, K. A., & Brunsma, D. L. (2002). *Beyond black: Biracial identity in America*. Thousand Oaks, CA: Sage.

7. Brewer, M. B. (1991, October). The social self: On being the same and different at the same time. *Personality and Social Psychology Bulletin*, *17*(5), 475.

8. Harwood, J. (1999, Winter). Age identification, social identity gratifications, and television viewing. *Journal of Broadcasting & Electronic Media*, *43*(1), 123–136.

9. Audit Bureau of Circulations Publisher's Statement (2009). Retrieved from http://img4.coastalliving.com/static/pdf/2009/abc_statement_10-7-08.pdf

10. Wolcott, J. (2009, August). What's a culture snob to do? *Vanity Fair*, *588*, 68–71.

11. Purdum, T. S. (2009, August). It came from Wasilla. *Vanity Fair*, *588*, 92–97, 139–144.

12. Lewis, M. (2009, August). The man who crashed the world. *Vanity Fair*, *588*, 98–103, 136–139.

13. Munk, N. (2009, August). Rich Harvard, poor Harvard. *Vanity Fair*, *588*, 106–112, 144–148.

14. *The Daily Show*. (2009, July 15).

15. The Pew Research Center for the People & the Press. (August 17, 2008). *Key news audiences now blend online and traditional sources*. Retrieved from http://people-press.org/report/?pageid=1353.

16. *The Wall Street Journal*. (2009, July 22).

17. *Harvard Business Review*. (2009, July–August).

18. Heifetz, R., Grashow, A., & Linsky, M. (2009, July–August). Leadership in a (permanent) crisis. *Harvard Business Review*, p. 64.

19. Ariely, D. (2009, July–August). The end of rational economics. *Harvard Business Review*, p. 78.

20. Reich, R. B. (2009, July–August). Government in your business. *Harvard Business Review*, p. 94.

21. About *RHM*. Retrieved from http://www.realhuntingmag.com/pages/about.asp

8

THE CO-PRODUCING EXPERIENCE

Ashlee Humphreys

- I contribute to the conversation on this site.
- This site does a good job of getting its visitors to contribute or provide feedback.
- I do quite a bit of socializing on this site.
- I often feel guilty about the amount of time I spend socializing on this site.
- I should probably cut back on the amount of time I spend socializing on this site.

WHERE DO THE MEDIA END
AND THE AUDIENCE BEGIN?

When results in Iran started rolling in on June 13, 2009, The Islamic Republic News Agency announced that Mahmoud Ahmadinejad had won the presidential election with 63 percent of the vote. On June 13, *The New York Times* reported that the second-place opponent, Mir-Hossein Mousavi, had issued a statement calling the results, "an amazing incident of lies, hypocrisy and fraud."[1] That same day, a Wikipedia entry for 2009 Iranian election protests was created and then updated 117 times within 24 hours by contributors all over the world. Streams of reports followed via Twitter: "Now more ppl here. Forces are harsher. Tear gas!" By June 21, traffic on the Wikipedia entry had spiked to 35,700 viewers and about 140 contributors daily. American blogger Andrew Sullivan disseminated tweets on his blog, "The Daily Dish," sponsored by *The Atlantic*.[2]

On July 9, more violence erupted. More tweets came out of Tehran: "Hundreds of Protesters chanting against the regime infron of Ploytechnic University, Near Azadi Sq. (not conf)," then "Heavy Clashes at Karegar Shomali St, (Near Enghlab Sq.) Tear gas, Fire and blockage...," as if by newswire. Blurry video of smoke and fire in a crowd of fleeing protesters was uploaded to YouTube by independent news network iNewsNetwork DE.[3] At Flickr, hundreds of pictures detailed the violence. Iranian Americans offered editorial comment from their extensive experience in the region. Organizations such as CNN picked up cell phone photos taken by protestors. Within hours, hundreds of dispatches circulated worldwide, including first-person accounts, vivid images, and informed opinion. When confronted with this flurry of activity, much of it aimed at producing and distributing reliable information to the public, one is forced to ask: Where do the media end and the audience begin?

Audience participation in the production of news has exploded in the last decade because readers are better able to contribute, and indeed often enjoy creating, what might traditionally be called "news." But the idea that readers contribute content to the news is not a novel one. The first newspaper in the New World, *Publick Occurrences both Forreign and Domestick*, offered a fourth page on which readers could simply write their own news.[4] Letters to the editor were printed in English newspapers as early as 1720, and "citizen journalism" took the form of early reports provided by amateur correspondents in villages near and far.[5] In essence, what we call a newspaper today originated from a conglomeration of reader-supplied materials, including personal letters, advertisements, and public notices. The newspaper was in its origin a co-produced document, one that came to be professionalized only in the late 19th and early 20th centuries.[6]

Audience contributions have had a rich history in other media as well. Radio call-in shows regularly featured audience content as early as 1945,[7] and public access television existed from the early 1970s until the deregulation of media companies in the 1990s.[8] Contrary to those who hype the newness of "new media," the idea that the audience provides content to the news source is practically built in to the idea of journalism, at least a journalism that serves the public.[9]

So what is "new" about new media? Today, the contribution of the audience to the news is perhaps more pervasive than at any other time in the last 200 years. Readers play a role not only in providing feedback to stories but also in rating and circulating headlines, offering comments to a community of other readers, and even doing reporting of their own. The co-creation can be captured by statements such as, "I contribute to the conversation on this site."

The reasons for this shift from passive to active readership have been widely touted—the weakening of traditional print journalism, the lowering of barriers to entry, and the reduction in costs of data storage and broadband distribution.[10] The real question, however, is not, "Why did this happen?" but rather, "What does this mean for journalism and how can professional journalists incorporate reader contributions in a productive and meaningful way?"

Experiences of co-production may include the many social experiences people have with and through media. After all, when the audience creates content, it is usually for other readers. Readers therefore can also describe it as "I do quite a bit of socializing on the site" and even "I often feel guilty about the amount of time I spend on this site socializing." This chapter focuses on the productive efforts of the audience that contribute value to media rather than the social experiences per se. (Chapter 9's exploration of the Community-Connection experience will detail more specifically the dynamics of social interaction via online communities.)

Although there is a growing and informed literature on participatory journalism, my goal in this chapter is to outline the concept of co-production in general and to apply it to the media context. In doing so, I hope to open opportunities for seeing the development of media co-production outside the boundaries of traditional media and into business contexts that deftly combine distribution, technology, and content. By delving into the contributive nature of the audience experience, we can better understand how to structure media products in order to cultivate audience contributions, align them with existing products, and increase value for both the reader and the community of readers.

MODES OF CONSUMER PRODUCTION

Audience participation in media production can be better understood as an experience of consumer production or co-production. First noted by Alvin Toffler in 1980, consumer production—also known as co-creation, co-production, or prosumption—occurs when consumers provide input into products that they consume.[11] The growing involvement of the audience in the production of media is congruent with this more general shift in consumer goods.[12] As suggested earlier, however, although co-production is not radically new, it does have an increasingly vaunted position in contemporary business strategy and a rising prevalence in the marketplace.

To understand how the experience of co-production can be valuable, we have to dig a little deeper. Co-producing is a further step in what marketers call the "value chain."[13] The value chain is the series of transformations per-

formed on a commodity that add value to the final product. These transformations can be done by either the producer or consumer. For example, the
value chain for an apple involves several steps: It must first be harvested,
then cleaned, packaged, distributed, sold, and then (sometimes) transformed
by cooking for consumption. Theoretically, the consumer could intervene in
any one of these steps in the value chain. There are orchards where consumers can go out and pick their own apples. What we call "co-production"
is when the consumer takes on one or more of these steps in the value
chain.[14]

We can use this model to understand the co-production of news. The
value chain for news runs roughly as follows: Raw data are first observed,
then selected and filtered, processed and edited, distributed, and finally
interpreted (Figure 8.1).[15] Theoretically, the consumer can intervene at any
point in the process. With citizen journalism, for example, the consumer
observes a newsworthy occurrence, writes and edits it, and then submits it
to the "producer" for distribution. If the citizen journalist owns the means
of production, he or she can even publish and distribute the news as well.
Understanding consumer interventions at each step of the news value chain
allows us to understand the different levels and types of co-production
experiences available in the news industry, and to assess the steps that professional news organizations can take to incorporate co-production into
current business models.

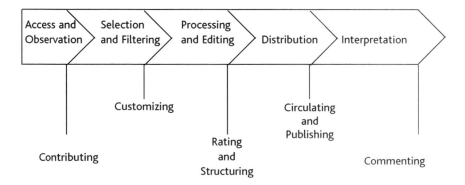

**Figure 8.1. Stages of the News Value-Chain and Co-Producing
Practices (Adapted from Domingo et al., 2008)**

THE ALPHA AND OMEGA OF NEWS: CREATING AND COMMENTING ON CONTENT

One of the most involved types of co-creation is when readers contribute to the content itself. This practice goes by many names—participatory journalism, citizen journalism, produsage—but in general it is defined as the production of content by members of what would traditionally be considered the "audience." In this analysis, I combine the first step in the value chain—creating content—with the last step in the value chain—commenting on content—because both practices amount to the same thing: creating the final product that is the news. If anything, the distinction between creating content and commenting on it is the (increasingly tenuous) distinction between fact and opinion.

Several online publications have pioneered the development of user-supplied news content. The Dutch Web site Skoeps (http://www.skoeps.nl), the progeny of major Dutch media entities PCM and Talpa, "asks users to upload their own pictures and videos of newsworthy events."[16] The organization then resells user-generated images to third parties and splits the profit 50:50 with the user who provided the image. This innovative business structure gives something back to contributors. In other words, if consumers are contributing to the value chain of the product, they get some of the profit.

More often citizen journalist sites are volunteer-only, and users eagerly contribute their labor. Korean-based OhmyNews (http://english.ohmy news.com/) is one example of a Web site in which all news is citizen journalism. Founded in 1999, the site publishes user-created stories about a variety of international topics from posters around the globe. Its staff consists of CEO/ Publisher Oh Yeon-ho, assisted by one paid newsroom employee and a volunteer staff of four editors. Contributions are largely fueled by a prestige system among users through the awarding of recognition, status designations, and awards. The payment system at OhmyNews was discontinued in 2009 in favor of awarding prizes of 300,000 won (or about $200) to one winning contribution each month.[17]

Wikipedia, the online encyclopedia, and its media partner, wikinews, are wholly constructed by amateur reporters and editors. On www.wikinews. org, users contribute to practically every step in the news value chain. They select, write, and report stories. They proofread, make editorial decisions about inclusion of content, and collectively fact check articles. According to an early study conducted by *Nature*, Wikipedia entries on scientific topics were almost as accurate as *Encyclopedia Britannica* entries.[18] (*Britannica* disputed the findings.)

Why do people make these contributions? One study of Wikipedians found that fun, an open-source ideology, and ego enhancement were three of the top motivations for contributing. The users surveyed spent an average of 8.27 hours per week contributing content to the site.[19] That's a part-time job! Some have suggested that the amount of time users spend contributing to these kinds of projects may arise due to an intrinsic enjoyment, a state marked by transportation, a loss of time, a sense of "flow" that one undergoes when deeply immersed in a task.[20] It's no wonder, then, that consumers may report spending "too much" time socializing or contributing content or "feeling guilty" about socializing. It's therefore important that the time spent co-creating be given some value—either by making the value of socialization salient to users or by monetizing it for contributors.

The openness to accepting citizen journalism demonstrated by these publications, however, is not common. A survey of 17 leading international news sites found that only 1 of them was "moderately open" to user-created content. Six of those news sites were "slightly open," while the rest—more than half of the sites—were strictly closed to reader-contributed content. Major news organizations have been reluctant to open their gates to amateur journalists, and consequently the distribution of this kind of news content remains institutionally "marginalized" to the blogosphere.

By far, the more common way that users create content is through comments. Commenting occurs at the end of the value chain as readers interpret the news content. On www.huffingtonpost.com, for example, visitors comment on the day's top stories, sometimes providing valuable analysis or insight. The comments become part of the story, part of the product that is The Huffington Post. Importantly, the site is only as good as its commentators, and the company has done a careful job of cultivating content that will attract informed readers and thoughtful essayists. If the media company wants to "co-opt customer competencies,"[21] then the customers must, of course, be competent. Contrast The Huffington Post's savvy commentators to those on a site like YouTube, where comments often digress to common cultural scripts, fights, or trivial "flame wars." (Chapter 9 has some specific suggestions for cultivating users and managing user input.)

There are, of course, a few pitfalls associated with the creation of news content by users. First, amateur reporters may not employ the same fact-checking standards and procedures as trained journalists. Second, large news organizations provide resources for travel, connection to sources, and editorial oversight that can increase the quality and reliability of news. Third, the integration of consumer and producer input into news presents a myriad of profit-sharing quandaries, especially when revenue is generated by advertising. Successful user-produced content can be accomplished if it is fairly compensated, carefully cultivated, and collectively monitored.

THE AUDIENCE AS MARKETER:
CUSTOMIZATION OF CONTENT

"Customization" describes co-production in cases where consumers choose preferences that enable the media product to be personalized, thereby increasing the value of the product for the end user (Figure 8.1). For example, when users set preferences for news on msnbc.com, they do the work of the company marketers by highlighting what is important to them and then enabling the news provider to distribute relevant information directly. Typically, market research would be conducted to determine the most preferred order of topics for particular segments, but co-production allows for narrowcasting of particular ideas if consumers will only first do the work of selecting their preferences. In some cases, preferences are automatically detected so that readers may not even be aware of their part in product customization. In this kind of co-production, the end value of co-production is retained by the reader rather than distributed to a community of readers. Consumers add value in the value chain by modifying the object to suit their needs.

As we see, the practice of customization has very different implications from the rating and selection of content. Specifically, the distinction between adding personal value for the end user and adding value for the community of users can be the distinction between putting the audience to work for themselves and putting them to work for the news organization. In some cases, it can be both. A study of photo "tagging" (identifying pictures with keywords for easy search) found that people tagged in order to organize — which they saw as benefiting both themselves and larger social groups. When it came to communicating with others, they said they tagged for their family and friends rather than for a wider public or for themselves.[22]

THE AUDIENCE AS EDITOR:
RATING AND STRUCTURING CONTENT

Another way in which the audience can contribute to the media product is by playing the role of the editor. As Figure 8.1 shows, the audience can intervene in the story-selection process by rating and structuring news content. In this type of co-creation, called "structuring," the audience takes on some editorial role, usually culling good content and weeding out bad content.

Many sites, such as Yahoo! News, compile a list of "Top-rated," "Most e-mailed," and "Most viewed" stories. These lists are based on the idea that if visitors share, recommend, or view a news story, then it must be important and can be used by other readers to sort out interesting, useful, or "front page" stories from others. Still, a survey of 17 major international newspapers found that online versions often allow users to rate stories but rarely allow them the freedom to create content.[23] The sites surveyed were selected as "slightly," "moderately," or "very" open to letting readers rate and structure the content of the site. Although only three sites were "very" open, the majority were at least "moderately" open to consumer ratings.

Note, however, that these ratings are often only used to determine lists of stories and rarely allow the audience to filter out or remove content. Perhaps one reason for not relying more on them is that customer ratings of stories often produce odd lists: often trivial or quirky stories float to the top at the expense of serious or important stories. This is not, as some commentators have suggested, because the audience is dumb. Rather, the norms that prevail online dictate that one would not email or circulate an average, unsurprising, or depressing story. People are more likely to send a funny, odd, or uplifting story to their friends because communication norms often place a priority on positive information.[24]

To remedy the problems associated with pure user ratings, selection criteria can combine both user and editorial input. At the comedy Web site FunnyorDie.com—begun in 2007 by Will Ferrell, Judd Apatow, Adam McKay, and Chris Henchy—content is chosen only in part by the audience through a rating system that immortalizes or kills a video. The system divides videos into three levels. Editors anoint some videos as "Chosen Ones," which means that they will remain on the site irrespective of viewer ratings (they have "diplomatic immunity"). In the second category, videos are classified as "Immortal" if at least 80 percent of 100,000 viewers rate them as "funny," and they remain on the site indefinitely. Last, videos are sent to "The Crypt" to die if at least 1,000 page views result in a user rating of only 20 percent funny.

Through this system, a combination of editorially sanctioned content and user-rated content is presented on the site. This hybrid model allows editors to draw attention to some content while still empowering the audience to rate their own videos and structure the media experience. With this innovative system, the Web site has garnered media attention,[25] attracted the interest of venture capital investors,[26] and become 1 of the 15 most popular privately owned, U.S.-based video sites on the Internet,[27] reaching more than 1 million people a week worldwide.[28]

Some sites use "featured" videos on the home page as a way of selecting some "front page" content that is editorially controlled rather than user-dictated. The perhaps-ironic pitfall here is that editorial control can often lead to lower perceived authenticity, especially if advertising and promotions are also included in the model. Users are often very savvy about discerning sub rosa motives for "featuring" content on the front page and will often develop habits of overlooking the choices. Selecting users as editors can be one way to make the process seem more authentic.

THE NEW NEWSIES: CIRCULATING AND PUBLISHING CONTENT

The audience can also publish and circulate news stories. In this sense, the audience co-creates through entrepreneurship, becoming an agent that not only produces but also owns and distributes content (Figure 8.1). Citizen journalism can take this a further step by publishing content on a user-owned blog. This allows the creator to retain the rights to the material, but it comes with the challenges associated with publishing in a sphere that in many cases is not well trafficked. As barriers to entry have been reduced by Internet technology, more and more "journalists" have been born, writing, publishing, and promoting online publications wholly of their own creation.

Blogs are one common way that citizen journalists can self-publish, and this once-marginalized space is quickly growing and has gained some legitimacy. Between 2004 and 2008, the number of blogs grew from 4 million-plus to 133 million.[29] Despite this growth, many bloggers quickly tire of producing content and maintaining a fresh page. As *The New York Times* reported, "[according to a 2008 survey by Technorati, which runs a search engine for blogs, only 7.4 million out of the 133 million blogs the company tracks had been updated in the past 120 days. That translates to nearly 95 percent of blogs being left to lie fallow on the Web, where they become public remnants of a dream—or at least an ambition—unfulfilled."[30] The job of citizen journalism, it appears, may be too much for a one-man blog operation. The best models for co-production operate with some combination of organizational resources and user input.

CREATING THE CO-PRODUCING EXPERIENCE

What are some suggestions for the successful creation and implementation of the Co-Producing experience? First, the news organization should consider the type and level of involvement it wants from the audience. What step(s) in the value chain should be given to the readers? This is perhaps the most important decision in creating the Co-Producing experience because it determines the structure of the organization, the type of content produced, the costs of producing content, and the resources devoted to maintaining and monitoring reader involvement in the future.

The news organization still brings a lot to the table. In a 2009 publicity stunt, celebrity Ashton Kutcher set out to gain more Twitter followers than CNN's breaking-news feed.[31] The celebrity did win (although CNN maintains 45 official Twitter accounts, with more than 1.3 million followers), and the claim, endorsed by some social-media hypesters, was that Twitter could not only provide breaking news but would replace the functions of the traditional news organization. But many of them missed an important fact, hidden behind the tweets of individual people: News is not produced simply by typing on a computer; the value chain runs much deeper than that.

Theoretically, any normal person can do the tasks of a professional journalist, but the very concept of a profession means claiming (or, better yet, earning) jurisdiction over some set of tasks.[32] Here news organizations have three key assets: social and financial resources, a staff of professional journalists cognizant of sound procedures for reporting news, and the ability to edit with authority. In what follows, I discuss three ways in which media organizations can use their resources to create and structure the Co-Producing experience for their audiences.

LEAVING ROOM FOR PLAY

Openness is one key component to attracting an engaged audience in the world of social networking and co-creation. Yet, ironically, one of the hardest things for a medium or company to do is to leave room for the independent development of content without censorship. For example, Wal-Mart attracted negative attention in July 2006 with its foray into social networking, a project called The Hub. The site was intended as "an online destination for students to preview the latest back-to-school fashions and merchandise at Wal-Mart while engaging in a creative contest to express their personality and style."[33] But the company's attempt to maintain tight control over the activities of users left the site largely fallow of user interaction and activity. As one blogger, Joseph Weisenthal, reported, The Hub did "not allow messaging between users, and will alert parents when their child signs up for the site." This kind of tight control, Weisenthal argued, meant that "the only way teens will ever take to the site is if it becomes a competition to slip subversive images or messages onto a profile."[34] Wal-Mart's policy of strict control over the site in combination with the unclear alignment of the tool with Wal-Mart's overall family-values strategy led The Hub to be widely regarded as a failure.[35] In October 2006, the site was shut down without much notice.[36] Organizations wishing to create a Co-Producing experience must become comfortable with the uncontrolled and uncontrollable nature of co-production. Important tradeoffs between brand identity and company liability, on the one hand, must be considered against the potential gains from encouraging consumer participation, on the other hand.

A sense of play is one of the most important factors in increasing interest, attitude, and involvement in consumer experiences.[37] A few companies have harnessed the capacity of social network play. Mozilla and Apple, for example, utilize the spirit of consumer play to generate advertising content[38] and even product development.[39] These companies have harnessed consumer interest and engagement by encouraging participation to build fierce loyalty. Studies show, for example, that people place a higher value on things they create.[40] This kind of participation, therefore, increases involvement in and evaluation of company products.

Applying what we know about play and consumption can improve the construction of participatory media environments. Specifically, environments should be set up so that users can customize their experience and easily connect with others in new ways around objects or information that is valuable to them. Innovative modes of exchange can encourage continual back-and-forth communication, which drives traffic to the community. For example, Facebook has successfully used gifting norms—the idea that a gift should be reciprocated—to encourage users to exchange symbolic objects that, of course, require them to sign onto the site repeatedly, thereby setting up habits of site usage. The "status update" feature was initially panned by users,[41] but the company stuck with it, and it now drives regular traffic to the site as users get updated on "news" of their friends' make-ups, break-ups, and other life events.

It is important that the media provider cultivate space for play. Not all user-created content will be directly relevant to the news, and it often may not contribute to value in any obvious way. A survey of Wikipedia users found that a sense of "fun" was one of the only factors associated with a high level of contribution. When people are intrinsically motivated to contribute, they contribute more and for longer than if they were motivated by ideology, values, or social esteem.[42] Very often, these incidental uses may simply provide an autotelic experience,[43] one in which the reader enjoys contributing for its own sake, not because of some further value. Where play is intuitive for users, it is important for the media provider to cultivate a space for it.

MAKING A STRUCTURE

Although user creativity is at the heart of what makes co-production valuable, it is useless if the content consumers produce is not valuable, clear, and cleanly presented. Customization should not give way to a chaotic structure or destabilize the perceived legitimacy of the organization. Chapter 9 elaborates more specifically on the importance of structure—setting up a clear purpose for the site and rules for user interaction—for facilitating a clearly defined and harmonious social community. Here I briefly detail the ways in which aesthetic structure may help or hinder co-production.

MySpace, for example, is known for its innovation of the ability to incorporate HTML code into user pages. However, this has left room for user-created content that is hard to read, hard to access, and generally nonsensical. Many users are turned off by the cluttered and incongruent content of member pages, preferring the clean interface of sites such as Facebook or LinkedIn.[44] Site structure led to segmentation by social class, income, and age.[45] Younger users and users in lower socio-economic classes network on MySpace, whereas their college-educated comrades flock to Facebook[46] partly because a clean minimalist structure tends to be preferred by individuals with more cultural capital.[47]

Coherent and consistent site architecture can be an important component for achieving legitimacy. Audience members trust information that is presented in a clear, direct way. For news, this kind of trust is perhaps more important than anywhere else on the Internet. Trust is paramount not only for producers of "hard news" but for opinion pages as well. Writers of opinion pages make arguments that they want readers to believe, so they too are likely to benefit from the legitimacy conferred by a clean and clear structure. Sites such as the Drudge Report, for example, have an idiosyncratic style that may confer authenticity, but this presentation often falls prey to suspicion that the contributors are not professional. Some have suggested that the Drudge Report, despite its initial success, might now be giving way to competitors who present information using a more up-to-date interface.[48]

GETTING DEEP

Last, deep area-specific expertise and cultural knowledge are imperative when trying to understand why people co-produce. Attaching a community like The Hub to the Wal-Mart megabrand clearly struck cultural discord with many Internet users. Although some social networks have built success around the idea that people like listing desired goods,[49] an explicitly branded attempt at doing this failed because it seemed too instrumental to company interests. (Chapter 9 has some suggestions for applying an understanding of cultural and social dynamics in order to provide relevant content.)

One of the most valuable things a news organization must know about its users is what they *do not* want to do. The organization should thus consider what steps in the value chain would be a hassle for users and what steps can inspire passion and involvement. Co-production is not merely a way of getting "free content"; it must engage consumers on a deeper level, not simply take ideas. To be viable, consumer participation must contribute value to the media product as well. Ultimately, both parties can benefit from co-production—if equal and fair exchange occurs.

CONCLUSION

The Co-Producing experience gives media properties value that cannot be gained in other ways. Users enjoy participating in the production of news content, and luckily they also like consuming the products of others. Although attracting and retaining a group of dedicated participants can be costly and difficult, bringing consumers into the value chain—inviting them into the production of media by reporting, rating, editing, or commenting on news—enhances memory and instills loyalty and engagement beyond traditional boundaries of passive readership. Providers of Co-Producing experiences should be aware that opportunities exist to create or enhance other experiences through co-production, such as "Makes Me Smarter" or "Talk About and Share." As Chapter 9 shows, building a framework for co-creating experiences is intricately related to community building with the media. The ultimate goal is to create a fulfilling experience for the audience while maintaining the legitimacy, trust, and authenticity that journalism requires.

NOTES

1. Retrieved from http://www.nytimes.com/2009/06/14/world/middleeast/14iran.html
2. Sullivan, A. (2009, June 13). *The daily dish.* Retrieved from http://andrewsullivan.theatlantic.com/the_daily_dish/2009/06/the-revolution-will-be-twittered-1.html
3. Retrieved from http://www.youtube.com/watch?v=22kBCqgIBig, with multiple Iran protest videos: http://www.youtube.com/user/iNewsNetworkDE
4. Burns, E. (2008). *Infamous scribblers: The founding fathers and the rowdy beginnings of American journalism.* Paw Prints. Harris, R. P. f. B. (1690). *Publick occurrences both forreign* and domestick, in *Publick Occurrences both Foreign and Domestick.* Boston.
5. Wahl-Jorgensen, K. (2007). *Journalists and the public: Newsroom culture, letters to the editor, and democracy.* Cresskill, NJ: Hampton Press. Wiles, R. M. (1958).

Freshest advices, foreign and domestic, *Dalhousie Review.* Printed (1775, November 13). Newport, RI: Solomon Southwick.

6. Deuze, M. (2005). What is journalism? Professional identity and ideology of journalists reconsidered. *Journalism: Theory, Practice, and Criticism,* 6(4), 442–464.

7. Gillmor, D. (2004). *We the media: Grassroots journalism by the people, for the people.* Beijing; Sebastopol, CA: O'Reilly.

8. Fuller, L. K. (1994). *Community television in the United States: A sourcebook on public, educational, and governmental access.* Westport, CT: Greenwood Press. Kellner, D. (2009). *Public access television.* Retrieved from http://www.museum.tv/archives/etv/P/htmlP/publicaccess/publicaccess.htm.

9. Rosen, J. (1999). *What are journalists for?* New Haven, CT: Yale University Press.

10. Gillmor, D. (2004). Ibid.

11. The "co-" in "co-production" carries the double meaning of "cooperative" and "consumer." See Toffler, A. (1980). *The third wave.* New York: William Morrow & Company.

12. Prahalad, C. K., & Ramaswamy, V. (2000, January). Co-opting customer competence. *Harvard Business Review,* 78(1), 79–88.

13. Porter, M. E. (1985). *Competitive advantage: Creating and sustaining superior performance.* New York: London: Free Press; Collier Macmillan.

14. Humphreys, A., & Grayson, K. (2008). The intersecting roles of consumer and producer: A critical perspective on co-production, co-creation, and prosumption. *Sociology Compass,* 2, 21–28.

15. Domingo, D., Quandt, T., Heinonen, A., Paulssen, S., Singer, J. B., & Vujnovic, M. (2008). Participatory journalism practices in the media and beyond: An international comparative study of initiatives in online newspapers. *Journalism Practice,* 2(3), 326–342.

16. Deuze, M., Bruns, A., & Neuberger, C. (2007). Preparing for an age of participatory news. *Journalism Practice,* 1(3), 322–338. Rosen, J. (1999). *What are journalists for?* New Haven, CT: Yale University Press.

17. OhmyNews (2009). FAQ. Retrieved from http://english.ohmynews.com/ reporter_room/qa_board/qaboard_list.asp?page=1&board=freeboard. http://english.ohmynews.com/reporter_room/qa_board/qaboard_list.asp?div_code=54" Payment system retrieved from http://english.ohmynews.com/reporter_room/qa_board/qaboard_list.asp?div_code=54

18. Giles, J. (2005). Internet encyclopedias go head to head. *Nature,* 438(7070), 900–901.

19. Nov, O. (2007, November). What motivates wikipedians? *Communications of the ACM,* 50(11), 60–64.

20. Csikszentmihalyi, M. (1975). *Beyond boredom and anxiety.* San Francisco: Jossey-Bass Publishers. Lakhani, K. R., & Wolf, R. G. (2003). *Why hackers do what they do: Understanding motivation effort in free/open source software projects.* MIT Sloan School of Management working paper 4425-03.

21. Prahalad & Ramaswamy (2000).

22. Ames, M., & Naamen, M. (2007). Why we tag: Motivations for annotation in mobile and online media. *CHI 2007 Proceedings,* 1, 971–980.

23. Domingo et al. (2008). Via Internet.
24. Taylor, S. E., & Brown, J. D. (1988). Illusion and well-being: a social psychological perspective on mental-health. *Psychological Bulletin, 103*(2), 193–210.
25. *Washington Post.* (2007, June 27). *TIME.* (2007, July 31). *Times Online.* (2008, August 10).
26. *Reuters.* (2008, December 22). Retrieved from http://www.reuters.com/article/peopleNews/idUSTRE4BL4P820081222
27. Wylie, P. (2008, October 1). *Fierce 15.* Retrieved from http://www.fierceonlinevideo.com/story/top-15-movers-and-shakers-online-video/2008-10-01
28. Quantcast. (2008). Retrieved from http://www.quantcast.com/funnyordie.com. See also http://www.funnyordie.com/about/ratings and http://www.quantcast.com/p-19gN3EBNl7sTw#traffic
29. Technocrati. (2008). *State of the blogosphere.* San Francisco, CA. Retrieved from http://technorati.com/state-of-the-blogosphere/
30. Quenqua, D. (2009, June 9). Blogs falling in an empty forest. *The New York Times.* Retrieved from ht tp://www.nytimes.com/2009/06/07/fashion/0/blogs.html
31. Sutter, J. (2009). Ashton Kutcher challenges CNN to Twitter popularity contest. Retrieved from http://www.cnn.com/2009/TECH/04/15/ashton.cnn.twitter.battle/. See also http://www.cnn.com/2009/TECH/04/15/ashton.cnn.twitter.battle/index.html
32. Abbott, A. D. (1988). *The system of professions: An essay on the division of expert labor.* Chicago: University of Chicago Press.
33. French, A. (2006, August 3). Wal-Mart defends The Hub. *The Morning News.* Retrieved from http://www.publish.com/c/a/Online-Media/WalMart-Closes-MySpace-Clone-The-Hub/
34. Weisenthal, J. (2006). Even Friendster looks good next to Wal-Mart social-networking site. In M. Masnick (Ed.), *Culture.* Retrieved from http://www.techdirt.com/articles/20060718/1058226.html
35. Garfield, B. (2006, August 23). Retrieved from http://adage.com/garfield/post?article_id=110673
36. Staff at PCMag.com. (2006, October 4). Wal-Mart closes MySpace clone "The Hub." Retrieved from http://www.pcmag.com/article2/0,2817,2024268,00.asp
37. Holbrook, M. B, & Batra, R. (1987). Assessing the role of emotions as mediators of consumer responses to advertising, *Journal of consumer research, 14*(3), 404–420. Holbrook, M. B., & Gardner, M. P. (1998). How motivation moderates the effects of emotions on the duration of consumption. *Journal of Business Research, 42*(3), 241–252.
38. Muniz, A. M., & Schau, H. J. (2007). Vigilante marketing and consumer-created communications. *Journal of Advertising, 36*(3), 35–50.
39. Thomke, S., & von Hippel, E. (2002). Customers as innovators: A new way to create value. *Harvard Business Review, 80*(4), 74–82. Von Hippel, E. (1988). *Sources of innovation.* Oxford: Oxford University Press.
40. Norton, M. I., & Ariely, D. (2007). *Psychology and experimental economics: A gap in abstraction.* Association for Consumer Research conference, Memphis, TN.

41. Thompson, C. (2008, September 5). Brave new world of digital intimacy. *New York Times Magazine.* Retrieved from http://www.nytimes.com/2008/09/07/magazine/07awareness-t.html?pagewanted=all

42. Nov, O. (2007, November). What motivates wikipedians? *Communications of the ACM, 50*(11), 60–64.

43. Holt, D. B. (1995). How consumers consume: A typology of consumption. *Journal of Consumer Research, 22*(1), 1–16.

44. Boyd, D. (2006). Identity production in a networked culture: Why youth heart MySpace. *MédiaMorphoses.* Boyd, D. (2007, June 24). Viewing American class divisions through Facebook and MySpace. *Apophenia Blog Essay.*

45. Boyd, D. (2006). Identity production in a networked culture: Why youth heart MySpace. *MédiaMorphoses.* Boyd, D. (2007, June 24). Viewing American class divisions through Facebook and MySpace. *Apophenia Blog Essay.*

46. Boyd, D. (2006). Identity production in a networked culture: Why youth heart MySpace. *MédiaMorphoses.* Boyd, D. (2007, June 24). Viewing American class divisions through Facebook and MySpace. *Apophenia Blog Essay.*

47. Holt, D. B. (1998). Does cultural capital structure American consumption? *Journal of Consumer Research, 25*(1), 1–25.

48. Reagan, G. (September 8, 2009). *The New York Observer.* Retrieved from http://www.observer.com/2009/media/are-days-drudge-over

49. Zhao, X., & Belk, R. W. (2007). Live from malls: Shopping blog (Web log) and consumer desire. *Advances in Consumer Research* (Vol. 34, pp. 131–137). Valdosta, GA: Association for Consumer Research.

9

THE COMMUNITY-CONNECTION EXPERIENCE

Rich Gordon

- A big reason I like this site is what I get from other users.
- I'm as interested in input from other users as I am in the regular content on this site.
- Overall, the visitors to this site are pretty knowledgeable about the topics it covers.
- This site does a good job of getting its visitors to contribute or provide feedback.
- I'd like to meet other people who regularly visit this site.

On a November Sunday in 1983, readers of *The Miami Herald* got a glimpse of the future. Inside their newspaper, they found a special section promoting an amazing new service that could deliver to them—on their TV sets—something resembling what we would recognize today as the World Wide Web.

The cover read:

TOUCH THE FUTURE
Futuristic Way of Living Arrives in South Florida
VIEWTRON SERVICE BEGINS
THE WAITING IS OVER
WHAT YOU WANT—WHEN YOU WANT IT

Viewtron, a subscription service launched by newspaper publisher Knight-Ridder, offered national, state, and local news, email and live chat, e-commerce (from dozens of local merchants and the J.C. Penney catalog), airline ticketing and rental car reservations, sports scores updated throughout the game, online banking, e-learning (SAT test preparation and Spanish lessons), the *World Book Encyclopedia*, coupons, games, and horoscopes. One of many "videotext" services launched around the world in the 1980s, Viewtron was a remarkable technical achievement, differentiated by its broad range of content and by its use of graphics—which look crude today but were a significant advance over the simple text delivered by other such services of the time.

The developers of Viewtron assumed that its users would relish the chance to get high-quality news and information on demand—an assumption that was still prevalent a dozen years later when newspapers and other content providers launched their first Web sites. The Viewtron pioneers were surprised to discover, however, that the majority of users—even those who said they liked the service—dropped it within six months. Among those who remained active subscribers, it wasn't information that drove their usage—it was the email and live chat capabilities.

"What we sold them was Information on Demand—a Mighty Wurlitzer of knowledge," Reid Ashe, chairman of Viewtron's parent company, would write later. "People bought it. We delivered. They were satisfied. But they quit using it because they didn't really want it."[1] It wasn't more news or more information that users wanted, Ashe wrote. "It was communication— interaction not with a machine, but with each other."[2]

This lesson from Viewtron has been relearned with each generation of interactive technology: from videotext to dial-up bulletin boards, Usenet, CompuServe, America Online, GeoCities, Slashdot, and Facebook. It's a lesson that was reinforced powerfully by Northwestern University's research on online experiences, released by the Media Management Center in 2005. The Center's research has found that many experiences that consumers have with media apply across platforms. For instance, the Makes Me Smarter experience is a powerful driver of usage for newspapers, magazines, and Web sites. So are the experiences we describe as Timeout, Utilitarian, and Entertainment and Diversion. With Web sites, however, two experiences unique to the online environment emerged from the researchers' conversations with online users.

The Co-Producing experience (Chapter 8) can be encapsulated in statements such as:

- I do quite a bit of socializing on this site.
- I contribute to the conversation on this site.
- I should probably cut back on the amount of time I spend socializing on this site.

And the Community-Connection experience can be summarized by the statements at the top of this chapter.

These experiences are, of course, closely related. The first addresses the motivations for a user's participation in online conversations, and the second speaks to the value that users derive from the conversations and content supplied by others. Although there are ways to deliver these experiences through traditional media—a newspaper's letters to the editor or a trade magazine's hosting of in-person events—the Northwestern researchers concluded that these are Web sites' true differentiators as media properties. As Calder, Malthouse, and Schaedel put it, "Items such as 'I do quite a bit of socializing on this site,' and 'I contribute to the conversation on this site,' would not characterize a newspaper or magazine, and we did not hear such statements in our qualitative interviews for these media."[3] The researchers' analysis further concluded that experiences with Web sites can be grouped under two broad categories: "Personal Engagement," which encompasses experiences that have counterparts in newspapers and magazines, and "Interactive Engagement," which is specific to Web sites and is driven by the "participation & socializing" and "community" experiences described above.

"ONLINE COMMUNITY": HISTORY AND DEFINITIONS

The evolution of online communities is inextricably linked to the history of computer-mediated communication. The first such communities, dating to the late 1970s, were bulletin board systems (BBS) that users accessed through telephone lines and a computer maintained by the BBS operator. As the Internet became available through universities and government institutions, it spawned email lists (or listservs) and, in 1979, the Usenet discussion system. By the 1980s, commercial online services (America Online, Compuserve, Prodigy) were competing, in part, by providing discussion boards and real-time chat. In the early 1990s, the World Wide Web provided a new platform that, to a great extent, absorbed and diminished the others. With the 21st century came social networks such as Friendster, MySpace, Facebook, and Twitter.

"Online community" is a relatively ancient term; the *Oxford English Dictionary* dates it to 1988. But I think it is superior to more contemporary alternatives such as "Web 2.0" or "social media." It also more accurately captures the flavor of successful conversation-driven Web sites than terms such as "user-generated content" and "citizen journalism," which imply motivations ("generate content" or "be a journalist") that are not necessarily common or typical. In a report for the Newspaper Association of America,[4] I developed a definition of "online community" that sought to be comprehensive enough to encompass the communities of the past—as well as those built with tools or technologies yet to come:

> Online sites and services that allow multiple people to create and share content, communicate with one another, and build relationships with other participants.

Although technologies change, what endures is the value that people derive from interacting with others.

As far back as the mid-1980s, Howard Rheingold first encountered the community experience via the WELL dial-up bulletin board system which attracted a mix of counterculture types, journalists, Grateful Dead fans, and others in the San Francisco area:

> People in virtual communities use words on screens to exchange pleasantries and argue, engage in intellectual discourse, conduct commerce, exchange knowledge, share emotional support, make plans, brainstorm, gossip, feud, fall in love, find friends, and lose them, play games, flirt, create a little high art and a lot of idle talk.... To the millions who have been drawn into it, the richness and vitality of computer-linked cultures is attractive, even addictive.[5]

By the late 1990s, as the Web began to dominate interactive media, *BusinessWeek* contrasted "Internet communities" with content-driven Web sites. A quote from one executive captured the distinction: "It's not the content. It's the people, stupid. Content may be why people visit a site. But community is why people stay."[6] The same demand for human interaction has driven the success of Web sites as diverse as:

- IndyMoms, a site for mothers in Indianapolis, developed by the *Indianapolis Star* and later replicated nationwide (under the name of MomsLikeMe.com) by Gannett Co., the *Star*'s parent company;
- Slashdot, where technology professionals share and comment on the news—and can generate the so-called "Slashdot effect" by driving massive traffic to the site where that news was originally published;
- Vorarlberg Online, a widely popular portal associated with a broadsheet daily newspaper in Austria, which builds social connections through photos of social events and community forums for each town in its region;[7]

- "Nashville Is Talking," a blog-based conversation site from WKRN-TV that, nine months after its launch in 2006, had more monthly page views than the station's original Web site;[8]
- Spotted, a service offered by dozens of U.S. newspapers that combines newspaper-generated photos of social events with a photo-sharing service for local residents—and generated five times the number of page views per visit as the papers' news sites.[9]

And, of course,

- Facebook, which started as a social network for college students but has quickly grown to become one of the most widely used sites on the Web.

Even YouTube, which consumers use mostly as a searchable archive of broadcast video and which TV executives lament as a distributor of illegally copied content, has actually become a powerful hub for interpersonal interaction, especially among young adults. YouTube users have created hundreds of thousands of "vlogs" (video blogs), in which users record personal messages using webcams, enabling others to respond in text comments as well as their own videos.[10]

BUILDING AN ONLINE COMMUNITY

For every successful online community, there are countless others that fail. They can become conversational free-for-alls, in which participants insult one another, make racist or otherwise objectionable comments, fail to stay on topic—or just provide such a volume of content that they overwhelm the site's capacity to organize or present it. Or they can become digital wastelands, places that fail to attract enough contributors to make the site compelling for other participants.

Just like real-world communities, however, online communities can be built successfully based on a plan. That's what happened with IndyMoms.

For years, the *Star*'s leaders—like those at other newspapers—had been "bombarded with research study after research study about how poorly newspapers performed with moms," recalled Kevin Poortinga, vice president of product development for the *Star*.[11] Mothers, especially those with young or multiple children, had trouble making time for the paper and didn't find enough of the content valuable or relevant. Research found there were 180,000 women in the Indianapolis market who fit into the target demographic: ages 25 to 44, with children ages 17 and younger.

A critical step in building any online community is determining its purpose, its reason for existing. A few examples from Jenny Preece, a scholar who has studied online communities, are: to exchange information, to provide support to others, to enable informal chatting and socializing, and to discuss ideas.[12] Closely related to a community's purpose are the benefits that members expect to derive from participating. In the case of the IndyMoms project, the *Star* convened focus groups and found that mothers were particularly interested in advice from other moms and ideas for things to do with their children in the Indianapolis area.

Why do people participate in online communities? Perhaps the most basic reason is the human desire for self-expression. Other drivers of participation include:[13]

- *Anticipated reciprocity*: A person can be motivated to contribute in hopes of receiving useful information in return at some point in the future;
- *Increased reputation*: A user may contribute, at least in part, out of a desire to become known as an expert or valued participant in the community;
- *A sense of efficacy*: Users may contribute out of a belief or hope they are having an impact on other users;
- *Attachment or commitment*: Over time, a sense of affiliation can develop among participants in an online community, driving members to contribute to improve or strengthen it.

Online communities can be built around news (via commenting on articles, as on most news Web sites), around geography (sites such as Vorarlberger Online's "Bürgerforums" or FredTalk, a discussion board in Fredericksburg, VA, operated by the *Free Lance-Star* newspaper), or around common interests (such as Craftster.org, an online community where people share hip, off-beat, crafty do it yourself [DIY] projects). Online communities can also be built around participants' social relationships—the basis of social network sites such as MySpace, Facebook, and LinkedIn. Social networks are different from earlier online-community forums, in that they are based on relationships among users—typically, starting with relationships that already existed offline. By tapping first into existing social ties, rather than focusing on bringing together people who don't already know one another, social networks have been able to grow rapidly and develop tremendous loyalty. In March 2009, for instance, Facebook had more than 91 million users—three times the user total for CNN.com and more than five times the total for NYTimes.com, according to Compete.com. Just as important, Compete.com reported that Facebook users visited the site more than twice as often as users of NYTimes.com and CNN.com and spent more than twice as much time per visit (16 minutes for Facebook compared with 8 minutes for NYTimes.com and 7 minutes for CNN.com).

TECHNOLOGY APPROACHES

There are many possible technologies for enabling person-to-person inter-action, and the choice can influence whether a community succeeds. In the case of IndyMoms, because the Indianapolis mothers were particularly interested in advice from their peers, the *Star*'s team chose a discussion board model. Discussion boards or forums make it easy for one participant to ask a question and for others to respond.

Other technology options include:

- Commenting on articles or posts;
- Weblog hosting to enable members to create their own content (and solicit reactions from other users);
- Photo and/or video sharing (examples include Flickr, YouTube, and the local Spotted sites);
- Ratings and reviews (e.g., Yelp and Angie's List);
- Collaborative editing, ranking, and link sharing (such as Digg, reddit, and Newsvine);
- Social networks, in which users create profiles and "friend" or "follow" others.

Beyond the overall technology platform selected, there are decisions to be made about features and functionality. For instance, should users be required to register before posting a comment? Although required registration can deter participation, it also can reduce the volume of "fly-by" participation by people who don't understand the needs and expectations of longtime community members. And registration yields vital information for data mining, lead generation, and site analysis.

Similarly, should user comments be reviewed by an editor, or perhaps a volunteer moderator, before going live? Although prescreening contributions can improve the overall tone of the conversation, this practice requires staff time and attention that many site managers aren't prepared to commit. Furthermore, given contributors' desire to see that their posts are visible to others, even short delays in posting can inhibit further participation.

A community site also needs policies or rules that govern or guide user behavior. Often, as in the case of registration requirements, these policies are inextricably linked to the functions of the software that powers the community. Preece describes the establishment of policies as a key part of designing a community's "sociability." Policies can include how people become members, what codes of conduct they are expected to follow, how comments or posts are reviewed, and by whom.

MANAGING COMMUNITIES EFFECTIVELY

Building an online community is something like growing a garden. Leave it untended for too long and it may die, become overgrown, or fill up with weeds. Successful communities need gardeners—people whose job it is to plant seeds of conversation, add water or fertilizer to nurture interaction, or pull out the weedy, unpleasant comments that might deter others from participating. These functions can be performed by employees or members of the community. In the case of IndyMoms, the role of community manager was shared by the site's editor and by "discussion leaders"—moms whom the *Star* paid $25 a week. *The Bakersfield Californian* newspaper chose to hire a community manager—Jason Sperber, a former teacher who had gained experience managing user interaction through his blog about being a stay-at-home dad.

Community managers require an unusual mix of skills—"part psychologist, part social worker, part police officer,"[14] as I put it in the Newspaper Association of America online community report. In Bakersfield, Sperber is a constant presence on the site, praising, cajoling, and sometimes coming down hard on people who post objectionable material.

In general, the more cohesive (and, typically, the smaller) the community, the less necessary it is for community managers to intercede. "Broadly-based communities tend to experience more interpersonal confrontations because participants have different expectations," Preece writes.[15] This is a key reason that commenting on news Web sites can often get much more contentious than on a site like Craftster.org, where users have more in common.

Communities with high participation require underlying software that leverages human participation—and human nature—effectively. Slashdot, for instance, has built a variety of interesting tools that improve the user experience and make the site easier to manage. To encourage participation but also encourage people to log in and establish consistent user IDs, Slashdot allows people to comment without registration—but their user name shows up as "Anonymous Coward." To prioritize the best comments, Slashdot has developed several mechanisms. Every comment has a score from –1 to 5 based, first, on the volume and quality (as rated by other users) of comments made by each user. Beyond that, Slashdot randomly selects members—all of them frequent contributors—to serve as site moderators. The moderators have the power, for a limited time, to bump up the score for high-quality posts or deduct points for low-quality posts. Then there is a second layer of people—"meta-moderators"—who are asked to review a selection of moderators' ratings.

The end result is that high-quality posts, and posts from highly rated users, end up with high scores. These scores give every Slashdot user the ability to filter what's visible on the site. Each user can choose a threshold score that determines which comments they are able to see. Choose a threshold of –1 and you see every comment; choose 5 and you will see only the ones that are most highly rated.

MOTIVATING USERS TO CONTRIBUTE

On most sites, even those built for the primary purpose of enabling user participation, the great majority of visitors contribute irregularly, if at all. Jakob Nielsen, a well-known writer and consultant on Web site usability, refers to a "90-9-1" rule. This means that 90 percent read or observe but don't contribute, 9 percent contribute from time to time, and 1 percent account for a majority of the content.[16]

Here are a few ways to motivate participation:

- *Make it as easy to participate as possible, while recognizing that there can be a tradeoff between ease of participation and volume of objectionable content.* Topix.com, which hosts some of the Web's most active discussions related to local news, allows anyone to post without registering. But some news sites that used Topix technology to power their comments ultimately decided to use a different platform because the volume of objectionable content became too high.
- *Communicate policies and expectations prominently.* For instance, BlufftonToday.com, a site launched by Morris Communications to serve a South Carolina suburb, created a prominent mission statement that said, in part: "With your help, we will provide a friendly, safe, easy to use place on the Web for everyone in Bluffton.... In return, we ask that you meet this character challenge: be a good citizen and exhibit community leadership qualities."[17]
- *Require registration and consistent user IDs and let users create personal profiles so others will get to know them.* Some sites, such as MinnPost.com, a Web-based news site in Minnesota, require commenters to register with their real names. Others let users create "handles" or site-specific identities and tie them to the user's email address to encourage them to use the same ID consistently.
- *Actively recruit the first participants.* Seeding a site with content and registered users before it launches—and beyond—can increase the likelihood of participation. In the case of IndyMoms,

"discussion leaders" who are paid $25 per week are required to start four new discussion threads each week and to comment on five other threads.

- *Offer different options to participate, from simple to more complex.* In general, the more time-consuming and complicated the process of participating, the fewer people will do so. Many more people, for instance, will click "thumbs up" to rate a restaurant positively than will write a lengthy review.
- *Reward people who make high-quality contributions.* This can be as simple as posting a compliment or as sophisticated as building a system for rating posts or contributors. At vita.mn, an entertainment site in Minneapolis, users accumulate "karma" points when others save, tag, or comment on their content. Media sites such as Gawker, Jezebel, and Gizmodo gives staff the power to designate "Tier 1" commenters—prioritizing comments from participants "who have proven themselves to be engaged, intelligent, humorous, fair-minded, thoughtful, rational, etc."[18]
- *Connect the virtual world to the physical world.* Connections established online can be strengthened through opportunities to interact in person and vice versa. One way to accomplish this is to hold conferences and trade shows, traditionally a major component of business-to-business magazines and Web sites. The Spotted photo-sharing sites build these virtual-to-physical connections by sending photographers to community events, shooting pictures of participants to be posted on the Web, and handing out "You've Been Spotted" cards to people who were captured in those photos. IndyMoms has a "mom squad" whose members are paid $15 per hour to attend events that attract mothers to promote IndyMoms, take photos, and create photo galleries about the events for the Web site.

DEALING WITH OBJECTIONABLE CONTENT

Sometimes it's possible for a site to have too much participation—or too much of the wrong kind of participation. News sites, which bring together users who may have little in common and deliver content on controversial topics, can often generate hostility, racism, and personal attacks. Over time, the managers of a community-oriented site can predict the types of topics that have the greatest potential to generate unpleasant comments.

In some cases, a light touch in advance can defuse problems. The editor of IndyMoms, Epha Riche, will post a comment any time a user refers to spanking, a controversial topic among moms. Her post typically reminds members to "respect each other's opinions," she said. "If it's not something you would say to a room full of people you just met, you should think twice about posting it to our forum."[19] At newsday.com, editors decided simply not to allow comments on articles related to certain topics known to generate objectionable responses, such as crime, accidents, immigration, race, religion, children, and death.

Technology can also play an important role in screening out objectionable content. "CAPTCHA" software (an acronym for Completely Automated Public Turing Test to Tell Computers and Humans Apart), for instance, screens out automated postings by requiring a human being to interpret an image (typically a sequence of letters)—something a computer can't do. And automated "dirty word" filters can delete or alert the staff to posts containing profanity or other unpleasant content (although it is usually pretty easy to evade the filters by misspelling or inserting extra characters).

If such content clears these automated systems, it is still an option for a manager or moderator to delete it. And many sites have empowered users, implementing an "alert to objectionable post" button that allows them to flag inappropriate comments for review. In some cases, the post is immediately removed but can be reinstated, after review, by a manager. In other cases, the post stays online until a manager decides whether the complaint is warranted. The most sophisticated community-building tools provide a dashboard that can alert a manager to topics that often prove controversial or to areas of the site where there is a lot of posting or traffic.

SOCIAL NETWORKS AND THE FUTURE OF ONLINE COMMUNITIES

Social networks such as MySpace, Facebook, and Twitter are, on the surface, just contemporary examples of online communities. But as they evolve, there are indications that they are fundamentally different from their ancestors. One difference, mentioned previously, is in the way social networks are used to strengthen digital connections among people who have previously established ties rather than strangers who share a common interest. Beyond that, the social networks—Facebook, in particular—have begun providing capabilities that could allow them to subsume some of the older community formats; Facebook allows users to create groups and forums, to share photos, and to chat in real time with other members. Facebook also has embarked on a strategy to turn itself into a platform rather than just a site. For instance, it allows developers to build applications that users can add to their profile pages. Applications can be frivolous (the "Pass a Drink" application allows users to buy a virtual beverage for their friends) or more serious (*The Washington Post* built a "political compass" application that positions users and their friends along a liberal–conservative spectrum).

The most successful applications seem to tap into the users' social network—sharing content or enhancing communication with friends. This is why the "friends list" is the most fundamental component of an online social network. "What makes social network sites unique is not that they allow individuals to meet strangers, but rather that they enable users to articulate and make visible their social networks," say danah boyd [sic] and Nicole Ellison, two academics who have studied these sites.[20]

The core functionality of social networks can be extended successfully to sites whose primary purpose is something other than social connections and to sites catering to niche or business interests. In 2007, for instance, USATODAY.com was redesigned to enable users to register, establish profiles, and designate "friends" among other site users. Adding these functions, along with other design changes, enabled the site to increase the average number of page views per visit from two to eight, according to Compete.com.

Some examples of sites that use social-networking approaches to build community include:

- Bakotopia.com, a site for young adults created by *The Bakersfield Californian* newspaper that helps its audience "find cool events, meet up, buy and sell stuff, find jobs, and more";[21]
- FastCompany.com, relaunched in 2008 as a social network for the community of users interested in the forward-thinking topics covered by *Fast Company* magazine;
- School Matters (http://schoolmatters.knoxnews.com/), a social network created by the *Knoxville News Sentinel* for people interested in a broad array of education issues.

Online social networks also are becoming an important tool for content sites to alert online users to interesting content and to build their audiences. *TV Guide*, for instance, designated a staff member to serve as its ambassador on Facebook, Wikipedia, and sites geared to fans of various TV shows. And the *Chicago Tribune* has created a "social media" persona named Colonel Tribune, who has hundreds of thousands of Twitter followers. The Colonel posts regular updates about interesting content on the *Tribune*'s Web sites, interacts with individual users, and convenes "tweetups"—in-person gatherings of his Twitter followers.

As technology evolves, social networks have begun to challenge the very idea that a community needs to be based at a particular Web site. Increasingly, both Facebook and Twitter are becoming services that can influence users' experiences throughout their use of the Web. Facebook does this through "Facebook Connect," which allows other sites to log in users through their Facebook IDs and cross-post to Facebook. HuffingtonPost. com used "Facebook Connect" to launch "HuffPost Social News," which enables logged-in users to see what their Facebook friends have viewed, recommended, and commented about on the site.

Twitter, which is more of a communications protocol than a Web site, has sparked a huge amount of innovation by opening up "tweets" to be accessed by developers at other sites. This allows Web sites to display tweets next to relevant content, as well as aggregating tweets on a particular topic. Beyond that, software developers have created a wide variety of tools (e.g., Twhirl and TweetDeck) that make it easier for users to keep tabs on topics being discussed via Twitter.

Media sites have begun to try to capitalize on these capabilities. For instance, during the presidential inauguration of Barack Obama, CNN used "Facebook Connect" to display, next to video of the event, the Facebook updates of users watching in real time. And huffingtonpost.com has begun displaying relevant Twitter "tweets" next to articles.

WHERE'S THE MONEY?

Despite plentiful evidence that community building is a valuable strategy for driving online usage and loyalty, some companies have chosen not to make this a priority. A common justification is the supposition—based on feedback from potential advertisers—that it's harder to generate revenue from communities than from sites populated with professional content. Some advertisers fear that community members will not be receptive to ads if they are engaged in conversation; others don't want their ads to appear in such an uncontrolled environment. Even Facebook and Twitter, despite their success in attracting users, have failed (as of this writing) to translate their massive usage into a significant flow of any revenue.

It may well be that banner advertising—the core online revenue source for most content Web sites—may not translate well to online-community sites. But that doesn't mean there aren't ways to generate revenue from community. IndyMoms derives a significant portion of its revenue from a monthly print publication, distributed free in mom-friendly places, that draws most of its content from the Web site's discussion board. And when Gannett transformed its newspapers' moms sites into a national network called MomsLikeMe, it found national advertisers such as Post Grape-Nuts, Procter & Gamble, and Unilever interested in creating sponsored groups and discussion forums on the network. Unilever, for instance, runs "Living

Beautifully for Less" groups across the 80 communities served by
MomsLikeMe.[22] Newspapers run by Lee Enterprises have begun rolling out
"commercial social marketplaces," which mix business directories with
social networking capabilities.[23]

CONCLUSION

Technology, consumer behavior, and the world around us have changed dramatically since the first online communities were born in the 1970s. The lessons of history suggest, however, that community building may always be
the key driver for usage of interactive services. Reid Ashe, the former chief
executive of Viewtron, summarized these lessons nicely as far back as 1991:

> When seers describe the media of the future, they usually envision a per-
> sonalized newspaper, covering the individual's specific interests, updat-
> ed continuously and delivered electronically. Next to each story is a but-
> ton marked, "Tell me more."
>
> They may have the technology right, but the application wrong. Think
> of a medium, any medium, as a window through time and space. We're
> beginning to learn what people want to see in it. They don't want to see
> a machine, a library. They want to see other people.[24]

NOTES

1. Ashe, R. (1991, September). The human element: Electronic networks succeed
    with relationships, not information. *The Quill*, p. 13.
2. Ashe, R. (1991, September). The human element: Electronic networks succeed
    with relationships, not information. *The Quill*, p. 13.
3. Calder, B. J., Malthouse, E. C., & Schaedel, U. (2009). Engagement with online
    media and advertising effectiveness. *Journal of Interactive Marketing*, 23(4).
4. Gordon, R. (2008). The online community cookbook: Recipes for building audi-
    ence interaction on newspaper Web sites. *Newspaper Association of America*.
    Retrieved from http://www.naa.org/Resources/Articles/Digital-MediaCook
    book/Digital-Media-Cookbook.aspx
5. Rheingold, H. (2000). *The virtual community: Homesteading on the electronic
    frontier* (pp. xvii–xviii). Cambridge, MA: MIT Press. (Original publication 1993
    by Addison Wesley.)
6. Hof, Robert D. (1997, May 5). Internet communities: Forget surfers. A new class
    of netizen is settling right in. *BusinessWeek*, pp. 64–80.

7. Berger, P. (2007, November). Innovation in action: Vorarlberger Nachrichten: Regional Media Company Reports on all Its Readers. *Newspaper Association of America*. Retrieved from http://www.naa.org/docs/Audience/innovation-in-action-v.pdf

8. Heaton, T. (2007) *Another milestone for WKRN*. Retrieved from http://donata-com.com/archives/00001560.htm

9. Gordon, R. (2009). *Audience building initiatives: Spotted at Morris Communications*. Retrieved from http://www.growingaudience.com/Best Practices/CaseStudies/AudienceBuilding/Spotted-at-Morris-Communications. aspx

10. Wesch, M. (2008, June 23). *An anthropological introduction to YouTube*. Presentation at the Library of Congress. Retrieved from http://www.youtube. com/watch?v=TPAO-lZ4_hU

11. Gordon, R. (2007, September 1). Audience building initiatives: IndyMoms draws busy parents with discussion niche content. *Newspaper Association of America*. Retrieved from http://www.growingaudience.com/BestPractices/ CaseStudies/AudienceBuilding/IndyMoms-Draws-Busy-Parents-with-Discussion-Niche-Content.aspx

12. Preece, J, (2000). *Online communities: Designing usability, supporting sociability* (p. 114). Chichester, UK: Wiley.

13. This list is drawn from Kollock, P. (1999). The economies of online cooperation. In M. A. Smith & P. Kollock (Eds.), *Communities in cyberspace* (pp. 227–229). London: Routledge.

14. Gordon, R. (2008). The online community cookbook: Recipes for building audience interaction on newspaper Web sites. *Newspaper Association of America*. Retrieved from http://www.naa.org/Resources/Articles/Digital-Media-Cook book/Digital-Media-Cookbook.aspx

15. Preece, J, (2000). *Online communities: Designing usability, supporting sociability* (p. 81). Chichester, UK: Wiley.

16. Nielsen, J. (2006, October 9). *Participation inequality: Encouraging more users to contribute*. Retrieved from http://www.useit.com/alertbox/participation_ inequality.html

17. Retrieved from http://www.blufftontoday.com/about.html

18. Holmes, A. (2008). *Fasten your seatbelts...it's gonna be a bumpy sight*. Retrieved from http://jezebel.com/5310875/fasten-your-seatbeltsits-gonna-be-a-bumpy-sight

19. Gordon, R. (2007, September 1). Audience building initiatives: IndyMoms draws busy parents with discussion niche content. *Newspaper Association of America*. Retrieved from http://www.growingaudience.com/BestPractices/Case Studies/AudienceBuilding/IndyMoms-Draws-Busy-Parents-with-Discussion-Niche-Content.aspx

20. boyd, d. m. [sic lower case], & Ellison, N. B. (2007) Social network sites: Definition, history, and scholarship. *Journal of Computer-Mediated Communication*. Retrieved from http://jcmc.indiana.edu/vol13/issue1/boyd. ellison.html

21. Retrieved from http://www.baketopia.com/home/StaticPage/2

22. O'Malley, G. (2009, July 27). Brands using Gannett's ripple6 social media platform to reach customers. *MediaPost* News. Retrieved from http://www.media-
post.com/publications/?fa=Articles.showArticle&art_aid=110542
23. Gordon, R. (2008). The online community cookbook: Recipes for building audience interaction on newspaper Web sites. *Newspaper Association of America*.
Retrieved   from   http://www.naa.org/Resources/Articles/Digital-Media-
Cookbook/Digital-Media-Cookbook.aspx
24. Ashe, R. (1991, September). The human element: Electronic networks succeed
with relationships, not information. *The Quill*, p. 13.

10

THE ANCHOR CAMARADERIE EXPERIENCE

Beth Bennett

- I enjoy watching the people doing the news talk with each other.
- I feel like I get to know the anchors on the news programs I watch.
- The anchors and reporters on the programs I watch are qualified professionals.
- I look forward to reading certain writers in this magazine/newspaper.
- I feel like I get to know the anchors/people writing the articles.

Job recruiters sometimes use the "airport test" to consider an interview candidate's personality. For the recruiter, it boils down to: "Would I want to be stuck in an airport with this person?" In the same vein, television news viewers apply the "living room test" to news anchors: "Do I want this person in my home night after night?"

Many viewers become loyal to an anchor without much conscious thought. They can't describe exactly why they watch, but they can describe how they *feel* about their anchor. This chapter examines the ways that anchors create the experience of camaraderie with their viewers and how it is evolving.

It seems only natural that we should connect with the folks we watch every evening at 5, 6, 9, 10, or 11. In the most intrinsic way, news anchors help us make daily decisions about how we live—from matters of national importance (such as voting) to personal comfort (such as whether to wear a heavy or light jacket). They are with us during public crises and moments in history. The anchors we love and respect seem to know exactly what to say during bad times. Their words can help us heal or drive us to action.

Although it is not spoken or written, news anchors and their viewers share a covenant. It's a silent agreement that requires viewers to do just one thing: watch. In exchange, anchors must deliver useful and meaningful information in short, easy-to-understand language. Plus, anchors (and the news teams behind them) must provide information that is well sourced, vetted, and relevant to the audience. As part of this covenant, anchors convey trustworthiness in both their on-air and off-air appearances. They are role models for their communities. Viewers expect anchors to be authentic and not "acting"; in other words, viewers want to believe that the caring, trustworthy anchor on the screen possesses the same qualities off screen.

The relationship between the anchor and viewer is built on an overall sense of trust; however, it is not particularly democratic. The anchor does all the talking, and the viewer has little opportunity to participate in the conversation. In fact, often the anchor is paternalistic—picking and choosing what news will best suit the viewer in a finite amount of time. Even attempts at more open conversation through Facebook and other social networking sites leave the viewer as more passenger than driver.

That said, the viewer is not totally passive. He or she can (and often does) end the relationship. When the anchor breaks the covenant, viewers may go elsewhere for their news or simply not watch news at all. But when an anchor fulfils this covenant, the viewer is most likely happy and willing to continue watching.

This sense of trusting the anchor as a qualified news professional leads some viewers to report a feeling of friendship with their favorite anchor. Their day is not complete unless they've had time with "their" anchor. This sense of friendship can lead them to participate (in a small way) in the overall conversation. They may read the anchor's blog or RSS feed, email him or her, or respond when the anchor posts to Facebook or Twitter. Viewers may be disappointed when the anchor is on vacation or maternity leave. It is as if viewers feel like they get to know the people behind the news. The connection is far more than that with an acquaintance.

Viewers often cite trustworthiness as a reason that they follow an anchor. But audiences have shown an enormous capacity for forgiveness even when an anchor does something that could be perceived as challenging the viewer-anchor bond. It is not uncommon for viewers to vehemently defend their favorite anchor when she or he faces potential shame.

The local Chicago news market has featured plenty of examples of such forgiveness. In 2006, it came to light that anchor/reporter Marion Brooks (NBC 5) had had a relationship with former Atlanta Mayor Bill Campbell. Brooks had been a reporter in Atlanta, and she was called to testify at Campbell's corruption trial.[1] This story was covered in national and local daily newspapers, but it wasn't a career-ender, and at least some viewers defended Brooks and continued to watch her. When an audience sees an anchor take a few public blows, it can help to humanize him or her even further. We all make mistakes, right? So if our anchors make mistakes, too, it can make them that much more likable.

Engagement with the audience is a driver of television viewership, and anchor camaraderie has been shown to be a component of this loyalty. The Media Management Center looked at this impact during its 2007 study on broadcast media. Researchers asked 1,400 viewers to watch randomly selected newscasts in Chicago and answer a series of questions about their experience. In particular, respondents were asked to rate the statements about anchor camaraderie that led this chapter.

The results showed that the Anchor Camaraderie and the Makes Me Smarter experiences were ranked highest as drivers or predictors of program viewership. The findings confirmed what industry professionals have long believed—that viewers often pick news programs based on their anchors.[2] Anchor camaraderie, when mixed with strong content, causes viewers to watch because they feel connected to both the stories and the professionals delivering them.

So how does an anchor, or news manager, create a product in which the viewer is totally engaged? It's not an easy question to answer because audiences vary widely in taste, attitudes, and needs. Plus, anchors also vary in style and substance. Camaraderie does not come in neat packages or one-size-fits-all approaches. Moreover, much of the camaraderie that an anchor creates with co-anchors and viewers is difficult to manufacture. It has to do with intellect, wit, good looks, talent, personality, charm, and so on. Remember the airport test.

When we factor audience age into the mix, it becomes clear that a one-size-fits-all or "A plus B equals C" approach really won't work. According to the State of the News Media Report 2009, the Pew Project for Excellence in Journalism's annual report on American journalism, evening network newscasts have failed to attract younger viewers. The median age for nightly news viewers was older than 60 for CBS, NBC, and ABC in 2008, which showed little improvement over 2007.[3] It would seem that putting younger news anchors at the desk would help. But the study also noted that younger anchors at two networks had not been able to attract a younger audience. Young anchors do not equal a young audience.

To complicate things, one form of camaraderie might appeal to a select group of the audience but disengage another. For instance, some viewers prefer a lighter approach from their anchors. They want "happy talk" or cross-talk between the anchors. One of the largest television consulting firms, Frank N. Magid Associates, has for years sent consultants into newsrooms to help anchors with their delivery and inter-broadcaster "cross-talk." Consultants often encourage anchors to share personal stories about their families and experiences, when appropriate, but this lighter "banter" might not appeal to viewers who prefer straight talk from their anchors. The "straight talk" group appreciates an anchor's sense of professionalism and news judgment. This group trusts that its anchor is reporting factual information and bringing them the most important news of the day.

The existence of such segments creates opportunities for news organizations to differentiate themselves from others in their markets. The approach followed by, for example, *PBS NewsHour with Jim Lehrer* doesn't have to appeal to everyone. It should have a strong appeal to its targeted viewers, but the producers and journalists should not be concerned if non-target viewers don't care for it. Is Fox News concerned when those who are not part of its target complain? This chapter attempts to transcend the particular characteristics of individual news programs and discusses general approaches to achieving camaraderie. The next sections address the different approaches that broadcasters have taken to grow and maintain audience—approaches that are evolving with new technologies and changing attitudes among generations of viewers.

"BRINGING IT"

As a young television news reporter, I constantly sought feedback from veteran journalists. Their criticisms were often so nebulous: "Work on your delivery," "Build a bigger presence." Huh? How do I do that? Once, I gave my resume reel to a reporter in the Chicago market and asked him how I could improve. He called me a few days later to say that I just wasn't "bringing it." He couldn't offer any specifics.

Audiences want anchors who "bring it." But viewers can't exactly define what that means, so the challenge for news managers and anchors is to know what an audience wants even when the audience isn't sure. They can articulate what the audience is thinking even when the audience can't.

The most successful anchors of today and the past have (even unintentionally) struck a chord with their viewers in a fixed moment of history. It should come as no surprise that Walter Cronkite, once called the "most trusted figure" in American public life,[4] was the grandfather of creating engagement. As anchor of *CBS Evening News* from 1962 to 1981, he did more than bring viewers compelling stories; he helped viewers understand why they should care about stories.

For example, Cronkite and many journalists of his time made Vietnam personal for viewers by offering heart-wrenching pictures, context, and commentary. But Cronkite took it one step further and leveraged his power with the public to push for negotiations between the American government and the North Vietnamese. He famously told his viewers in 1968 that "the bloody experience of Vietnam is a stalemate."[5] President Lyndon Johnson was watching that newscast and reportedly told an aide, "If I've lost Cronkite, I've lost Middle America."[6] After that, President Johnson opened negotiations and decided not to run for another term in office.

Cronkite was tough on politicians, especially when they abused public trust. He is often credited with keeping the Watergate story alive by providing a two-part overview about the scandal. His 22-minute explainer piece made the complex political story relevant for millions of Americans. Cronkite's push to keep politicians honest and give Americans the real story is perhaps one of the most noteworthy ways that he built an enormous following. A week after Cronkite's death in 2009, Frank Rich wrote in *The New York Times*:

> If he was the most trusted man in America, it wasn't because he was a nice guy with an authoritative voice and a lived-in face. It wasn't because he "loved a good story" or that he removed his glasses when a president died. It was because at a time of epic corruption in the most powerful precincts in Washington, Cronkite was not at the salons and not in the tank.[7]

IMPASSIONED ANCHORING

Cronkite figured out what worked for his audience. He was stoic and booming in his approach, but occasionally paused for emotion, as he did when he announced the death of President John F. Kennedy. That was the right approach for his audience in the 1960s and 1970s. His delivery style was the Voice-of-God approach, which was later used by Peter Jennings, Tom Brokaw, and Dan Rather. In short, Cronkite knew how to "bring it" for his time.

But what works for anchors now is different. Reading news copy with the Voice of God is too old-fashioned for many audiences and sometimes off-putting in its paternalistic approach. Today, anchors who seem to build and maintain audiences find tangible ways to claim emotional (or even political) stakes in a story. I consider this to be an "impassioned" approach to reporting—one in which the anchor is fully invested as a news professional, but also as a critical thinker and an emotional storyteller.

Anderson Cooper's work during Hurricane Katrina is a telling example of this impassioned approach. He took his CNN show, *Anderson Cooper 360*, to Louisiana to report first-hand on the disaster and won respect nationwide for his in-the-trenches reporting.[8]

Like many other world-class journalists, he held elected officials accountable for the dismal federal response to Katrina, and he provided viewers with compelling pictures and stories.

But here's the difference between Cooper and anchors of the past: Cooper became emotional during live reports. After four days of covering the storm and its aftermath, Cooper erupted on the air. His emotive outburst happened during a live talkback interview with U.S. Senator Mary Landrieu (D-LA). The interview was contentious from the start. Cooper asked, "Does the federal government bear responsibility for what is happening now, should they apologize for what is happening now?" Landrieu dodged Cooper's first question and launched into a long pat-on-the-back for President Bush and other politicians in Washington. With what appeared to be a war zone behind him, Cooper took Landrieu to school. He interrupted her and said:

> To listen to politicians thanking each other and complimenting each other, you know, I've gotta tell you, there are a lot of people here who are very upset, and very angry, and very frustrated. And when they hear politicians…thanking one another, it just, you know, it kinds of cuts them the wrong way right now. Because literally there was a body on the streets of this town yesterday being eaten by rats, because this woman had been laying on the streets for 48 hours. And there's [sic] not enough facilities to take her up. Do you get the anger that is out here?[9]

The interview is still a hit on YouTube—it had 142,000 views as of January 2010.

Jonathan Van Meter just happened to be writing a piece about Cooper for *New York* magazine when Katrina hit. After the Landrieu interview, he called Cooper and asked if he'd gone too far. Here's what Cooper told Van Meter: "Yeah, I would prefer not to be emotional and I would prefer not to get upset, but it's hard not to when you're surrounded by brave people who are suffering and in need. I feel like the people here deserve to have some answers."[10]

That's exactly how the audience felt. Cooper intuitively knew what they were thinking and feeling. He was not just an instant success, but an instant hero among his viewers. Cooper said what *they* wanted to say but in a far more eloquent and decisive manner. His anger was palpable to the audience because he really, truly felt it. Cooper's emotive coverage prompted *The New York Observer* to call him "emo-anchor." It's a fitting title, but emotion was just part of it. Cooper was totally impassioned by the news—he felt sad because he was experiencing the aftermath personally. He wasn't just reporting about the victims, he was interacting with them and communicating their feelings to an empathic audience.

Cooper took his impassioned approach even further while covering the earthquake in Haiti. Cooper's reporting style was very much "point of view," in which he and other CNN anchors appeared to have even coordinated their dress for this disaster. Both Cooper and Dr. Sanjay Gupta often appeared in muscle T-shirts, as if they were heroes at the ready.[11]

Heroics were not just limited to dress. In one well-publicized CNN video clip, we see Cooper pull a bloodied boy from a crowd of looters turned violent.[12] In this scene, Cooper seems to step out of the role of reporter. However, as viewers, we expect this of Cooper; frankly, it would be odd if he didn't help. What's troubling is CNN's decision to air the clip— as if CNN recognized that heroics are part of Cooper's unique connection with the audience and worth playing up whenever possible as part of a wider branding strategy. Somehow the commercialization of Cooper's impassioned approach undermines it and (to me) makes it seem less genuine.

Not all anchors have to be emotional to strike a chord with viewers. Another approach is to take a position, which can serve as a powerful tool to bring like-minded viewers into the fold. MSNBC's Rachel Maddow is an example of this approach. A political analyst, former AIDS activist, and liberal radio host turned television pundit, Maddow clearly stands to the Left and makes her position well known. She is openly gay, which has appeal for younger, progressive viewers.

During the 2008 Obama campaign, she filled in for the vacationing Keith Olbermann on *Countdown*. She was such a hit that network executives gave her a show of her own, and during the 2008 election season she was regularly pulling in an average high of 1.9 million viewers.[13]

Maddow is just herself. She is passionate without emoting. She's fiery and says what she thinks about the news even if it's controversial or unpopular. Straight talk wows her audience.

In late 2009, Maddow had Richard Cohen on her show. Cohen had started the International Healing Foundation and written *Coming Out Straight: Understanding and Healing Homosexuality*, which argues that homosexuality can be "healed." Cohen said his organization promotes "loving people, loving all homosexual people...." However, in Uganda, Maddow said, Cohen's work had been cited as "inspiration" by drafters of legislation that resulted in a "kill the gays" bill.

"We disavow all relationship to it," Cohen said about the legislation. "Uganda got it wrong and, I'm sorry to say, you did too, Rachel." Undaunted, Maddow took Cohen through portions of his book in chapter-and-verse style, selecting passages that could be used to promote violence against gay people and questioning both their accuracy and their intent, with Cohen noting that one passage would be pulled from a future edition. In an exchange about a controversial source, she told Cohen, "This is made-up, fake-authoritative stuff that in other countries is being taken as science and used to justify quite literally killing gay people. Do you see now why you're being used in a political context here?"[14]

Besides being smart and witty, Maddow's timing is impeccable. She came onto the television scene when the nation, and her audience, was calling for change. As a host and pundit, she is not held to the same standards of many traditional anchors, who are often loath to share their opinions with viewers for fear of appearing biased even as polls show that many Americans believe their news anchors are biased anyway. And, there's something refreshing about Maddow just being herself. She's the diva of straight talk, and her audience eats it up.

Of course, one concern worth noting is this: If all anchors served up opinion a la Maddow, it might lead to an even greater political schism among the national audience. Viewers may watch only those anchors with whom they agree. Many viewers already follow anchors along political lines—Bill O'Reilly of Fox News and Keith Olbermann of MSNBC each have loyal followings. However, if all anchors across the medium spewed positions, it would risk fanning the flames of public rage without tempering emotions. In the national anchor mix, it is important to have anchors who take a middle-of-the-road approach, too.

And so, the Web site for *Anderson Cooper 360* tries to strike a balance between passion and position. In a multi-media presentation, Cooper walks onto the home page and says: "We don't take sides. We look at all the angles. Finding facts, holding people accountable, keepin' 'em honest."[15]

WHERE HUMOR AND NEWS INTERSECT

Humor is yet another way that anchors can be impassioned in their coverage. Comedy Central's Jon Stewart has a passionately loyal following for *The Daily Show* because he knows his audience so well: They appreciate irreverence, humor, and taking to task people in high places.

If Anderson Cooper's most engaging moment with the audience came during his Katrina coverage, Stewart's came during his interview turned inquisition with CNBC's host Jim Cramer in March 2009. Cramer apparently had no idea that he was walking into a virtual deposition. Jon Stewart and his staff did their research. Stewart would accuse Cramer of making bullish calls despite the floundering economy. Cramer would deny it. Then Stewart would show a clip from Cramer's show, *Mad Money*, in which Cramer made a bullish call. Cramer admitted multiple times that he could do a better job, but he seemed uncomfortable and victimized. Stewart told him, "Look, we're both snake oil salesmen to a certain extent. But we do label the show as 'snake oil' here. Isn't there a problem, selling snake oil as vitamin tonic saying that it cures impetigo?"[16]

Stewart called for video from a 2008 interview in which Cramer talks out of school about hedge fund market manipulations. At one point Stewart said, "I understand you want to make finance entertaining, but it's not a f&*#ing game, and when I watch that I get...I can't tell you how angry that makes me."[17] Stewart put into words what his audience was thinking.

Stewart's confrontation gave the audience what they wanted—some reckoning for the disastrous economy. And a few laughs. To get there, Stewart had to take risks and be controversial, as he does regularly. His impassioned and combative approach engaged the viewers and left many saying that he performed a great act of journalism. (Ironically, in fall 2008, Cramer had told *Today* show viewers to get out of the market if they needed money within five years. Given that, it seems he served his own audience yet was unable to defend himself against Stewart.[18])

Although Stewart plays mock-anchor, and it is clear that he is not a journalist, he does a better job behind the desk than many real anchors. Stewart takes an impassioned approach in every show. He reveals ironies and flaws in news stories (and the journalists who report them) that many real anchors don't feel comfortable exposing for fear of appearing biased. And it turns out that many Americans use *The Daily Show* as a source for news. According to a 2007 study by the Pew Research Center for the People & the Press, 16 percent of people interviewed reported watching comedy news shows like *The Daily Show* or its spinoff *The Colbert Report* regularly. (The corresponding figure for *The O'Reilly Factor* was 17 percent.[19])

A separate 2007 study from the same organization equitably compared the news agenda of *The Daily Show* with more traditional news programs:

> The program's clearest focus is politics, especially in Washington. U.S. foreign affairs, largely dominated by the Bush Administration's policies in Iraq, Washington politics and government accounted for nearly half (47%) of the time spent on the program. Overall, *The Daily Show*'s news agenda is quite close to those of cable news talk shows.[20]

CHANGING APPROACHES

Sometimes an anchor deeply entrenched in the past can find a new beginning with the audience. Katie Couric started her news career in the early 1980s, first working for ABC's Sam Donaldson. She rose during an era when the Voice of God was still the golden approach. That said, Couric has always had a softer side, which was especially clear during her tenure on NBC's *Today* show.

That softer side made it difficult for Couric to define herself when she took over *CBS Evening News* from Dan Rather in 2006. As a woman and former morning show anchor, Couric struggled to shake the image of "light-weight." It wasn't until the fall of 2008 that she found her launching pad, when she landed a coveted interview with Sarah Palin. Although it's possible that the Palin camp granted Couric time with the vice-presidential candidate with the expectation that it would be "soft," Couric showed real chops in questioning her. The multi-part interview included a number of moments in which it seemed that Couric was teaching Palin about her own running mate. In one exchange, Couric asked for examples of times when John McCain had pushed for financial regulations. Palin couldn't name a single example but promised to get some. In a painfully embarrassing moment, Couric pushed Palin for a deeper explanation of how Alaska's proximity to Russia translated into foreign policy experience. Palin's answer was rambling and convoluted.

Not surprisingly, the interview was parodied on *Saturday Night Live* and made plenty of news of its own; Couric herself saw a short-term ratings boost for *CBS Evening News*.[21] She did what many of her viewers fantasized about doing—exposing flaws in Palin's armor and making her squirm. Whatever her news obligations, Couric read her audience and knew what they were thinking. Viewers would not have tolerated a soft interview.

ABOUT-FACE TIME
FOR ASPIRING NEWS ANCHORS

Success with the audience is about far more than how anchors deliver stories. It's really about whether they can "bring it." Successful anchors must have that *je ne sais quoi*—a sense of intuition about what the audience wants and feels. It's nearly impossible to engineer that quality, but newer anchors can take some cues about what is generally playing well with audiences today.

Many young anchors try to sound like the Voice of God. But *sounding* like anchors of the past is a mistake. Younger audiences don't want their parents' news. And, they don't want any phony-baloney anchor stuff. Aspiring anchors should retain a sense of authority yet infuse it with passion and connection to both the audience and the news. In short, news anchors should sound more like real folks and less like professional newsreaders.

As we've seen, authenticity plays well in Rachel Maddow's case. One of the first and most important steps in sounding authentic is to find one's own voice. Of course, that's a bit nebulous. For starters, new anchors should learn to pay attention to the *meaning* of the copy. If a story is sad, the anchor should slow down and take on a saddened tone. Better yet, the anchor should actually *feel* sad during the read; that emotion will come through in his or her delivery. If the story is surprising, the anchor should deliver it in a way that sounds as if there's a surprise (or at least some mystery). Anchors should know when to pause for effect, just like when someone is telling a joke and pauses before the punch line.

The look and feel of television news hasn't changed much over the decades. New technologies have improved the window dressings (a green screen here, a virtual set there), but the physical, practical look of the program is not particularly innovative. Anchors still sit behind desks for the most part. At the very least, anchors should move away from the desk and try standing. For starters, it will help smooth out their delivery (less stoic and more human). Plus an anchor sitting behind a desk may be disengaging for the millennial generation—it's too much like their parents' news. Television by its very nature is a barrier between the anchor and audience, so why set up more barriers?

One way that anchors are reaching out to viewers is through social networking sites, including Facebook and Twitter. Mark Suppelsa, a co-anchor on Chicago's WGN-TV, often reads viewer comments on the air. Many anchors use social media networks to announce coverage and start conversations about news events. Viewers can vote stories up or down and can post photos and links to Facebook. Sometimes their content makes it on the air. Many anchors even exceeded the allowable number of "friends" on Facebook. In Cleveland, co-anchors staged a Facebook face-off to determine who could accumulate more friends; Stacey Bell defeated her colleague Bill Martin by 311 friends.[22]

In fact, the Web is becoming a nexus for building viewers both online and on-air. It's a perfect place to tease coverage because it's where younger audiences are spending their time. Plus it allows friends of friends to see posts so stations can tap into new viewers.

REAL FRIENDS

The relationship between the anchor and viewer may be described as a friendship of sorts, but in the end it's artificial. Although social networking provides the perception that the viewer can participate, the relationship is top down, with the anchor and/or producer filtering what appears on the air. Plus, until local *television* news is delivered on-demand and on-mobile with more frequency, it may always look dated rather than innovative.

For the audience to invite an anchor into their living rooms night after night, the relationship can be artificial, but the anchor's approach must be authentic. It requires that the anchor act, feel, and talk like him or herself, like a real person, even if it's controversial or means taking a position on the news. For their part, news managers must support anchors (and the overall news team) to deliver stories that can be told in a more impassioned way. This might mean tossing out that anchor desk, ditching the designer suit, or encouraging the anchor to report more controversial stories that demand an emotional commitment from the storyteller.

NOTES

1. Goodman, B. (2006, March 9). Atlanta jury to decide case of former mayor. *The New York Times*. Retrieved from http://www.nytimes.com/2006/03/09/national/09campbell.html?fta=y. Campbell was acquitted of bribery, racketeering, and wire fraud, but convicted of tax evasion. Retrieved from http://en.wikipedia.org/wiki/Tax_evasion. Chicago coverage included Feder, R. (2006, January 26). Atlanta trial dredges up anchor's past "mistake." Retrieved from http://freerepublic.com/focus/f-new/1566039/posts
2. Media Management Center. (1997). The local TV news experience: How to win viewers by focusing on engagement. Pp. 37, 39.
3. Retrieved from http://www.stateofthemedia.org/2009/narrative_networktv_audience.php?cat=2&media=6
4. Oliver Quayle and Co. poll, 1972. Retrieved from http://www.slate.com/id/2223288/
5. Retrieved from http://www.museum.tv/eotvsection.php?entrycode=cronkitewal
6. Nelson, V. J. (2009, July 18). Walter Cronkite, 1916-2009, a voice the nation trusted. *Los Angeles Times*. Retrieved from http://articles.latimes.com/2009/jul/18/local/me-walter-cronkite18
7. Rich, F. (2009, July 25). And that's not the way it is. Retrieved from http://www.nytimes.com/2009/07/26/opinion/26rich.html?pagewanted=1&_r=1&sq=rich%20cronkite&st=cse&scp=1
8. Learmonth, M. (2007, September 12). CNN makes major "360" tweaks. Retrieved from http://www.variety.com/article/VR1117971904.html?categoryid=1236&cs=1
9. Retrieved from http://www.youtube.com/watch?v=KsuRCXiYGO4
10. Van Meter, J. (2005, September 11). Unanchored. *New York Magazine*. Retrieved from http://nymag.com/nymetro/news/features/14301/
11. Retrieved from http://www.nytimes.com/2010/01/24/fashion/24tshirt.html
12. Retrieved from http://www.youtube.com/watch?v=UPyYapL.jBMA
13. Villarreal, Y. (2009, April 22). After election, liberal ratings flag; Maddow, left leaning host of MSNBC show, vows to keep asking the tough questions. *Los Angeles Times*. Retrieved from http://articles.latimes.com/2009/apr/22/entertainment/et-maddow22
14. Retrieved from http://www.youtube.com/watch?v=L2Pg22ow1e8
15. Retrieved from http://www.cnn.com/CNN/Programs/anderson.cooper.360/landing/

16. Retrieved from http://www.thedailyshow.com/watch/thu-march-12-2009/jim-cramer-pt—2

17. Retrieved from http://www.youtube.com/watch?v=dwUXx4DR0wo. Now available at http://www.thedailyshow.com/watch/thu-march-12-2009/jim-cramer-pt—2

18. Retrieved from http://today.msnbc.msn.com/id/27045699/

19. Pew research center for people & the press. (2007, April 15). Public knowledge of current affairs little changed by news and information revolutions: What Americans know: 1989-2007. Retrieved from http://people-press.org/report/319/public-knowledge-of-current-affairs-little-changed-by-news-and-information-revolutions

20. Retrieved from http://www.journalism.org/node/10953#fn3

21. Friedman, J. (2009, June 26). Katie Couric's Palin triumph didn't last. Retrieved from http://www.marketwatch.com/story/since-her-palin-triumph-couric-has-lost-the-buzz

22. Retrieved from http://www.fox8.com/news/wjw-news-facebook-faceoff-bill-stacey,0,7071393.htmlstory

11

THE TIMEOUT EXPERIENCE

Patti Wolter

- I lose myself in the pleasure of reading/looking at this magazine/newspaper/television programming/site.
- It is a quiet time.
- I like to kick back and wind down with it.
- It's an escape.
- The magazine/newspaper/television programming/site takes my mind off other things that are going on.
- I feel less stress after reading it.
- It is my reward for doing other things.
- I like to go to this site when eating or taking a break.

Stop. Pause. Breathe…. No, this isn't a yoga class. It's the beginning of a lecture to journalism students introducing them to the concept of magazines. The main idea? They've spent ample time learning to rush around to get the story, cut the video, and make the deadline. Now it's time to slow down the deliverable and concentrate on craft, on wordsmithing, on pictures and color, pace and flow, and the TOTAL package. This isn't to say that other forms of journalism don't value these items. Nor, as any magazine editor can tell you, does it mean that working at a magazine is relaxing (ahem!). It's a way of shifting students' thinking to the *whole* product they are creating—one that, when it appears in mailboxes around the country, should feel less like work or a "should read" and more like something created just for each person in the audience, something they'll collectively *want* to lose themselves in the pleasure of reading.

This experience isn't exclusive to magazines. It can be the part of the newspaper your reader wants to kick back and peruse with his morning coffee, the app he downloads to use on the subway, the article to which his Facebook friends direct him, and the online slideshow or video he indulges in while he's waiting for a conference call. So the creative question becomes: How do editors and producers craft media that consumers will seek out because the experience provided is transforming, indulgent, and immersive, whether for a moment or an hour?

Yet to assume that the Timeout experience is the equivalent of a bubble bath or a day lounging on a beach (on a remote island, surrounded by palm trees and blue water, *Condé Nast Traveler* style) is a folly. Most of us have time for a bubble bath once or twice a year at best, let alone that remote vacation. Rather, in our 24/7, access-to-everything world, we reward ourselves by grabbing mini-media respites all day long.

The essence of the Timeout experience is twofold. As the Media Management Center studies revealed, rather than engaging information for necessity (staying on top of world events), the Timeout experience engages for retreat and pleasure. For those who divide media into "lean-forward," actively engaged experiences and "lean-back," savored experiences, "timeout media" usually land in the latter category. However, without disagreeing with this split, we have to acknowledge that a timeout can be both. The subcategories that define the Timeout experience include the idea of "kicking back" or "losing oneself" in the medium of choice but also embrace using media for stress relief or simply as a reward. And in a ridiculously crowded marketplace of distractions, brands that appeal to people as a Timeout experience still have to get consumers to *actively* choose to spend their downtime moments first with a journalistic product and then with theirs.

Studies show that consumers faced with a barrage of news sources do not constantly seek more options, but rather tend to form a strong media habit that relies on a few trusted sources.[1] It stands to reason, then, that those media that strive to become a trusted source will have to offer consumers numerous opportunities and the widest possible aperture for consumers to choose their timeouts. With an unlimited number of media choices available, consumers lean in and lean back all throughout the day. Think of a good conversation with a friend, leaning in for the drama and leaning back for a laugh. How does your media product become that friend? What follows is a look at what works and who is doing it well.

KNOW HOW YOUR AUDIENCE
DEFINES A TIMEOUT

First and foremost, figure out how your reader defines his or her timeout. Learn what contact points encourage your reader/user/viewer to consume your product. Then look at your organizational vision and mission and stretch the boundaries of what you do. For example, do games on your Web site conflict with your mission or add to a community pillar? Do your circulation models offer heavy and light users different attractions? Do the tone of your writing and the mix of narrative and service pieces aptly reflect the ambitions and realities of how your audience uses your content?

Too often editors get caught up in what their content is offering to readers instead of how readers experience that content. At *Self* magazine, where I worked as features editor for 2 years, editors precisely tailor their service information to their audience. "[*Self*] is definitely a curl-up-and-read magazine," explained Carla Levy, the executive editor. "But a timeout isn't just a feet-up experience for our readers; challenging themselves is also a timeout. They get an hour to themselves, and they want to do something with it. They want to accomplish something, whether it's cook the perfect pasta, spend time with friends, or work out."[2] The magazine thus offers readers experiences to be used in both practice and vicariously, and it appeals to the idea of achieving goals—regardless of whether readers ever get off the couch to do so.

Editors at *Popular Science* have to keep audience experiences in mind, albeit with a different hook. With coverage of inventions and contraptions, scientific discovery, and engineering feats, the magazine feels chock full of "makes me smarter"-type content (see Chapter 3). But a couple of years ago, editors learned from focus groups that smarts were not only why readers buy the almost 140-year-old magazine. "This idea of *Pop Sci* as a downtime treat emerged really strongly," said former executive editor Mike Haney. Haney is now the deputy director of research and development for Bonnier Corporation, which owns *Popular Science.*

> I think that ultimately what *PopSci* is about is taking really complex and amazing topics and making them understandable to anyone. But hearing people tell us this was a leisure activity and not an educational tool reminded us to, for instance, make sure we weren't using jargon or were offering definitions when we had to, and not let our infographics get too ambitious.
>
> If any of our content feels like too much work to figure out, or makes the reader feel dumb, you suddenly shatter that "escape sensation." We should on every page deliver awe and inspiration first. That sense of

awe, delivered through images or through "radically clear display [copy] is what I think should get readers immersed into every page.[3]

As a result, *Popular Science* debuted the "Instant Expert" section, a two-pager in the feature well that deconstructs topics in an engaging, often visual, and almost encyclopedic manner, with smart infographics, timelines, and FAQs. It doesn't scream "escape" in that it doesn't *look* relaxing (not a lot of air or white space). Rather, the stories are less about timeliness and more inclined to wow with information, simplify tough topics such as stem cells, and arm the reader with a lot of impressive facts. Said Haney: "It aims to prepare readers to be the smartest guy around the water cooler when that topic comes up." This is a timeout for the curious mind.

The New York Times' approach recognizes that readers use the paper for a wide variety of experiences. It offers subscriptions in a variety of packages to accommodate those needs, differentiating between daily and weekend readers, by providing a special "weekender" package of just the Friday, Saturday, and Sunday papers. "We sell the product in two ways," said Todd Haskell, vice president of advertising, digital sales, and operations for *The New York Times.* "Our daily product is heavily focused on business and international news. Our readers view it [as fulfilling] a need or obligation to be as informed as they would like to be about the world. But our weekend product is very different. The weekender—Friday, Saturday, Sunday—is totally along the lines of escape. Whether it's Friday night and you want to immerse yourself in the paper or you read your favorite Sunday sections."[4]

Haskell said the fashion, photography, and culture of the "Sunday Styles" section plays directly to the idea of a timeout or an escape and, other than the front page, is one of the top-read sections of the weekend paper. Yet the paper offers other, more surprising, quiet-time Sunday options. "What's interesting is that on the weekend the other section that is right up there [with 'Sunday Styles'] is 'The Week in Review,' which is about as heavy as you can get," Haskell said. "Sunday Styles" is peppered with such regular well-known quick reads as "Weddings/Celebrations" and the "Modern Love" column, while "The Week in Review" contains longer commentary and op-eds on current events. "That's a good example of people looking for diversity. Both perform at consistently strong levels and they couldn't be more different," Haskell added.

Thus, the obvious corollary to "know your audience" is to "deliver as much as you can of what your audience needs." One reason to understand and deconstruct media engagement experiences is to figure out how to transform light users of a media brand into heavy users. A heavy user is one who returns to a media brand out of habit and to meet multiple needs, such as staying current on news trends and also reading for relaxation and stress relief. "We think our readers are looking for a diversity of journalistic experiences, especially our core readers," Haskell said, noting that CEOs are a prime example. "One of the most popular sections for C-suite executives in addition to business is culture. They are looking for high-quality journalism in the culture space. Movie reviews, theater, etc. People want hard news *and* culture and luxury," he said.[5] In other words, they want to turn to one source—or perhaps two if you consider the print and digital versions—for both information and Timeout experiences.

In the same vein is the classic *Wall Street Journal* "Middle Column," the regular front-page feature of quirky trends, events, or any other less-than-necessary but entertaining information. In the foreword to a collection of the articles, writer Michael Lewis explained the column in quintessential Timeout experience terms:

> How is it that the newspaper of record for the world's busiest readers has become a feature-writing showcase for pieces about catfish grabbing, or the absence of bananas in Greece, or a first-person account of a belly dancer? I do not know; but I can guess. Even the sort of business-people who digest their news in tiny paragraph summaries have a need in their lives for stories. And so a deal has been struck, between business writers and business readers. The readers agree to relax for a minute and read something that will not lead immediately to profits or professional achievement. In exchange they receive the little jolt of human interest we all require to get through our days—to chuckle knowingly, to make chitchat unrelated to work with our colleagues and spouses, to revive the usually dormant regions of our brains.[6]

APPEAL TO ASPIRATION

Part of what makes a media experience a lean-back versus a lean-in moment is the level of reality versus aspiration. Although a reader may "lean in" while reading a craft magazine's 1-2-3 steps on a new knitting stitch, she may never lift a spoon while relishing a *bon appétit* recipe for a sumptuous chocolate torte. Instead, the evocative photography and airy design set a tone for the kind of dessert we can all dream about. It is, in a word, aspirational.

Likewise, *National Geographic Adventure's* coverage varied from go-this-weekend travel tips to writerly, narrative tales of the kind of adventure most readers would only experience in an armchair. "Adventure shouldn't be all about what's attainable," said Michael Benoist, the former features editor of the magazine, which published for almost a decade before closing its print edition at the end of 2009. Acknowledging that armchair travel was a big part of *Adventure's* appeal, Benoist continued: "Most of our longer narratives weren't anything that anyone would ever try to do, other than our writers. A certain amount of it is envisioning yourself as stronger or braver or more open to new experiences than you really are. So our writers were your braver avatar."[7]

Benoist cited Kira Salak as one of the magazine's more popular adventure writers. "A lot of people love to think of themselves as Kira. They live vicariously through her trek across Papua New Guinea or her 600-mile solo paddle to Timbuktu." This meant investing in expensive (and dangerous) travel adventures and running stories with high word counts and large visuals for a "lose-yourself-in-the-narrative" read. "Longer stories almost serve as a replacement for a book. A lot of people are reading books and longer stories for escapism. That's kind of the point. And I don't think the passing of *NGA* is a death knell for long-form journalism. Plenty of magazines remain that do the genre quite well," said Benoist, now a senior editor at *GQ* magazine.

Again, however, it's important to recognize that aspiration does not just belong to media featuring faraway jaunts and 12-course meals. For *Popular Science*, the point is to show aspiration in terms of future technologies, gizmos, and creative engineering. *Pop Sci* strives in every issue to balance what editors refer to as "the relevant now" with the "aspirational future," Haney said. "One thing that was really instructive to me was to look back at the magazine during the Depression and realize that the covers were fantastical recreational vehicles. It was an escape for people even then. And while the hardcore journalist in all of us would sometimes rather that we did more hard-hitting investigative or relevant news-based coverage, it's good to remember that people come to us for an optimistic vision of what's possible, grounded in reality."[8]

That idea informs the magazine's "How 2.0" section, which showcases do-it-yourself engineering feats. After focus groups showed editors that readers wanted a downtime treat, the editors morphed the "How 2.0" design from small concept illustrations to bigger photos and more audacious undertakings. "Although we try to have a number of easily actionable tips in there, many of the projects are pretty ambitious because we know that almost none of our readers actually do the projects, but they like to see what's possible. It's aspirational DIY [do-it-yourself]," Haney said.

PLACE A HIGH VALUE ON VISUALS

Nothing is more immersive than gorgeous imagery, nothing more captivating than the voyeurism a picture or video/film clip can provide. Part of the appeal of television news shows involves the real people who viewers "meet" in interviews. The window into other people's homes, lives, and tragedies can make a viewer stop mid-click with the remote and get sucked in. Gone is the arms-length tone of a journeyman newspaper story, replaced with palpable emotion and relatable visuals. This is an advantage for television as a Timeout experience, especially in terms of entertainment (although the Internet is now a legitimate challenger to television in that regard).[9]

Pictures, moving *and* still, make stories feel real and provide a mental place to visit during the timeout media escape. Indeed, *The New York Times'* Haskell noted that one of the only regular weekday features that prompts immersive viewing is the classic online slideshow.[10] In January 2009, *The Times* ran a 52-photo slideshow online (by photographer Nadav Kander) of President Obama's incoming administration (it also ran in print in the *Sunday Times Magazine*).[11] "The average person—average—went through 40 of 52 slides," Haskell said. "That means the vast majority went through the whole thing, which is crazy. When we [cover] Milan and Paris fashion shows and original coverage, people sit there and go through lots of slideshow content as well. People get sucked in and continue to turn page after page and there it absolutely is an escape."

Integral to visual immersion are the cues readers get along the way—the explanations, voiceovers, captions, and what *Popular Science*'s Haney called "really clear, direct display."[12] The *Times* slideshow featured both captions on each photo and voiceover from the photographer referencing photos still to come. YouTube has right-hand summaries for videos (whether news content, nature content, or someone making a Jell-O cake).

Perhaps no vehicle does visual immersion better than *National Geographic*, the parent title of *Adventure*, which runs lengthy features, many of which are driven by full-spread, painstakingly captioned photos. Take the 22-page "Ice Paradise" feature that ran in the April 2009 issue.[13] The actual story doesn't start until the 9th page, after four double-page, full-bleed photos of polar bears, guillemot birds, and an amazing underwater shot of an Atlantic walrus. Eleven more pages of photos complete the package, each with captions that convey both the definitional richness of the Arctic area and its decline due to global warming. No reader has to complete the two-and-a-half pages of text by writer Bruce Barcott to understand what the story is about or to feel invited in for a visual escape to the far north.

National Geographic's Web site capitalizes on its brand dominance in the area of photography with an entire portal for photos. Here users can search the seemingly infinite universe of the brand's photo library by topic ("Animals," "Science and Space," etc.) or color (photos with red tones, blue tones, etc.), or even browse users' favorite picks, and then use the photos for screen savers and desktop backgrounds. Users can upload, share, and vote on their own photos, and they can create puzzles out of their favorites to assemble online or send via email to friends. It's a deeply immersive interactive experience—one that takes place less with journalism than with the brand, but one that keeps users on the site and unquestionably offers an "escape" experience exploring the visual world of the National Geographic Society.

CONSISTENT VOICES

Andy Rooney, the famous curmudgeonly television columnist, has filled the final segment of CBS news program *60 Minutes* with "A Few Minutes With Andy Rooney" since 1978. He keeps viewers engaged with the investigative news show for an entire hour, just with the promise of his familiar face, voice, and oftentimes controversial, generally entertaining opinions. Columnists, regular features, and bloggers are crucial to the Timeout experience, with the understanding that readers will return (i.e., make a habit) so they can take their timeouts with media they trust to deliver the same experience. "Nobody needs to read a columnist. You do it because you are intellectually curious," said *The New York Times'* Haskell. He called the print newspaper's longtime voices "the murderer's row of columnists," but said that online bloggers play an equally if not more important role. "Dick Cavett is the classic example. He has a huge following online." Indeed, Cavett doesn't even blog every day ("a feast or famine thing," Haskell said), but when he does, he gets hundreds of comments for every post. "The comments on his blog are crazy. You're not talking about one or two sentences. People are writing paragraphs of commentary," Haskell said.[14]

This is the participatory timeout, largely unique to the online experience. Indeed, Salon.com and Slate.com have built their online news and commentary sites on regular contributors offering new voices, at times snarky or tone-heavy opinions, and solid reportorial research—all with the opportunity for users to engage in the conversation.

But columnists are not just the purview of the serious-minded journalist. *Glamour* magazine's "Smitten: Daily Sex & Relationships Blog" doesn't feature a singular voice posting, but it promises daily content and almost always asks a questions back to the viewer (e.g., "Can you teach a guy to be a better kisser?"). Users can post their own opinions and keep checking back on the ensuing conversation in micro-timeout bursts. Fashion, health and fitness, beauty and finance (living on a budget), sex, and love blogs are among the daily followings, along with the faux pas of the day in the trademark "*Glamour* Dos & Don'ts." Similarly, one of *Self*'s most popular blogs is its "Eat Like Me," written by registered dietitian Cristin Dillon-Jones.[15] She blogs about what she eats all day, every day as a mom, dietician, and regular woman trying to eat good food, healthfully, on the run, at restaurants, and at home. It's not deep thinking, but it is voyeuristic, service-oriented, and an easy five minutes with the site. "The blog offers a very literal engagement that you can't achieve with print," Levy said. "Readers actively seek it, talk to each other, and to the blogger."[16]

THE ELEMENTS OF CRAFT

Aside from creating reasons to habitually bring readers and viewers to a given news medium, several classic strategies for crafting the perfect story are crucial to the immersive Timeout experience—namely, tone, pacing, and storytelling. Done well, these elements keep the reader engaged and allow him to willingly "escape" with the story or, in the words of the subcategories, seek it out as a "reward" or for "quiet time."

Tone. How a media product talks to the consumer can make or break his decision to spend time with it. The *Cooking Light* reader might want to wind down the evening with stories that feel like they are coming from her best friend. But the Gawker user who takes short timeouts for a laugh or reward doesn't want a voice anywhere near that sincere. Gawker.com's news and gossip—with a load of snark—don't appeal to everyone, but its casual, sometimes profane voice and attitude is a large part of the brand's identity. That level of consistency and humor helped build what began as a New York media gossip site into the irreverent national media and gossip watchdog site it is today.

Yet consistency is both important and a fine line to walk. "Tone plays into the timeout feeling a lot," said *Self's* Levy. "We are careful always to be supportive and inspiring. We don't want to finger-point. At the same time, we can't have the same tone throughout the magazine: A homogenized voice feels inauthentic. If we had an upbeat, chatty approach to serious stories, they wouldn't feel weighty enough."[17] Overall, the tone has to achieve a level of trust, has to convey a sense that the magazine is talking uniquely to the reader as a sister, friend, or confidante, as someone worth escaping with. For *Popular Science*, the tone is authentic awe. "A phrase we use a lot around here is, 'Don't make it feel like homework,' " Haney said.[18]

Pacing and mix. The way media lead consumers through the product, start to finish, is another crucial strategy for maintaining the timeout (i.e., keeping customers vested in the product by creating an immersive—and thus escape-prone—experience). The order and flow of stories by type (interview, profile, narrative, infographic, chunked), tone, and visuals can change a light user into a heavy user by choice ("There's so much here, I *want* to spend an hour with this product") or by accident ("I just got sucked in").

Television news programs are perhaps the most transparently paced medium. Commercial breaks have forced their creators to master the tease or suspenseful pause in a narrative so the viewer will come back after the commercial distraction. A lineup that mixes hard news with personal interviews, feel-good success stories, and, when possible, dramatically told investigations, keeps the viewer on enough of an emotional roller coaster to stay engaged.

Plotting a magazine's feature well is much the same: "Start with impact. You have arrived at the heart of the book," Levy said. "You don't want quiet stories back-to-back. Keep the reader visually engaged, offer her a little surprise. It's about keeping them interested and making readers stop and pay attention. The worst thing that could happen would be for a reader to flip through the magazine and put it down in 5 minutes."[19]

Fashion magazines in particular mix bold multi-spread full-bleed fashion photos with pages of numerous short, item-driven copy. It's a visual and mental ebb and flow, in and out of visual content versus content that has to be read, and the drama of what comes next is what maintains the immersive experience. While some stories may run short, it's the visual differentiation that keeps delivering more page-turning surprises—and a larger escape—for the reader.

A look at the feature mix in *The New Yorker* reveals a more text-oriented attention to flow. Rarely does the magazine have more than one or two distinctly political/war-related stories. There is room for the classic "who knew?" feature (think Malcolm Gladwell on everything from ketchup to khakis to infomercials); regular arts and culture stories; and fiction, movie reviews, and event listings. Visually, cartoons pepper the gray text-heavy pages to offer moments of humor amid a serious story. Bold art opens each new feature even if text reigns supreme on the following pages. New art, cartoons, and poems remind the reader in quick bites that there are many rewards still to come. The blend of long stories and quick hits promises that there's an escape worthy of a five-minute stress reliever or an entire evening lost in the magazine's pages. Of course this is also about offering a timeout by satisfying numerous needs in one place, but the mix is crucial to presenting a magazine that feels like a combination of (extraordinarily well-written) "should reads" and immersive, writerly voices on more random topics.

Storytelling. It bears noting here that part of the mix is just plain good writing and the appropriate time, space, and length to do so. Nothing pulls a reader into a media product like evocative storytelling. Long-form narrative doesn't fit in every media product, but examples abound and not just in magazines—the *Frontline* documentary and the Salon.com feature count as well. It is the ultimate timeout because its very length demands the reader/viewer stop multi-tasking and invest in the experience.

Storytelling—with the goal of keeping readers, users, and viewers engaged—may just be one of the solutions for media trying to find solid ground in an upended industry. Michele Weldon, a journalist and professor at Medill/Northwestern University, analyzed the content of the front pages of 20 American newspapers from 2001 to 2004 for her book, *Everyman News: The Changing American Front Page*.[20] "What I found in my research was that there has been an astounding increase in the showcasing of compelling narrative on a multitude of topics, from national and local news to global stories that have no direct impact or consequence for a user's daily life. People will spend time on good storytelling whether it is a 2,000-word story on an individual halfway around the world or a profile of the local soccer coach who lives in the next block," she explained. "The good news for journalists is that the story is king, regardless of how it arrives.... This profound competition for eyeballs is not the death of journalism but the cattle prod to ignite the profession into a higher standard of excellence."[21]

Strong writing and strong visuals are crucial for prolonged engagement. Story type (e.g., personal narratives, "real people" true stories) and story editing make a difference as well. Any well-edited feature plays with pacing and mix within a given story by artfully mixing anecdotes, history, and reportage with logical section breaks, section heads, pullquotes, and signposts to give readers a mental chance to take a deep breath, feel suspense, and keep plowing forward.

GO WHERE YOUR READERS ARE "TIMING OUT"

It would be remiss to not comment on the obvious ways in which the online experience can particularly engage the timeout value. The medium's active context provides more of a lean-in than a lean-back experience; that makes it the ultimate workday timeout. Five minutes on YouTube is practically sanctioned TV-watching at one's desk; Gawker.com wants to provide users with coffee-break gossip, whether the gossip is at the literal coffee machine or just the figurative one created by its comments section. We've already discussed the "comments" function of blogs, which allows users to engage in the story itself and/or the community of opinions around that story. Puzzles, games, and other classic entertainment diversions also are cropping up on media Web sites. Such entertainment is integral to the Timeout experience because it's yet another way for the user to lose himself in the experience for a few minutes. (See the Entertainment and Diversion experience discussion in Chapter 12 for more on media as entertainment.)

Increasingly, media are realizing that what many consumers do for timeouts all day (and night) is to visit sites such as YouTube, Flickr, and

Facebook. So media meet their users where the users are. It's possible to "friend" *The New York Times* and NPR on Facebook and specify the kinds of stories you want to read. One can get updates on what's in the *Times* without having to navigate the site or even check the homepage. Radio, traditionally a medium for the audience held captive in the car, has used digital functionality to become a "timeout choice" for its fans. One can download MP3s of feature-driven NPR shows such as *This American Life*. The result: a user choosing a Timeout experience with a news medium that's portable enough to bring on a daily jog (adding media to a different timeout activity) or daily commute (turning to media to "escape" the drudgery of rush hour). This, of course, is the future of the Timeout experience—making sure the consumer's media of choice are available and accessible whenever he or she is ready for a break.

Special thanks for research to Chris Neary.

NOTES

1. Diddi, A., & LaRose, R. (2006). Getting hooked on news: Uses and gratifications and the formation of news habits among college students in an Internet environment. *Journal of Broadcasting and Electronic Media, 50*(2), 193–210.
2. Interview with Levy, C. (2009, October 15).
3. Interview with Haney, M. (2009, October 15). Via email.
4. Interview with Haskell, T. (2009, October 15). Via phone.
5. Interview with Haskell, T. (2009, October 15). Via phone.
6. Lewis, M. (2002). In K. Wells (Ed.), *Floating off the page: The best stories from the* Wall Street Journal's *"Middle Column"* (p. XIV). New York: A Wall Street Journal Book, Simon & Schuster.
7. Interview with Benoist, M. (2009, November 11). Via phone.
8. Interview with Haney, M. (2009, October 15). Via email.
9. Diddi, A., & LaRose, R. (2006). Getting hooked on news: Uses and gratifications and the formation of news habits among college students in an Internet environment. *Journal of Broadcasting and Electronic Media, 50*(2), 193–210.
10. Interview with Haskell, T. (2009, October 15). Via phone.
11. The caucus interactive feature: Obama's people. (2009, January 13). *The New York Times.* Retrieved from http://thecaucus.blogs.nytimes.com/2009/01/14/magazine-preview-obamas-people/?scp=4&sq=portraits%20of%20the%20incoming%20administration&st=cse
12. Haney, M. (2009, October 15). Via email.
13. Barcott, B., photographs by Nicklen, P. (2009, April). Ice paradise: The rich life of Svalbard, Norway's Arctic archipelago, faces a creeping thaw. *National Geographic,* pp. 66–87.
14. Interview with Haskell, T. (2009, October 15). Via phone.

15. Retrieved from http://www.self.com/fooddiet/2008/10/expert-bio-cristin
16. Interview with Levy, C. (2009, October 15).
17. Interview with Levy, C. (2009, October 15).
18. Interview with Haney, M. (2009, October 15). Via email.
19. Interview with Levy, C. (2009, October 15).
20. Weldon, M. (2008). *Everyman news: The changing American front page.* Columbia, MO: University of Missouri Press.
21. Weldon, M. (2008, November 19). Via e-mail.

12

THE ENTERTAINMENT AND DIVERSION EXPERIENCE

Josh Karp

- It often makes me laugh.
- This Web site always has something that surprises me.
- It is definitely entertaining.
- Once I start surfing around this site, it's hard to leave.
- I like stories about the weird things that can happen.

"Anybody can read you the news. I promise to feel the news to you."

—Stephen Colbert

In 1976 there were only two kinds of coffee: regular and decaf. Unless you count Sanka as its own thing; in that case, there were three. There were also three networks, a handful of UHF stations in each market, no cable, no Internet, and multiple newspapers in major cities.

It was against this backdrop that Paddy Chayefsky wrote *Network* and created Howard Beale, a traditional television news anchor who was having a nervous breakdown on the air. Beale's madness, distressing at first, quickly became entertaining to a bored and angry public. Before long, his rants of "I'm as mad as hell and I'm not going to take this anymore!!!" grabbed huge audiences, all of whom became so engaged that they stuck their heads out of their windows and screamed along with "the mad prophet of the airwaves."

Paddy Chayefsky was no dummy, and with this darkly comedic film he clearly understood that America was heading away from a culture that valued reassuring, avuncular anchors such as Cronkite and Brinkley toward one in which news and entertainment would merge. What Chayefsky probably couldn't have imagined, however, was Glenn Beck.

Although the three major networks continue to produce largely traditional news broadcasts, the truly engaged audiences are watching Fox News and Comedy Central, where the anchors are not venerable journalists or familiar talking heads but instead (whether they admit it or not) are entertainers like Beck, Bill O'Reilly, Jon Stewart, and Stephen Colbert. Toss in Keith Olbermann (MSNBC's yin to O'Reilly's Fox News yang), and you have a large swath of the popular news media/punditry who have changed the way audiences engage with their medium.

This group has put a priority on creating personalized Entertainment and Diversion experiences for a society in which the individual has become a priority and where most people wake up each morning expecting not a one-size-fits-all cup of regular or decaf but a tailor-made version of the "grande extra hot, soy, half-caff, skinny, caramel machiatto with no foam, but two Splendas."

In a broader sense, the approach of creating experiences that engage audiences through a fun, funny, entertaining, and often addictive (the "it's hard to leave" sub-experience) diversion from our increasingly complicated lives only deepens audience connections, making readers, listeners, viewers, and Web surfers feel part of something larger. Engagement with media comes to reflect their worldview and who they are as an individual in the same way that their clothes, home, and car do.

TELEVISION

In *Amusing Ourselves to Death: Public Discourse in the Age of Show Business*, media critic Neal Postman concluded that television was not an appropriate medium in which to foster "rational argument" or reasoned political discourse. Instead, Postman argued, television exists primarily to entertain, something it does in a highly targeted way.[1] Twenty-five years later, if there's not a network that reflects your worldview or interests (be they gardening, cooking, motorcycle repair, celebrity drug interventions, or watching doctors perform surgery), there is probably something wrong with you rather than the media.

Glenn Beck is the definitive example of how this has worked. After middling success in the world of morning radio, Beck discovered politics and became a one-man media empire, proudly declaring that he is indeed

Howard Beale. If one puts politics to the side, it's easy to understand the appeal. Beck is the car accident that you can't avoid stopping to watch, but that is just the beginning. The audience responds to Beck's style, which is warm, is familiar, and uses direct address. It connects to him on a large scale (as an audience) but also as individuals. By seeming to work without a script and engaging in a free-form emotional roller coaster that teeters between joy and tears, Beck becomes pure entertainment under the guise of news commentary. Thus, while Beck may be many things, he is primarily the embodiment of the "it's definitely entertaining," sub-experience.

Another important component of Beck's approach is the way in which he has so rapidly established himself as a 24/7 cross-media entertainment vehicle. Beck is a best-selling author of both fiction and non-fiction. He's on TV and radio, and he blogs. If for some reason you have missed a single thought that Beck expresses each day, simply go to his site and find streaming video of his podcast. The medium is no longer the message. The messenger is the message.

Or, as commentator/satirist Stephen Colbert said about having his set's décor converge on him: "That was the instruction I gave my designer. I said, 'I am the news. I translate nothing. I am not a medium. I am not a member of the media, because I'm not a vessel. I am it.'"[2]

The ability to create content that "often makes me laugh" is another sub-experience that has been played out through a redefinition of how we look at news.

Shortly after Walter Cronkite's death in July 2009, an online poll conducted by *TIME* magazine found that Jon Stewart was now America's most trusted newscaster—by a landslide. With 44% of the vote, Stewart crushed his nearest competition (NBC's Brian Williams) and left poor Charlie Gibson and Katie Couric lying in a ditch by the pop-culture roadside.

Stewart has penetrated the national mindset by making people laugh while delivering what his viewers perceive to be "the truth." Like Beck, his communication with his audience is deeply personal. Those who watch Stewart are drawn to the way in which he seems to reflect their mindset (as opposed to worldview or political stance) and translates events through a prism they believe is unique to them. Unlike Beck, Stewart also succeeds by communicating how preposterous it is that it takes a comedian to debunk the "official version" and to show time and time again that the emperor isn't wearing any clothes.

Cronkite took off his glasses and rubbed his eyes when Kennedy was shot—a spontaneous act that briefly edged towards breaking down the fourth wall and emitting a national emotion. Stewart does this on a nightly basis by making people laugh. Exhibit 1A of how this works can be gleaned watching the eight-and-a-half minutes in which he took apart CNBC financial reporter Rick Santelli (who was having a "Howard Beale moment") and that channel's coverage of the investment world.³ Along with Beck, O'Reilly, Olbermann, and Colbert, Stewart lives on this side of the fourth wall (where viewers gladly meet him), entertaining his audience by keeping them aware that they are always in on the joke—about as engaging an act as you can find on television.

PRINT

The Onion engages in the "often makes me laugh" vein by taking another convention of traditional news media—the classic AP story—and turning it on its head. The result is humor that is often insightful in the same way as Hunter Thompson's work often has been deemed "the least factual" but "most accurate" account of the 1972 presidential election.⁴ In late September 2009, the *Onion*'s "American Voices" (a mock "man on the street" format) asked three "average citizens" (always the same three pictures but always different names and occupations) the following: "A clarification of law makes it less likely that relatives of terminally ill people will be prosecuted in England for helping a loved one end his or her life. What do you think?"

"Systems analyst Paul West" responded this way: "Won't this lead to a rash of terminally ill people being put out of their misery?" This said as much as many Sunday opinion pieces, but it did so in a way that engaged the reader through humor and a sense that the editors know them and how they think about the world.

Perhaps the most remarkable example of the intersection between humor and audience engagement would be *National Lampoon* magazine between 1971 and 1978. At a time when general interest magazines were dying out and narrowly defined audiences were the rage, the *Lampoon* was the unthinkable: a general interest humor magazine startup. Hefner had tried it. So had H. L. Mencken and innumerable others. Only *Mad* had survived this formula for disaster.

Politically incorrect in the extreme, *National Lampoon*'s content was usually offensive (at best) to most advertisers and media buyers. Yet, somehow the *Lampoon* became a phenomenon by tapping into a market and a mindset. The market was the post-1960s male baby boomer in all of his jaded glory. The mindset? Nothing was sacred so long as it was funny. Not sex, not race, not even Norman Rockwell, whose reputedly "lost" pornographic work was displayed in one issue.

This slaughtering of sacred cows, and even the not-so-sacred kind, resonated with young men in a way that is almost inconceivable today. With a circulation of more than a million, the magazine was passed around at high schools, fraternities, and God knows where else—until each copy had been devoured by an estimated eight readers per. And to drive home that connection even further, *Lampoon* editors frequently appeared in photo essays, letters to the editor, subscription ads, notes in the margin, and even as characters in a story or two.

Thus, readers not only felt deeply engaged with and connected to the content, but also that they were in on something: a conspiracy of bright, juvenile, nihilistic smartasses who knew that everyone was full of crap and held Humphrey and Nixon in equal contempt. *Lampoon* fanatics felt as if they had a personal relationship with the editorial staff. It would be hard to find an audience more engaged than that.

In the non-humor print world, audience engagement can be achieved through straight, everyday staples of the magazine and newspaper trades — features, department pieces, and sections that take a look at the less newsy side of a publication's mission. Just about any magazine published by *Condé Nast* does a masterful job of entertaining and creating diversion experiences, often doing so by providing a sense of vicarious participation in an unattainable world. In *Vanity Fair*, they folded the dirty laundry of the rich and famous via the late Dominick Dunne's monthly accounts of murder trials and other mysteries, or through Evgenia Peretz' behind-the-scenes take on a scandal at Jackie O's prep school alma mater, Miss Porter's. Yes, these are stories about "the weird things that can happen" sub-experience, but they are also pure, entertainment-driven frivolity that can suck you in and spit you out hours later feeling like you were just at the world's best upscale cocktail party.

In *Architectural Digest*, you get to see the inside of Diane Keaton's home as well as an endless tour of lavish country estates, private islands, and summer homes. These all are destinations that most readers will likely never visit, much less acquire. But, *Architectural Digest* (as well as less upscale titles such as *Hollywood Life* and *InStyle*) creates a sense of being entertained simply by observing the way other people are able to live. And to a large degree it does so in a manner that is every bit as important as the title's service and utility aspect unless you desperately need to acquire the same bed sheets as Dennis Quaid.

Fitness magazines provide a similar diversion. It would be difficult to quantify how many men (myself included) and women you will see in airports reading *Men's Fitness*, *Shape*, and *Men's Health*. Even without the analysis of a TSA X-ray, very few of these people seem to have six-pack abs, and I suspect very few of them will get down to 5% body fat after reading those magazines. But, pretty much everyone enjoys reading about the possibility (however remote) that they can attain the holy trinity: drinking all the beer they'd like, getting all the sex they need, and still having Mark Wahlberg's stomach — all of which are usually leaping off the covers.

Similarly, when it comes to golf magazines, chances are that few readers hit 300-yard drives or one-putt more greens as the result of a tip in *Golf Digest* (in fact the average handicap has been basically unchanged for 50-plus years). But reading about success on the greens is an irresistible diversion from both everyday life and a 20-something handicap.

Pick up the "Sunday Styles" section of *The New York Times* and the diversion is this: A housewife in Omaha or a lawyer in Montana can spend an hour on a day of rest with a cup of coffee and take a tour of what is cool and worth knowing about. Towards the back there are the wedding announcements, pored over by people who know neither bride nor groom—and by prospective brides all over the country who are using the featured wedding to redefine expectations and desires for their own nuptials.

"A Night Out With" features everyone from actress Julianne Nicholson in Manhattan to mystery writer James Ellroy visiting his hometown of Los Angeles. Again, there's a vicarious thrill of hanging out with interesting people in interesting places. One week you're peeking in on *Juno* screenwriter Diablo Cody's female Hollywood Rat Pack, the next you're an expert on the waning years of late punk poet Jim Carroll's life. Toss in a hipster New Orleans bar and the cool new trend of drinking coconut milk from the shell, and you've created an experience that, like Jon Stewart, Glenn Beck, and *The Onion*, becomes part of your self-definition. You may be stuck in an office in Minneapolis during the day. But deep within lurks someone who knows what's what.

"Sunday Styles" has been derided by some as soft or "not real journalism." That criticism certainly has some basis in fact. Slate, for example, mocked one story about a "trend" in which straight men were expressing an increased preference for cats as house pets. The source for that information seemed to be the writer's wishful thinking and interviews with a cat therapist.[5]

Still, my colleague Patti Wolter has pointed out the power of "Styles" as a Timeout experience in the previous chapter. Also, it's foolish to believe that newspapers aren't in the entertainment business via lifestyle sections, comics, crosswords, and advice columns, to name a few. Pick up a copy of the *Chicago Tribune's RedEye* (styled in a less glossy version of *ESPN The Magazine*'s "We'll entertain you or die trying" format), read the headlines of any tabloid, or see how *The Wall Street Journal* treats many of its features, and you realize that entertainment is not only part of the mix, it's a vital component. That's because engaged readers increasingly need a reason to pick up the newspaper. Although sections such as "Sunday Styles" might not be breaking Watergate each weekend, the entertainment value they provide is a reason to pick up the paper in a world where the Internet is more than filling the void for immediate news and analysis.

RADIO

While local radio, in the form of political and sports talk, has been the media equivalent of hour-later-you're-hungry Chinese food, it has also become a venue for diversion and experiences that engage listeners on a basis that is far deeper than informational. The most significant example of this is National Public Radio, with its rabidly loyal followers who take everything they hear to be the god's-honest, undiluted truth as easily as those who listen to Beck or Limbaugh do. But NPR does this through different, less personal methods, which seem to have almost the same impact.

Few shows demonstrate this as well as *Marketplace*, a nightly business broadcast that does anything but "feel the news to you." Instead, by employing the conventions of good long-form journalism (unique slants on topics, strong, plain language, good storytelling), *Marketplace* takes seemingly dry and complex subject matter and makes it enormously entertaining. Listeners are treated as being intelligent, but the topic is treated as if it's clouded in jargon that the *Marketplace* reporters find unnecessary. You get the sense that they are curious about the exact meaning—or even the components of—the consumer price index. So, when host Kai Ryssdal (from neither a traditional business nor a business reporting background) talks to a management consultant about the road towards economic downturn, he does what we would do, asking, "How did we get into this mess?" The impact of this approach, and the show's ability to explain complicated ideas and systems without talking down to listeners, enables a feeling of deep engagement among a diverse audience, many of whom find *Marketplace* as entertaining as *This American Life* (if not more so).

INTERNET

About two days after my first foray into social media (a Facebook account), I asked my wife the following question: "What the hell is the point of all of this?" There were several, she told me, but most importantly it was "something for people to do all day at work when they hate their jobs." Although that may be a somewhat pessimistic view of a significant trend, it did speak to the Internet's unique ability to engage (as well as divert) visitors by providing raw, unfiltered opinion and information with an immediacy and specificity that even Starbucks couldn't replicate. It is the very essence of the "once you start surfing this site it's hard to leave" sub-experience.

Even when using the Web for completely Utilitarian experiences (buying clothing, doing research, checking stock prices), it is difficult not to be sucked into the vortex of information that is at your fingertips.

Here's how that works.

Say you're arguing with a friend over what year the Stones album *Exile on Main Street* was released. Immediately you go to Wikipedia, where you get the answer (1972). But as you read on just a bit more, you realize that you've never seen the film *Gimme Shelter*. Seeking to learn a little bit about the film, you follow the link to realize that the Maysles brothers directed it. Darn if you don't recognize that name from somewhere. So again, you follow the link. "That's right," you say, "they directed *Grey Gardens*," which gets you nostalgic about that movie, and again, you follow the link and find that the home which serves as the backdrop for the camp classic is now owned by Ben Bradlee, who apparently is a graduate of the Dexter School, where your cousin from Boston graduated in the mid-1980s. You get the idea. It can go on for hours. The information has become the entertainment and diversion, and your access to that information tosses you down a rabbit hole from which you may not emerge for hours. The online movie resource imdb.com and other sites that aggregate information about a certain topic have the same impact and turn information into its own form of diversion.

The link-following pattern can also dovetail with the endless stream of opinion available on the Web. If you want a wry take on sports, go to dead-spin.com and one story will inevitably lead to another. ESPN.com does the same from another angle, bringing its successful entertainment-based attitude to both its print magazine and its Web site. Left-wing politics? Try The Huffington Post. Annoyed or amused by celebrity fashion disasters? Visit Go Fug Yourself and find invective from a two-woman editorial staff that embodies your smartest, cattiest friend. By providing a respite (restful or not) from life, they allow the reader to engage deeply (or broadly) with a subject or worldview that matches theirs.

One of the most significant changes in American culture in the past 30 years has been the move away from a collective society that values the mass into one that values each and every idiosyncratic aspect of who we are as individuals. That's why we can all have our coffee the way we want it, as well as our entertainment, information, and even the design-your-own-color-scheme shoes you can buy from Nike. And when it comes to media engagement, the more entertaining and personal the messenger can be, the deeper the connection that can be forged.

All of this means that Chayefsky was practically clairvoyant about everything in *Network* but the ending—where Beale is assassinated by the network because of low ratings. In 2010, Howard Beale is reality several times over. He's a multimillionaire diversified across all media, with an audience that is deeply engaged in his every thought and action. Today, no network in its right mind would kill Howard Beale because he's not a crazy newsman but instead a gifted entertainer in a world where engaged audiences are *not* amusing themselves to death. It's the opposite: They are amusing themselves to life.

NOTES

1. Postman, N. (1985). *Amusing ourselves to death: Public discourse in the age of show business.* New York: Penguin. See also http://en.wikipedia.org/wiki/Amusing_Ourselves_to_Death
2. Strauss, N. (2009, September 17). The subversive joy of Stephen Colbert. *Rolling Stone, 110.*
3. Retrieved from http://thinkprogress.org/2009/03/05/santelli-show/
4. Variously attributed. See Mankiewicz, F. (2008). In G. Carter (Producer) & A. Gibney (Director). *Gonzo: The life and work of Dr. Hunter S. Thompson.* London: BBC Storyville.
5. Shafer, J. (2008, October 7). Press box: Bogus trend of the week: Dudes with cats. "As a mélange of fashion notes, celebrity reporting, personal essays, and piffle, 'Sunday Styles' resembles the old-fashioned supermarket tabloids in that it knows that it's a stinking pile of entertaining trash and makes no apologies for it...." Retrieved from http://www.slate.com/id/2201764/

13

THE VISUAL EXPERIENCE

Jeremy Gilbert

Matt Mansfield

- I look at the pictures in it and think "Wow."
- Most often I look at the pictures/videos before anything else.
- I like to look at the pictures/videos even if I don't read the story.
- I sometimes show a picture in it to someone else.
- I like to look at the pictures for a while.
- I love the photography on this show.
- The photography is one of the main reasons that I watch this show.

Henri Cartier-Bresson, the famous French photographer, believed in the power of the real, the calling to reveal life through the lens of his camera in ways not done before the early part of the 20th century. He started a movement. "To me," he said, "photography is the simultaneous recognition, in a fraction of a second, of the significance of an event as well as of a precise organisation [sic] of forms which give that event its proper expression."[1]

Cartier-Bresson coined the term "decisive moment" in 1952 to describe that instant when a photographer knows to click the camera and "see" something that will only exist in that one frame. The resulting picture takes you to that very second. Cartier-Bresson's work influenced a generation of photojournalists who aimed for the reality of that moment. Photographers started to "show" in a way that words had not done before.

But as "decisive" as Cartier-Bresson's epiphany was, the idea that visuals can transport us, can take us places (or make us remember them), became another milestone along one of the oldest paths of understanding. "Images and the art of storytelling have a lengthy and intertwined history: more than 30,000 years ago, humans were using images on cave walls to tell stories and to report on their own world and experiences," explained Fiona Carroll. She described how the ancient cave paintings in Lascaux, France, created an "illusive and convincing narrative." This "new technology," cave painting, helped record events, instruct children, and illustrate folktales.[2]

Now, technologies from newspaper infographics to elaborately directed television shows make visual expression easier and more pervasive than ever. Technology dispersion has turned formerly passive recipients into active participants; as the experiences that people have with images become more personal, more interactive, and more communitarian, they are sharing more about what moves them, with great consequence for media brands.

NEWS PHOTOGRAPHY AND THE NARRATIVE "WOW"

The imagery that transports people inside complex stories works best when woven into a singular story that powerfully allows the viewer to make the photographer's experience his or her own.

Consider the *St. Petersburg Times'* 2009 Pulitzer Prize-winning "The Girl in the Window," a story about Danielle, a six-year-old who had grown up feral, locked in a filthy room the size of a closet, covered with roaches. Danielle might have never seen the sun, and she was unable to speak or laugh when she was adopted by a family in nearby Fort Myers, Florida.

Times photographer Melissa Lyttle, who also won a 2009 National Press Photographers Association award for her work over five months, photographed all phases of Danielle's life: going to the beach, figuring out school, learning to ride horses, attending church services. Lyttle described the process of capturing these emotional images to the Poynter Institute's Steve Myers this way:

> You just let this moment come. Especially the picture at the very end, of Bernie holding her up and Danielle looking out the window with this beautiful light on her—[a lot of times it's a] total surprise. I was in there long enough and they had forgotten me, and they went about themselves, and it just became this really beautiful, beautiful surprise.[3]

The photojournalist needed to become invisible to bond with her subject and allow audience members to experience Cartier-Bresson's "decisive moment." And *Times* readers made an immediate emotional connection with the story—and with Danielle, through the power of the photos: "The photos are so gripping. I would love to know more," Kate from St.

Augustine said. And the package made Brenda from Clearwater extremely angry:

> I have never been so "outraged" by an article in the newspaper! I can't get Dani's little face out of my mind. She and her new family are wished the very best. As for her mother...lock her up in a room with the same conditions she gave to Dani![4]

The eloquent words of the story, written by Lane DeGregory, drew the audience in, to be sure. But the powerful photos actually showed what Danielle's vacant stare looked like in the bubble bath—or the joy she and her stepfather felt as they basked in the sunlight. Those were the moments of Danielle's evolution that stuck with readers, many of whom did exactly what the Calder/Malthouse research suggests: "I look at the pictures in it and think, 'Wow.'"

WHAT READERS WANT TO SEE IN THEIR NEWSPAPERS

The Poynter Institute's 2007 EyeTrack study sought to clarify the relationship that audience members forge with visual storytelling in newspapers. Although the study did not directly address engagement, its results confirmed that "readers preferred live action photos" and seemed to indicate that readers of news preferred documentary photojournalism.[5] Yet, as many North American newspapers cut back on space in print because of current economics, they often downsize photography without taking into account the connection between readers and photojournalism. The past few decades saw a shift toward photos, infographics, and other visual storytelling, so this "solution" needs to be explored to determine how best newspapers can meet their mandate to deliver a critical mass of information and enlightenment.

The importance of the "I like to look at pictures for a while" sub-experience is illustrated by the emphasis on large-scale photos by London's *Guardian*. The paper is printed in Berliner format (18.5" x 12.4", which is smaller than the traditional American broadsheet), and it paces its news packaging with fewer images at larger sizes—reserving space each day for a single center-spread image that tells a news story. The paper has gained international design acclaim as a "World's Best-Designed Newspaper"™ from the Society for News Design and applause from the Design Museum (they named the team behind the paper's transformation from broadsheet to Berliner as one of four nominees for the 2006 "Designer of the Year.")[6] In addition to keen writing and commentary, this display is seen as a key competitive advantage. By dramatically presenting these images, the *Guardian* causes a "Wow" sub-experience and helps the tabloid stand out within the crowded London newspaper landscape.

"The *Guardian*'s daily 'doubletruck' photo is a perfect example of catering to the strength of the print platform," said Dennis Brack, deputy assistant managing editor for news art at *The Washington Post*. "A couple of square FEET of newsprint allow readers to get up close and personal with amazing scenes from around the corner...and around the world. We have an even more-expansive physical format at *The Washington Post*, and we've devoted the broadsheet doubletruck spread of our Sunday 'Style & Arts' section to visually driven storytelling for nearly three years."[7]

ARCHITECTURAL DIGEST AND VISUAL TRANSPORTATION IN MAGAZINES

On the pages of *Architectural Digest*, we're transported into multi-million dollar dreams through carefully composed scenes crafted via creative collaboration between top-notch editors, photographers, and designers. Save for obligatory opening pictures with the main characters (who are delighted to show off their possessions, status, and joie de vivre), the rooms portrayed are shot mostly without people in them. Richly rendered, glorious color spreads allow us to match our aspirations to theirs. The audience completes the experience; it's easier to "see" ourselves in those luxurious spaces without the "clutter" of actual humanity.

Photography in less tony shelter magazines enables us to match our rehab plans with the successes that are shown; travel magazines make us feel that we are "there"; food shots take us into famous kitchens or allow us to create sumptuous or simple dishes well. And the seemingly ever-expanding universe of celebrity chronicled in the pages of *People, US Weekly,* and the like provide "talkabout" material composed of equal parts wannabe and schadenfreude—photos we can "show...to someone else," as the sub-experience puts it. Said *The Washington Post*'s Brack:

> The weekly news magazines, in a glorious past life, capitalized on the strength of their canvas, to present scenes from distant, mysterious worlds to tens of millions of readers. Today, a slimmed-down, unfortunately "right-sized," version of this tradition endures. Jim Nachtwey is still transporting 20 million *TIME* readers to the world's most desperate locales several times a year.[8]

Henry Luce wrote the credo for empowering magazine audiences to "see," which he expressed in his famous mission statement for the long-time queen of weekly magazines, *Life*:

> To see life; to see the world; to eyewitness great events; to watch the faces of the poor and the gestures of the proud; to see strange things— machines, armies, multitudes, shadows in the jungle and on the moon; to see man's work—his paintings, towers, and discoveries; to see things thousands of miles away, things hidden behind walls and within rooms, things dangerous to come to; the women that men love and many children; to see and to take pleasure in seeing; to see and be amazed; to see and be instructed....[9]

DOCUMENTARIES AND TELEVISION: REALITY AND BEYOND

The documentary images of war are a different kind of transportation, taking us to places we could never access on our own and asking us to contemplate the reality of what we're seeing. The modern war photographer James Nachtwey, mentioned above, talked at the 2007 Technology, Entertainment, Design (TED) Conference about what it meant for him to come of age in the 1960s, as documentary photography was playing a pivotal role in the social movements of his lifetime:

> Our political and military leaders were telling us one thing, and photographers were telling us another. I believed the photographers, and so did millions of other Americans. Their images fueled resistance to the war and to racism. They not only recorded history, they helped change the course of history. Their pictures became part of our collective consciousness and, as consciousness evolved into a shared sense of conscience, change became not only possible, but also inevitable.
>
> In the face of poor political judgment or political inaction, it becomes a kind of intervention, assessing the damage and asking us to reassess our behavior. It puts a human face on issues, which from afar can appear abstract or ideological or monumental in their global impact. What happens at ground level, far from the halls of power, happens to ordinary citizens one by one.[10]

Fictional Visual experiences also can illuminate real-life events. Professor Gary Olson, who chairs the Political Science Department at Moravian College in Bethlehem, Pennsylvania, described his experience of seeing the 2008 film *Stop-Loss*. Directed and co-written by Kimberly Peirce (who also directed the award-winning *Boys Don't Cry*), the film is about the Iraq war and the problems facing vets returning to life in Texas:

> It's fiction but more than a few scenes have remained with me, especial-
> ly an indelibly affecting scene with a hospitalized Iraqi vet. In some
> respects the film felt more authentic than the "embedded" media cover-
> age or, in truth, the total lack of coverage of the actual war.[11]

At the same time, authenticity is a crucial value in the experience of consuming visual media. The spread of professional-quality photo and video
editing tools in recent years means that the credibility and honesty of images
and video are increasingly difficult to assume and prove.

Since the 19th-century advent of news photography, image manipulation has been a common problem. In the 1860s, early news photographers
married President Abraham Lincoln's head from one photo with John
Calhoun's more regal body.[12] But these days, news professionals and news
consumers alike are regular users of powerful tools, raising the veracity bar
even higher. "…Visual journalists and their viewers share a set of assump-
tions that provides the foundation for photography's long-lived credibility,"
explained University of Oregon journalism professor Tom Wheeler.[13] Visual
journalism must assume the same responsibility for authenticity as written
content, and straying from visual honesty betrays users' trust. Although tennis player Andy Roddick may be able to laugh off his own digitally
enhanced biceps,[14] altering images distorts the "Wow" sub-experience. In a
world of digital photo manipulation, a stunning photograph or video runs
the risk of being unbelievable instead of amazing.

To preserve the integrity of visual images, news organizations must
become more open and transparent about their standards. This means labeling illustrations more clearly and in larger type and also including a Web link
or excerpt from the organization's policy on photo manipulation to answer
viewer questions. This need for transparency also extends to user-submitted
video or images. Organizations such as Current TV already have and post
clear ethical guidelines for user-submitted content, and the Creative
Commons community has created standards for how video and photography should be shared and credited.[15] More need to follow suit.

THE PHOTOGRAPHY TAKES ME THERE

Some of the best cues on engagement and branding on television don't come
from news programming. Take the case of *Mad Men*, Matthew Weiner's crit-

ically acclaimed AMC series, which employs its own evocative visual language to conjure up the 1960s world of Madison Avenue advertising and the (often sexist) milieu that accompanied it.

The agency at the heart of the show, Sterling Cooper, resembles something we know (advertising) yet also something to which many of us are just being introduced (the process behind creative decisions). *Mad Men* is an exercise in transportation, through everything from its pitch-perfect set design to the meticulous attention to historical detail in clothing and book choices—even the drinks the characters are holding in their hands. The ad men of the show's title are selling ideas, often visual ones, so it makes sense that it succeeds by engaging us in its world, by taking us back to a time at once very different yet not all that long ago.

One episode of *Mad Men* (2007) is built around the naming of the Kodak slide projector, a bit of meta-commentary on nostalgia that comes from the connection people have to photographs. Don Draper, Sterling Cooper's creative director, tells the guys from Kodak what they should call the thing in an eloquent speech aimed at selling all of us:

> This device isn't a spaceship. It's a time machine. It goes backwards. Forwards. It takes us to a place where we ache to go again. It's not called The Wheel. It's called The Carousel. It lets us travel the way a child travels, around and around, and back home again, to a place where we know we are loved.[16]

Mad Men has built an avid fan base through scenes just like that one, which by their "reconstructed veracity" evoke two visual sub-experiences: "I love the photography on this show," and "the photography is one of the main reasons why I watch this show."

VISUALS AND THE INTERNET

Audiences are more in control than ever. They can almost instantly choose any videos they want to see—and they can share their own Visual experiences with others. Popular sites such as YouTube or Flickr gather user-generated content and take the sub-experience, "I sometimes show a picture in it to someone else" to new levels of engagement. These sites alter the "ownership" of experience.

Much of the visual content being shared online now is not professionally made—it's not a controlled world like *Mad Men* but a playground for self-expression. Users can now easily see themselves in this kind of Visual experience. The smartest sites encourage collaborations between professionals and users, designing interfaces that allow users to submit their own work and mix it with the work of the pros.

One question in this space becomes how the size of images starts to play out on computer monitors, smaller laptop screens, or the even tinier screens we now all carry around on our mobile devices. These varied shapes and sizes present new challenges to visual display and audience perceptions.

Mario Garcia, who has designed hundreds of publications, including papers as diverse as *The Wall Street Journal* and *Gulf News* (Dubai), has argued that the seasoned skill sets honed over many years working in print are easily transportable to changing demands. In fact, his viewpoint echoes that of Cartier-Bresson and his decisive moment: "The role of a photo editor has never been more important in an age in which we are bombarded by images everywhere, starting right on the screen of our mobile telephone," Garcia said. "There is a certain immunity that comes with the constant barrage of visuals we are exposed to the moment we open our eyes. So, the good art director/photo editor is forever searching for that one image that stops us cold in our tracks, and makes us look. That is, in essence, what the job of the visual journalist is all about."[17]

NEW WAYS TO COLLABORATE VISUALLY

A little more than a week before the November 2006 U.S. midterm elections, the blog "Design Observer" and AIGA, the professional association for design, launched an online initiative in citizen journalism—voters across the country were asked to submit photographs of the election process at the polls. People took it seriously and sent in almost 450 images.[18] Continuing into the 2008 presidential primaries and general election, and supported by a partnership with *The New York Times* that helped it find a wider base, the "Polling Place Photo Project" began to suggest the power of an active, engaged audience to co-create its own compelling Visual experience. By the time both elections were over, almost 6,000 photos had been uploaded to the AIGA Web site from all 50 states.

As discussed in the chapter on the Co-Producing experience (Chapter 8), that audience impulse has recently sparked the hybrid of pro-am collaboration via Web and mobile devices. Here we further discuss how audiences, by supplying their own images and video, increase engagement and ambient intimacy.

During the 2007 shootings at Virginia Tech in Blacksburg, Virginia, some of the first footage of the campus shootings came from CNN's iReport submissions. In nearly all cases, these visuals augmented other kinds of professional visual journalism, but they added to the viewers' sense of community and loss.

Crowdsharing, in which professional journalists or community groups gather/upload still images in bulk, also allows people to see themselves in both the creation of the work and the work itself. *New York Times Magazine* columnist Rob Walker, who writes the "Consumed" column, engaged his audience by asking them to upload their own images of their local Martin Luther King, Jr. Boulevard as a test of stereotypes. Walker's group photo pool on Flickr amassed more than 500 images from around the country. The use of a public, free photo site like Flickr gave average readers a chance to show a picture to someone else, only this time, instead of finding the picture in a traditional publication, the users had their own chance to tell and share a story.

The professional journalist felt that the result was enriched by its collectivity. "I'm already a journalist, I can already write something with my point of view," Walker told Mark Glaser for the *Online Journalism Review*. "With Flickr, I can say, 'Here's an interesting subject,' and throw it open to others. . . . I think there's an advantage to having it open-ended, because I could have an unlimited number of people contributing to this in an unlimited number of places over an unlimited amount of time."[19]

THE KIDS ARE ALRIGHT

The generation of young people growing up now is "digital natives," a term coined by Marc Prensky in "Digital Natives, Digital Immigrants."[20] And they are again altering the rules for media brands. Their expectations of what creates authenticity are shaped by the always-present role of technology in their lives. They know no other way.

In a 2008 Media Management Center study titled "If It Catches My Eye,"[21] Northwestern University researchers interviewed a cohort of teenagers and concluded that visuals "are an appealing entrée into the news for teens." The study cited several teens' experiences of how they engage with media:

> Kirstie, 16, liked MSNBC's "The Week in Pictures" features because:
> They have short news clip videos. If there was an important address made by the President, then I'd have 30 seconds for that...I probably wouldn't sit down and watch the entire "State of the Union," but I'd watch maybe a minute of it on the Web site.

> Mark, 16, praised yahoo.com's "eye appealing" slide shows and videos:
> Say there's something about the news on there and I'll watch the video and it will give me a story and I'll kind of want to get involved. I just

watched the video last week about the Saddam hanging and, I don't know, I was like thinking it over if it was right or wrong.

Many of these young people are fiercely critical of established conventions for news and information that ignore the increasingly visual media culture in which they have come of age. As *New York Times* media critic David Carr put it, "...students...don't have to think out of the box because they were never in one to begin with."[22] Media companies need to harness and collaborate with this new creative energy.

THE BOTTOM LINE:
VISUAL STORYTELLING MATTERS

Media brands, we believe, should consider these three criteria when working to establish engagement with visual storytelling:

- Create, as we have discussed, compelling transportation experiences by believing in the power of visual language to take audience members places they cannot access or help them escape to places they'd like to go—with an emphasis on informing in ways other than text.
- Create a visual-content environment that extends across the entire brand. Make certain that audiences can rely on the Visual experiences they both expect and will get when they return.
- Create an internal culture that respects visual storytelling, plays by the rules of visual language as they relate to audience engagement, and works to manage creative resources. This culture should empower both staff and audience members who seek to collaborate—in a way that benefits everyone involved.

Brands are at their own "decisive moment" as they strive for survival—strive to matter—and attempt to reinforce a mindset that encourages audiences to "see" in new ways. The engagement that people have with visual content can be a driving force for attention (and time) if treated with some level of primacy. News and information companies will have to be agile and adaptive in responding to advances in technology that will inform how visual stories will and should be told. Without a strategic visual language, we believe, the opportunity to build a compelling visual transportation experience may be lost.

The next five years will be crucial for media brands. "Today, human beings work and think in fragmented ways, but visual language has the potential to integrate our existing skills to make them tremendously more effective," wrote Robert E. Horn in 2001 while serving as a visiting scholar at Stanford University. "With support from developments in information technology, visual language has the potential for increasing human 'bandwidth,' the capacity to take in, comprehend, and more efficiently synthesize large amounts of new information. It has this capacity on the individual, group, and organizational levels."[23]

Immersion in emerging visual storytelling tools — and how they are used to engage audiences — will be critical on the path ahead.

NOTES

1. Knowles, K. Henri Cartier-Bresson. Oxford University Press Inc. via Oxford Reference Online. Retrieved from http://www.oxfordreference.com.turing.library.northwestern.edu/views/ENTRY.html?entry=t91.e503&srn=1&ssid=854521522

2. Carroll, F. (2008). The spatial development of the visual-narrative from prehistoric cave paintings to computer games. In P. Turner, S. Turner, & E. Davenport (Eds.), *Exploration of space, technology, and spatiality: Interdisciplinary perspectives* (2nd ed., pp. 141–154). Hershey, PA: IGI Global.

3. Myers, S. (2008, August 7). Looking through "the girl in the window." *Poynter Online*. Retrieved from http://www.poynter.org/content/content_view.asp?id=148190

4. DeGregory, L. (2008, July 31). The girl in the window. *St. Petersburg Times*. Retrieved from http://www.tampabay.com

5. Quinn, S., & Stark Adam, P. (2007). EyeTracking the news, a study of print & online reading. *Poynter Online*. Retrieved from http://eyetrack.poynter.org/keys_07.html

6. The Design Museum. (2006). *Designer of the year*. Retrieved from http://designmuseum.org/designeroftheyear/

7. Interview. (2009, August 3). Dennis Brack, deputy assistant managing editor for news art. *The Washington Post*.

8. Interview. (2009, August 3). Dennis Brack, deputy assistant managing editor for news art. *The Washington Post*.

9. Janello, A., & Jones, B. (1991). *The American Magazine*. New York: Harry N. Abrams, Inc. p. 113.

10. Natchwey, J. (2007). *James Nachtwey's searing photos of war. TED talks, ideas worth spreading*. Retrieved from http://www.ted.com/talks/james_nachtwey_s_searing_pictures_of_war.html

11. Olson, G. (2008). The emotional power of photography. *ZNet*. Retrieved from http://www.ww.zcommunications.org/znet/viewArticle/17064

12. Farid, H. (2009). *Photo tampering throughout history*. Retrieved from http://www.cs.dartmouth.edu/farid/research/digitaltampering/

13. Wheeler, T. (2002). *Phototruth or photofiction? Ethics and media imagery in the digital age* (p. 131). Mahwah, NJ: Lawrence Erlbaum Associates.
14. *People.* (2007). Andy Roddick laughs off doctored magazine cover. Retrieved from http://www.people.com/people/article/0,,20040515,00.html
15. *Creative Commons, License your work.* Retrieved from http://creativecommons.org/choose/
16. *Mad Men.* (2007). Internet Movie Database. Quotes for Don Draper are from *Mad Men*: The wheel (#1.13). Retrieved from http://www.imdb.com/character/ch0031457/quotes
17. Interview. (2009, July 31). Dr. Mario Garcia, Garcia Media founder.
18. AIGA. *Citizens at the polls, cameras in hand.* Polling Place Photo Project. Retrieved from http://www.pollingplacephotoproject.org/
19. Glaser, M. (2005, November 15). Flickr, Buzznet expand citizens' role in visual journalism. *Online Journalism Review*. Retrieved from http://www.ojr.org/ojr/stories/051115glaser/
20. Prensky, M. (2001, October). Digital natives, digital immigrants. *On the Horizon, 9*(5) 1. MCB University Press. Retrieved from http://www.marcprensky.com/writing/Prensky%20-%20Digital%20Natives,%20Digital%20Immigrants%20-%20Part1.pdf
21. Vahlberg, V., Peer, L., & Nesbitt, M., (2008, January). *If it catches my eye: An exploration of online news experiences of teenagers.* Media Management Center, Northwestern University. Retrieved from http://www.mediamanagementcenter.org/research/teeninternet.pdf
22. Carr, D. (2009, December 21). After a year of ruin, some hope. *The New York Times*, pp. B1, B6.
23. Horn, R. (2001, December 3–4). Visual language and converging technologies in the next 10-15 years (and beyond). National Science Foundation conference on converging technologies (nano-bio-info-cogno) for improving human performance.

14

THE TALK ABOUT
AND SHARE EXPERIENCE/
IMPLEMENTING EXPERIENCES

Steven S. Duke

For newspapers: Something to talk about

- I bring up things I've read in this newspaper in conversations with many other people.
- I like to talk about national news and current events I read about in it.
- I like to give advice and tips to people I know based on things I've read in this newspaper.
- I show things in the newspaper to people in my family.
- Part of my role among friends or family is to keep them informed because I read the newspaper.

For online: Something to talk about

- This site often gives me something to talk about.
- I bring up things I have seen on this site in conversations with many other people.
- I use things from this site in discussions or arguments with people I know.
- I like for other people to know I look at this site.

For magazines: I build relationships by talking about it

- I like to have the magazine around so that others might read it.
- I show some things in the magazine to people in my family so they will understand.

- I bring up things I've read in the magazine in conversations with many other people.
- Reading this magazine is a little like belonging to an organization or a group.
- A big reason I read is to make myself more interesting to other people.

I once had a boss whose driving passion was sports. A natural athlete, he participated in some athletic activity almost every day. He followed and was knowledgeable about everything from football to tennis to horse racing. Naturally, his social conversation—whether in the elevator, at a party, or as the icebreaker before a business meeting—turned to sports.

In contrast, I have never played, enjoyed, or followed sports. Other than work, we had little in common, which meant unscripted meetings could be awkward and silence-filled.

My salvation: the newspaper, of course. Through it, I gained at least a superficial understanding of that day's hot sports topics, and I could join the conversation. It also gave me fodder to offer up other topics when sports talk ran dry. Not all conversational gaps are as awkward as those with the boss, but everyone except those living under vows of silence uses conversation as a social lubricant. Having things to talk about enables us to engage in human society, feel informed, look smart, feel good about ourselves, and draw others out.

After all, news—of the family, the clan, the community, and the world—has been the primary conversation-starter since before the written word. What began with something probably like, "How did you bag that mastodon?" has evolved to "Did you hear? Madoff got 150 years! What do you think?"

So news media have played a central role in fueling conversation from Julius Caesar's *Acta Diurna* in 59 B.C. through handwritten news sheets in 8th-century China to today's *New York Times*.

Research by the Readership Institute and the Media Management Center shows that this social experience—the Talk About and Share experience—is a top driver of usage for most media.[1] When people believe that a media brand satisfies their appetite for things to talk about, they will want to use it.

TALK ABOUT WHAT?

The Talk About and Share experience drives usage for newspapers, magazines, and Web audiences, but it ranks higher in importance for newspapers than it does for the others. It is third in impact on readership for newspapers, behind the experiences of being "a regular part of my day" and "looks out for my interests." It's 12th for online and 14th for magazines—still worth driving, just not as high a priority for these media. (The Talk About and Share experience did not show up as a factor for television audiences.)

So if we're going to drive the experience, what kind of things do people want to talk about? What do you talk about? Things that are important to you or your friends or things that make you more interesting to other people.

Big news is an obvious conversation-starter. When the collapse of Bear, Stearns and Lehman Brothers signaled the beginning of an international economic free-fall, it was a hot topic. So were pirates holding an American sea captain hostage, terrorists rampaging through Mumbai, and the spread of swine flu around the world.

Sports, celebrities, and scandals are prime candidates for sharing. "Do you think Letterman's affair will hurt him with women viewers?" "Do you think Brett Favre will finally retire?"

In some cases, "talk-able" topics can be about strange or silly things: "Did you see that a burglar is suing a homeowner because he fell through the guy's skylight and broke a leg?" "Did you see there's a town that's got a crosswalk for migrating salamanders?"

Stories that align with the Makes Me Smarter experience (Chapter 3) are good prompts for sharing, as are many watchdog stories from big investigations to "action line" columns.

Magazines have long run talk-about-it stories, and the notion is so well embedded at newspapers that newsrooms have jargon for it. They are "talkers" or "Hey Martha!" stories, and they are discussed in daily news meetings everywhere.

The challenge is to deliver the experience consistently, throughout the medium, and over time. We can't count on big news happening every day. Relying too heavily on sports, celebrity, scandal, and silly stories can diminish the value of our brand. So we have to approach every piece of content from concept to final execution with the intent of creating a "talk-able" medium. We do this by asking: "Is this something people will talk about?" "What tools and techniques can we use to enhance the sharing experience?" "How do we play this to take advantage of it as a conversation-starter?"

The key to applying experiences is understanding that they do not describe the editorial content itself, but rather the consumer's reactions to it. Applying experiences requires an unwavering attention to audience.

As then-editor of the Minneapolis *Star Tribune*, Anders Gyllenhaal, said, "Experiences are a way of converting traditional news judgment from editors' definitions (what's most interesting, what's important, what you just can't believe happened) to readers' definitions of how they react (what makes readers feel informed, what gives them something to talk about, what tells them the paper is looking out for their interests)."[2]

So how do we apply what we know about experiences, and in this case the Talk About and Share experience? We can do it at three levels: micro, product, and strategic.

MICRO-LEVEL APPLICATION

At the micro level, it's a way of making news decisions—which stories to pursue, how to approach them, and how to present them.

The daily search for a page one "talker" at newspapers is an example of applying the Talk About and Share experience at the micro level. Here editors are looking to give prominent play to the quirky or offbeat story. The Associated Press RSS feed of Top 10 stories does this. Along with the serious takes about politics, government, war, health, and economics—often stories that people will talk about—AP always includes one "talker." It might be a prominent sports or entertainment story, such as:

- "Armstrong jumps from 10th to 3rd at Tour de France"
- "Ex-'Idol' contestant struck, killed by car in NJ"

Just as often, the AP "talker" is quirky, ironic, strange, or silly, as in these from mid-2009:

- "Woman Jailed after Man Complains about her Cooking"[3]
- "Dimwitted Thieves Steal Fake Cell Phones in Mexico"[4]

Magazines are all about micro-level attempts to drive talk. Just look at cover lines, often posed as questions to promote reader conversation: "Does Iran Have the Know-how to Build the Bomb?"[5] "Can the Future be Built in America?"[6] "What Size Should Models Be?"[7]

Finding and publishing stories of human drama, humor, and pathos are a micro-level application of the Talk About and Share experience. David Johnson, a reporter for the *Lewiston Morning Tribune* in Idaho, has been doing this consistently since 1984, when he launched his now widely copied column "Everyone Has a Story." Johnson picks people at random from the area's telephone book, interviews them, and tells their stories.

Twenty-five years after its birth, the column gets prominent display every Friday on the front page of the newspaper and continues to generate conversation.

"Today's story was about an 11-year-old boy and his pet tree frog, Ricardio," Johnson told me in July 2009. "Last week's story was about a guy and his wife who are in the process of selling everything they own, moving to Israel, and preparing for the second coming of Christ. Week before that was about a 73-year-old guy who was born with one arm shorter than the other and continues to cope. Never know what will be next...that's the beauty of the random process."[8]

Johnson turned these human stories into a book in 2002, *No Ordinary Lives: One Man's Surprising Journey into the Heart of America.* However, long before the book, other newspapers had mirrored his idea, and from 1998 through 2004, CBS correspondent Steve Hartman replicated the concept on air with his "Everybody Has a Story" segment on the *CBS Evening News*, eventually producing more than 100 segments.[9]

MAKING NEWS "TALK-ABLE"

While useful for creating the sharing experience, hunting for the "talker" or relying on a single columnist to produce the quirky or unusual is an inconsistent, unpredictable approach. Editors need to create the experience intentionally.

For example, the *London Free Press'* editors enhanced the talk-able nature of an already intrinsically share-worthy local crime story by how they told it.

During the course of a year, there had been a large number of busts for homegrown marijuana in Ontario. What made the story particularly interesting was that the arrests took place in neighborhoods representing every economic stratum.

The story was inherently a conversation-starter, even were it to be presented with a traditional "Pot busts span London economic spectrum" approach, with a couple of photos of homes that had been raided. Smart editing enhanced the "buzz" elements of the story. The front-page headline addressed readers directly in a style common to magazines, asking, "Do your neighbours grow POT?", with a leafy sprig of cannabis hovering over photos of four raided homes spanning poor-to-rich neighborhoods. A map inside covered two-thirds of a page, with keys locating the 40 busts by date and address.[10]

Imagine the kitchen-table and water-cooler conversations generated by this map, created with a little extra editorial effort. "Who knew the neighbors were up to that?" "Look how close to the kids' school that one is!"

Magazine editors are often intentionally provocative, as *Sports Illustrated* is with headlines such as, "The best way to rule the NL? Start signing AL players"[11] and opinionated "Who's hot, who's not" features designed to generate dispute. All of this is layered on *SI's* "Did you see that...!?" photography, which catches moments that shriek for conversation, such as the stop-action shot of a pitched ball ripping the shirt out of Ranger Derek Holland's pants that ran in the September 14, 2009, issue.

OPPORTUNITIES ONLINE

This micro-level application is even easier online with searchable databases and Google mashups. The *Chicago Tribune*, in one of its continuing watchdog efforts, reported that, "the often sloppy use of perchloroethylene [used widely by dry cleaning stores] has poisoned hundreds of sites in Illinois." A map showing the worst sites accompanied the print story, but online the *Tribune* had a searchable database of all dry cleaning stores in the state. I entered my address and learned that 11 of the 20 cleaners nearest me were contaminated. Of course, I talked about this with family, friends, and neighbors.[12]

Chain-wide, Gannett newspapers have made a virtue of databases to provide information that generates conversational buzz. Gannett's *Des Moines Register*, as one example, has searchable databases on home foreclosures, million-dollar homes, parking tickets, state salaries, school graduation rates, lake water quality, attorney disciplinary records, most popular pet names, and scores more.[13]

Where pertinent, *The Register* supplements databases with PDF files of related documents, such as the contract of University of Iowa football coach Kirk Ferentz.[14] If you aren't a seven-figure wage earner, that one will get you talking.

Magazines, with their niche audiences and targeted content, have been quicker than newspapers to enhance the social experience online. Most facilitate sharing with buttons for emailing articles or linking them to Facebook, Digg, Delicious, reddit, and similar sites. Many others, such as *TIME*, provide buttons that link articles automatically to readers' blogs.

Some periodicals have developed forums where robust reader interaction takes place. *Cosmopolitan*'s online message boards in October 2009 hosted nearly 20,000 threads and multiple times that number of comments on topics ranging from fashion to sex. In the same month, *Better Homes and Gardens* showed more than 24,400 discussions with 400,000 posts on just its "Family Issues" forum.

REAL-WORLD EXPERIMENT

An unintentional comparative experiment in editing for the Talk About and Share experience took place in Canada on February 23, 2006, during the Turin Olympics.

Canadians are hockey-crazy, so when the highly touted Canadian hockey team, coached by the great Wayne Gretzky, was defeated 2–0 by the

Russians in the quarter finals, not even qualifying for a bronze, it was wrenching front-page news across the country.

On the same day, in what some papers treated as a footnote, Canadian Cindy Klassen took the gold in the women's 1,500-meter speed skating, countrywoman Chandra Crawford snared gold in a women's cross-country sprint ski event, and two other Canadian women took Olympic silvers.

The Globe and Mail sandwiched the headline "Sweet Victory, Sour Defeat" below a photo of a smiling Klassen and above one of dejected hockey players. Using similar editorial judgment, the *Toronto Star* put "ELATED" over a picture of Klassen in the embrace of a teammate and "DEFLATED" over a photo of a grimacing Gretzky (see Figure 14.1, p. 184).

Both were accurate, fundamental, solid journalism—but neither got at the heart of the national conversation. The editors of these two papers hadn't gone beyond the news that everyone got from television the night before.

However, two other editors tried intentionally to drive conversation. *The National Post*, using the same Klassen picture chosen by the *Star*, along with a photo of grim-faced hockey players, wrapped the images with "4 MEDALS AND A FUNERAL," playing off the title of the popular movie *Four Weddings and a Funeral*. This simultaneously invoked pop-culture resonance and an idea worth sharing (see Figure 14.2, p. 184).

Even more pointedly, the *Toronto Sun* paired a tight photo of a beaming Klassen with, "Hey, can SHE play hockey?... cuz Team Canada can't."

Each newspaper had the same information and images to tell the story, but each applied different sensibilities. Two newspapers took a "just the facts" tack, while two others recognized the story was the talk of Canada and looked for ways to encourage and drive the conversation.

We can disagree over elements of the *Sun's* headline and whether it works in all markets. The larger point remains that the *Sun's* editors knew what people would be talking about, and they tried to drive the Talk About and Share experience with intent.

Figure 14.1. *The Toronto Star* delivered solid, well-executed journalism in this attractive page 1 package on Canadian success and failure in the previous day's Olympics. However, with a little imaginative editing, the newspaper could have capitalized on the Talk About and Share experience that drives readership.

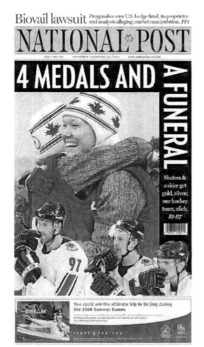

Figure 14.2. Editors at the *National Post* not only created an attractive Olympics package on the front page. They tapped into the Talk About and Share experience with a clever allusion to the movie *Four Weddings and a Funeral*. They contributed an additional conversation point to a natural, "talkable" topic.

PRODUCT-LEVEL APPLICATION

Experiences can also be applied one step up, at the product level, in which one or more experiences become the focus of the title. At this level, editors not only intentionally drive an experience at the story level, as the *London Free Press* did with the pot story or the *Sun* did with the Olympics story, but do it throughout their title with as many stories and in as many ways as possible so it becomes part of the brand identity.

Highlights applies the Talk About and Share experience at the product level. Designed to be a family experience, this magazine for children and their families has conversation-starters built into nearly every page: puzzles, read-to-me stories, jokes, and riddles, and hidden pictures.

For adults, *The Week* is created for readers who want to make themselves interesting to other people. It is both informative and a conversational, "bite-sized" news digest.

For a non-traditional media example, consider Fark.com, a Web site built entirely around aggregating stories people will talk about. Each is designated "scary," "silly," "cool," "asinine," or something similar. You'll find headlines such as:

- "Neighbors of a farm upset that the farm smells . . . like a farm"[15]
- "India christens her first nuclear submarine with a coconut"[16]

Fark.com has established its brand as the place to find tidbits that help you relate to others. If you want guaranteed conversation pieces, you can head to Fark before you head to the party.

That's the kind of go-to brand you can build, but you don't have to turn your publication into a humor site to activate the Talk About and Share experience. The Minneapolis *Star Tribune* joined the Readership Institute in a March 2005 test to see whether editing choices could make a difference in the reader experiences of those under age 30, including the Talk About and Share experience.[17]

The project team chose a typical issue with no extraordinary news and then rethought the editing choices and approaches, keeping the Talk About and Share experience and two others in mind. The team used only stories that had been available to the original editors.

The resulting "Experience Paper" was still driven by hard news. The front page was dominated by stories about a state legislative initiative to collect DNA samples from every person arrested for a felony, a proposal to legalize gambling on poker, and an article about identity theft. But the stories were chosen for the intrinsic "talk-about appeal" and were shaped through headlines, breakouts, images, and story forms to enhance the experience.

Testing stories in the "Experience Paper" with 340 adults ages 21 to 29 revealed that these readers were nearly five times as likely to talk about them as they were the original paper.[18]

OUT OF THE LAB AND INTO THE WORLD

Of course, the *Star Tribune* effort was a one-off controlled experiment, and the obvious question is whether such an effort can be sustained and with what results. A couple of examples provide some answers.

In Santiago, Chile, *Las Últimas Noticias* "is a newspaper designed to start a conversation among its readers," editor Agustin J. Edwards told the International Newspaper Marketing Association World Congress in May 2009.[19]

Las Últimas Noticias is the second-largest print and online newspaper in Chile, with a national edition and a city edition, as well as a Web-first product cycle. Editors and reporters apply the principles used in the Minneapolis experiment throughout the paper, determining story choice, approach, play, headlines, and images with an eye to giving readers things to discuss.

As soon as the earlier and smaller-circulation national edition is ready for the presses, its content is published online, where editors monitor hits and comments, getting real-time data on the effectiveness of their news decisions. This feedback informs the content in the city edition that comes off the presses a few hours later.

As a result of this intense focus, the print newspaper's circulation remained steady from 2005 through 2008, whereas online unique visitors increased by 50 percent. The increased total audience allowed *Las Últimas Noticias* to raise its advertising rates from below market average to above market average over the same period, yielding another valuable payoff.[20]

STRATEGIC-LEVEL APPLICATION

At the strategic level, marketing and promotion efforts are aligned with product-level initiatives to enhance one or more of the experiences as your core mission. You can do this to differentiate your title from competitors or differentiate between your print and Web products.

After the newspaper experience research appeared in 2003, the *Journal Times* of Racine, Wisconsin, began to focus on the Talk About and Share experience, first at the product level and then at the strategic level.

Adopting an idea from that research, the staff at this mid-sized Wisconsin daily began identifying local stories with high potential for con-

versation, writing them to enhance their talk-able nature, labeling them with
a "Debatable" icon and a note inviting readers to think about and discuss
them. Half a dozen "Debatable" stories appeared in every edition, scattered
in all sections, with one on the front page most days. "Debatable" stories
ranged from local sports coaching decisions to a proposal to install parking
meters in the central business district to decisions about U.S. troop deployment levels.

The idea was to make community conversation a primary aspect of the
Journal Times brand. In 2005, the *Journal Times* extended the idea to its Web
site, JournalTimes.com. With its interactivity, connectedness, and sense of
community, the Web is the natural place for the full flowering of the Talk
About and Share experience.

"I realized that not only could we give people something to talk about,
we could provide the forum for them to talk about it," then-editor Randy
Brandt told my Medill colleague Rich Gordon, who writes about the
Community-Connection experience elsewhere in this book (Chapter 9).[21]

In its move to the strategic level, the *Journal Times* aligned its marketing with its content. The brand tag became "Make a Connection." The print
product devoted 20 percent of its front-page banner to its Web address,
where conversation could take place, and flagged topics throughout the
paper that people could comment on. Editors published stories about online
comments.

In the first five months of the online experiment, user comments on
Journal Times blogs and stories went up almost 800 percent and total audience more than doubled, with most of the growth coming from people who
previously had been infrequent visitors. A year later, the increase had held,
with the number of online users who visited the *Journal Times* Web site regularly (once a week or more) more than double what it had been before the
change and monthly page views more than triple, Gordon reported in a case
study he wrote for the Newspaper Association of America.[22]

Driving the Talk About and Share experience with intent, providing a
forum in which the conversation could take place, and using these tactics
strategically to reposition the brand had increased conversation, traffic, and
audience size.

NEXT FRONTIER

The next frontier for journalists trying to enhance the Talk About and Share
experience is, of course, mobile, the ultimate social sharing environment.

The numbers show the importance of mobile. About one third of all
American adults have gone online wirelessly with a cell phone, smartphone,
or PDA.[23] Teen use of mobile phones, which previously had lagged behind

that of adults, grew from 45 percent in 2004 to 71 percent in early 2008, and more than a quarter of teens use these devices to send messages through social networking sites daily.[24]

Asahi Shimbun, the giant Japanese newspaper, was one of the earliest news operations to move into mobile delivery, and today it has more than a million paid mobile subscribers. But development of the iPhone, other smartphones, the Kindle, and the iPad has moved mobile way beyond a simple delivery platform to an interactive, sharing medium that can drive the Talk About and Share experience.

InstantEncore provides a Yelp-like experience in the niche news category of classical music (for more about Yelp, see Chapter 5 on the Utilitarian experience). Through its iPhone application, InstantEncore provides classical music news, concert updates, and podcasts, but it also enhances the Talk About and Share experience with tools to upload photos from concerts and write comments and reviews.[25]

On the general news front, Fwix, which launched in August 2008, has an iPhone application that gives users the ability to contribute news and photos to its news aggregation Web site, which at the time of my writing covered 85 cities.[26]

MAKING THE EXPERIENCE PREDICTABLE AND REPEATABLE

Efforts to contribute to consumers' desire to engage socially by sharing what they know abound these days. The challenge is to provide the experience so consistently that it becomes part of your brand, the way people think about you.

Glance back at the by-medium statements from consumers and co-creators that lead this chapter. Even if you think you are already doing a great job delivering the Talk About and Share experience frequently and consistently across time for your audience, some findings in the Media Management Center's research should give you pause. The study found that media executives thought readers' experiences, whether positive or negative, were far stronger than readers reported.[27]

The *Journal Times'* Randy Brandt experienced that disconnect firsthand after he and his staff made what they thought were dramatic changes in the content and design of the paper. During focus groups conducted in Racine by me and Medill colleague David Nelson (see Medill Innovation Study Projects, Chapter 16), we discovered that readers hadn't noticed the changes at all. Even when prompted, readers couldn't identify changes that Brandt thought were bold and risky.

The implication is twofold. First, readers' experiences with media can be tepid, at best, so it's important that we intentionally drive them. Second, journalists need to better understand how audiences use and respond to their products if they are to enhance the experience.

DELIVERING THE SOCIAL
EXPERIENCE ACROSS TIME

Here are 9 suggestions for consistent delivery:

- Formalize the process of targeting and driving the experience and unflinchingly make it part of editorial decision making, in both choosing and shaping content.

Take, for example, what happened in the newsroom at *Vanguardia Liberal*, the daily newspaper in Bucaramanga, Colombia. Sebastian Hiller, *Vanguardia*'s editor, worked with his staff and management team to select the experiences most relevant to young adults in Bucaramanga, according to Michael Smith, executive director of the Media Management Center. Number 1 on the list was "Gives me something to talk about."[28]

Then they set some guidelines for change in their newsroom. Among them was the creation of an "Experiences Planning Form" to guide all story discussions and planning. Reporters, photographers, and designers used the form at the point of story inception, so everyone focused on reader experiences from the outset. The journalists were asked to describe the central idea of the story and to consider whether it would make readers feel smarter, find value in it, give them something to talk about, or drive another of *Vanguardia*'s target experiences. (A copy of the form appears on Smith's blog.)[29]

At each step of the creation process, staff and editors referred back to the planning form to see whether they had delivered on their goal.

Vanguardia's approach may sound mechanical, but research has shown that formalized processes like this are necessary to change the way things are done—the culture–in any business or institution.

- Be tough-minded about what's "talk-able." You want to show-case content that is uniquely yours and that you can really imagine people chatting about. Be tough when asking, "Will people really talk about this? Why?"

In the *Star Tribune* experiment cited earlier, the newspaper already was aware of the need to provide conversation pieces for readers and tried to spotlight "talkers" every day. In the edition chosen for the experiment, editors of the original Page One had given centerpiece treatment to a story they considered a "talker." The article related the ambition of a local woman to walk every mile of every street in Minneapolis, a few miles at a time. However, then-deputy managing editor Monica Moses observed, "Once you've said that, what's left to talk about?" During the post-mortem of the study, Moses said one of the newspaper's prime needs was to be more rigorous and realistic regarding what people would talk about.

- Present the story in ways to stimulate thinking and discussion instead of a "just the facts, ma'am" approach.

Sometimes it's as simple as writing better headlines. For example, when the *Star Tribune* experience team remade an issue of the paper, it used a story reporting on a National Institutes of Health study about the region of the brain that inhibits risky behavior not being fully formed until the age of 25. The original headline read: "Do teens stay teens until 25?"

The story's lead, however, suggested that slow maturity of the inhibitor was why teens were having more auto accidents, among other things. So the team rewrote the headline more provocatively as, "Not fit to drive until 25?" with a deck asking, "Should the age be raised to vote, drink, or drive?"

The traditional journalism toolbox is loaded with conversation-drivers, including pull-quotes, charts, graphics, maps, photos, video, interactive Flash images, and more. Use them with intent to enhance the likelihood readers will talk about your content.

- Explain what the story means to me, if you want me to talk about it.

Too much journalism still deploys what I call "process stories." These pieces about budgets, legislative in-fighting, environmental arguments, and scores of other topics too often explore in not-so-gripping detail the workings of government and policy makers. What they lack is any hint of what it all might mean to me as a citizen, taxpayer, property owner, voter, or consumer.

Not many people become engaged in deep conversations about process. But they might talk about the tough tradeoff between maintaining free parking in the downtown business district at the expense of cutting hours at the municipal swimming pool.

That's the approach that reporter Bryan Gilmer took in a 2002 budget story in the *St. Petersburg Times*. The headline asked: "City has $548 million to spend: What do you want?" The main story and an array of breakout material laid before readers the hard, real choices that were up for discussion—to keep a beloved older neighborhood branch library or build a new shared library. The articles also explained how readers could express their preferences at the upcoming city council budget hearing.[30]

I have used Gilmer's story with hundreds of journalists at scores of workshops over the past few years, and I have gotten some instructive reactions from the participants.

The workshops were cross-functional, involving people from news, online, advertising, circulation, production, and marketing. Many, although not all, journalists disliked Gilmer's story. They didn't like the question headline or its use of the second person. They objected to the conversational tone of the story, the second-person direct address to the reader. They didn't like that it directly encouraged readers to go to the city council meeting to express their views.

The online staff, circulators, production managers, marketers, and advertising sales people in the workshops universally loved the story. They loved the conversational nature, the second-person address, the lack of formality, and the absence of jargon. They liked the graphics and breakout material that made it easier to understand. They said they learned about how budgets are made, how hard the choices are, and how to participate.

The non-journalists in these workshops are more representative of real readers, and their perspective on the story illuminates some other guides to consistently creating "talk-able" stories. Here is what these real readers are telling journalists they should do:

- Be more personal and connected with your readers.
- Use a conversational tone and don't be afraid to judiciously use second-person address.
- Use graphics liberally. Often they can tell stories more clearly than words, making the stories easier to remember and talk about. Use rollover relational databases online for the same reason.
- Don't be afraid to use question-mark headlines. Newspapers often follow an old-fashioned shibboleth against question headlines. Magazine editors aren't shy about talking directly to their readers this way and successfully convey a close, personal relationship.

As *Star Tribune* experience team leader Nancy Barnes observed: "Newspapers tend to talk about topics, keeping a distance between themselves, the topic, and the reader. In this experiment, we actively sought to talk to readers directly, and engage them every step along the way. That makes the newspaper seem more personal. It goes against our natural instincts, however."[31]

Another precept:

- Energetically join the conversation yourself.

If you want people to talk about what you've got, you have to let them know you've got it. Some of that is accomplished through traditional tools of play, placement, design, graphics, or icons.

However, you also have to use all the digital and social media tools at your disposal. Readers won't always come to you for news, but as Media Management Center research in 2008 found, if it "catches my eye," they'll read it.[32] That means you have to take the news to potential readers through the full roster of social networking tools.

The *Chicago Tribune* is a good current example of a news media company vigorously working to catch readers' eyes through social networking tools and at the same time stir up conversation. It started with the creation of "Colonel Tribune," a quirky Facebook avatar bearing the visage of legendary *Tribune* editor and publisher Colonel Robert R. McCormick topped with a folded newspaper hat. The Colonel—a nom de plume for a small cadre of 20-ish staffers—began by posting *Tribune* story links that his Facebook "fans" might find interesting and could attract interest on various other social network sites. Users then commented on and forwarded the links, continuing the conversation.

Today, in addition to his Facebook presence, Colonel Tribune has 640,000-plus followers on Twitter. Separately, ChicagoTribune is a Twitter Feed providing breaking news alerts (with 20,000 followers), and more than 80 *Tribune* executives, editors, columnists, reporters, and other staff contribute alerts through Twitter accounts under their own names. Some tweet infrequently, but others, such as columnist Eric Zorn and digital editor Bill Adee, tweet throughout the day, providing fodder in the forum created for conversation.[33]

In a Nieman Reports article, Adee said that 60 percent of chicagotribune.com traffic in 2008 came through search engines, Web sites, and blogs. "In all, more than 4,000 sites sent users our way—with 350,000 different clicks."[34]

To help get the most out of social networking, the *Tribune* employs a social media coordinator. "She is there to help our staff as much as it wants to be helped. I don't force Twitter or social media on anyone," Adee said. "You have to want to do it. Otherwise, it won't work. Then you have to understand it. That said, I don't hire anyone who doesn't understand it. I expect it to be part of the package by now."[35]

In mid-2009, the *Tribune* extended its endeavors to get "talk-able" content in front of readers' eyes by launching ChicagoNow, a blog network covering Chicago-focused niche topics. "We have evidence that there are plenty of people who don't use chicagotribune.com because they don't believe we have anything," Adee said. "But they might find chicagotribune.com content through their favorite ChicagoNow bloggers. Thus, it is a way of introducing the *Tribune* to a new audience."[36]

Remember that increasing the Talk About and Share experience correlates with higher readership. Do it better and people will identify with your brand and come back more often. But this experience, more than the others, comes with a free, added bonus: It is viral marketing, the best marketing that money can't buy.

Consumers under age 30 are skeptical of product advertising, have well-tuned antennae for marketing efforts, and take pride in resisting professional persuasion. What they trust are the recommendations of people they know. In today's fragmented media environment, the best endorsement you can get is a personal recommendation from one person to another.

That's an experience worth talking about.

NOTES

1. Peer, L., Malthouse, E., Calder, B., & Nesbitt, M. (2008). *Media experiences: A guide to research by the Readership Institute and Media Management Center*. Unpublished paper.
2. Nesbitt, M., & Lavine, J. (2005, April). Reinventing the newspaper for young adults: A joint project of the Readership Institute and *Star Tribune*. *Readership Institute*. Retrieved from http://www.readership.org/experience/startrib_overview.pdf
3. Top 10 stories via my.yahoo.com (2009, July 8).
4. Top 10 stories via my.yahoo.com (2009, July 7).
5. *Wired* online. (2009, October 5). Retrieved from http://www.wired.com/dangerroom/2009/10/does-iran-have-the-know-how-to-build-the-bomb/
6. *BusinessWeek*. (2009, September 21). Cover. Retrieved from http://www.businessweek.com/magazine/content/09_38/b4147046115750.htm
7. *Glamour*. (2009, October). Cover.
8. David Johnson, by email. (2009, July 10). Cover.
9. Bernbaum, B. (2009, July 11). Steve Hartman: Assignment America correspondent. CBS News Web site. Retrieved from http://www.cbsnews.com/stories/2002/05/16/broadcasts/main509349.shtml
10. Pedro, K. (2005, April 30). Do your neighbours grow pot? *London Free Press,* pp. A1, A10.
11. *Sports Illustrated*. (2009, September 14). Cover.
12. Hawthorne, M. (2009, July 26). Dry cleaners leave a toxic legacy, *Chicago Tribune*. Retrieved from http://www.chicagotribune.com/health/chi-dry-cleaners-pollution-bd26-jul26,0,5184515.story. Hawthorne, M., Mark, R., Germuska, J., Little, D., & Boyer, B. (2009, July 26). *Dry cleaners' toxic legacy: Find sites near you*. Retrieved from http://drycleaners.apps.chicagotribune.com/

13. *Des Moines Register* list of databases. (2009, July 26). Retrieved from http://data.desmoinesregister.com/watchdog/index.php
14. University of Iowa Head Coach Contract. Retrieved July 26, 2009, from http://www.desmoinesregister.com/assets/pdf/D2138899720.PDF
15. Fark.com (2009, July 26).
16. Fark.com (2009, July 26).
17. *Star Tribune* experience study: Overview page. Readership Institute. Retrieved from http://www.readership.org/experience/experiencepaper.asp
18. *Star Tribune* experience study: Overview page. Readership Institute. Retrieved from http://www.readership.org/experience/experiencepaper.asp
19. Edwards, A. J. (2009, May 13). Presentation to INMA World Congress, Miami, Florida.
20 Edwards, A. J. (2009, May 13). Presentation to INMA World Congress, Miami, Florida.
21. Gordon, R. Audience building initiatives: Online community at the *Racine Journal Times*. Retrieved from the Newspaper Association of America Web site at http://www.growingaudience.com/BestPractices/CaseStudies/Audience Building/Online-Community-at-the-Racine-Journal-Times.aspx
22. Gordon, R. Audience building initiatives: Online community at the *Racine Journal Times*. Retrieved from the Newspaper Association of America Web site at http://www.growingaudience.com/BestPractices/CaseStudies/Audience Building/Online-Community-at-the-Racine-Journal-Times.aspx
23. Horrigan, J. (2009, July 22). America unwired. Retrieved from http://pewresearch.org/pubs/1287/wireless-internet-use-mobile-access
24. Lenhart, A. (August 19, 2009). *More and more teens on cell phones. Pew internet & American life project*. Retrieved from http://pewresearch.org/pubs/1315/teens-use-of-cell-phones
25 InstantEncore. Retrieved from http://www.instantencore.com/
26. Fwix. Retrieved from http://fwix.com/about/cities
27. McCauley, T., & Nesbitt, M. (2003, May). *The newspaper experience study, Readership Institute*. Retrieved from http://www.readership.org/consumers/data/newspaper_exp.pdf
28. Smith, M. P. (2009, July 13). *Editing for experiences—one day at a time*. Readership Institute blog. Retrieved from http://www.readership.org/blog2/2006/09/editing-for-experiences-one-day-at.html
29. Smith, M. P. (2009, July 13). *Editing for experiences—one day at a time*. Readership Institute blog. Retrieved from http://www.readership.org/blog 2/2006/09/editing-for-experiences-one-day-at.html
30. Roy Peter Clark wrote in detail about this story at the Poynter Institute's Web site. Retrieved on July 13, 2009, from http://poynter.org/content/content _view.asp?id=52418
31. Nesbitt, M., & Lavine, J. (2005, April). Reinventing the newspaper for young adult. *Readership Institute*. Retrieved from http://www.readership.org/experience/startrib_overview.pdf
32. Vahlberg, V., Peer, L., & Nesbitt, M. (2008, January). If it catches my eye. *Media Management Center*. Retrieved from http://www.mediamanagementcenter.org/research/teeninternet.asp

33. For examples, search Twitter for ColonelTribune, ChicagoTribune, EricZorn, and Bill80. For a complete list of *Tribune* staff with Twitter accounts, see http://www.chicagotribune.com/community/chi-chicago-tribune-twitter-users,0,7337114.htmlstory

34. Adee, B. (2008, Winter). Digging into social media to build a newspaper audience. *Nieman Reports*. Retrieved from http://www.nieman.harvard.edu/report-sitem.aspx?id=100697

35. Adee, B. (2009, July 26). Facebook exchange with the author.

36. ChicagoNow is at http://www.chicagonow.com/

III

EXPERIENCE CASE STUDIES

15

CASE STUDY

Food Network

Ben Sylvan

It's not the easiest time to be in magazine publishing, let alone to be starting a new publication. The economic downturn, shifts to digital media, and a more general reluctance from ad buyers to purchase print advertising have led to a depressed state for the industry.

According to the Publishers Information Bureau, estimated ad page revenue dropped 3 percent in the first quarter of 2010 versus the same period in 2009. But this came after ad pages for major consumer titles dropped 17 percent in the fourth quarter of 2008 compared with the same time period in 2007, 26 percent in the first quarter of 2009 compared with 2008, and 30 percent in the second quarter of 2009 compared with the year before.[1] Accordingly, *VIBE*, *Blender*, *Condé Nast Portfolio*, *O At Home*, *CosmoGirl*, *Quick & Simple*, *Men's Vogue*, *Hallmark Magazine*, *Country Home*, and *Domino* were just a handful of the print publications that folded between 2007 and 2009.

Regardless, *Food Network Magazine* has thrived. A partnership between Scripps Networks and Hearst Magazines, the publication debuted as a newsstand-only test issue in October 2008 with a rate base of 300,000 (the circulation guaranteed to advertisers).[2] After newsstand sales hit that target within three weeks, the magazine released another test issue in January 2009 and then launched a May–June issue, both with a rate base of 400,000. When that circulation promise was carried forward to the August–September issue, it delivered a circulation of 900,000, more than doubling the exposure promised to advertisers. As a result of cooking up such success, executives announced the magazine would increase its rate base to 1 million in January 2010, six months ahead of schedule.[3]

Of course, high circulation isn't always indicative of advertising dollars. Engagement and demographics also influence ad revenue, meaning that plenty of high-circulation magazines struggle to bring in advertising. But with *Food Network Magazine*, everything worked together to create tremendous ad demand. According to the Magazine Publishers of America, the percentage of ad pages in magazines has ranged between 45 and 51 percent during the past 10 years, with ad pages dropping 11.7 percent in 2008.[4] But *Food Network Magazine*'s June–July 2009 issue closed with 61 full pages of ads — a 40 percent ad-edit ratio, quite credible for a new publication during a recession. If you include partial-page ads, the ratio moved closer to an impressive 50 percent. After releasing six issues in 2009, the magazine is slated to deliver 10 issues in 2010, thanks to both reader demand and ad support.[5]

The magazine's success as of early 2010 is indicative of Food Network as a whole. Again, despite the economic downturn and fractionating viewership facing the TV industry, Food Network's core product, its cable network, is also thriving. Launched in 1993 with a 6.5-million subscriber base, Food Network reached 98 million U.S. households as of August 2009 and consistently ranks among the top 10 cable networks in ratings among viewers 25 to 54 years old.[6] June 2009 was its highest-rated month to date, and the second quarter of 2009 was its best in terms of prime time and total day impressions.[7] Affiliate fees for the company increased 17 percent in the first quarter of 2009 compared with the previous year. Guy Fieri's Food Network-branded book, *Diners, Drive-Ins, and Dives*, became a *New York Times* bestseller.[8]

Clearly, Food Network must be doing something right. But what about it appeals to the palates of consumers and advertisers? By mirroring the process recommended in this book, Food Network has built a strong experiential media brand that translates well across platforms.

STIRRING EXPERIENCES

Recall that this book defines engagement in terms of experiences — a set of beliefs that people have about how a media brand fits into their lives.[9] Experiences are not about the brand itself but rather the relationship between the audience member and brand. Like most recipes on foodnetwork.com, Food Network's brand concept is alluring yet simple. Mix in one part Utilitarian experience (Chapter 5) with two parts Anchor Camaraderie (Chapter 10), then toss them with a dose of comfort and a dash of Makes Me Smarter (Chapter 3), and you start to explain the network's high concept.

Although Food Network has its identity locked down, it took time to find the right recipe. Upon its launch, the network consisted primarily of stand-and-stir shows where chefs deftly showed the audience how to cook gourmet meals. Back then the brand fit into people's lives in a utilitarian way—consumers simply learned recipes to perform at home.

As the Internet grew, Food Network loyalists found more places to replicate the Utilitarian experience. Thus, a network dedicated to demonstration shows started to become less sustainable and differentiated. After Scripps Howard purchased Food Network in 1997, it was determined that long-term success hinged on adding more meaning to consumers' lives. Erica Gruen, CEO of Food Network in the late 1990s, once said, "People don't watch television to learn things."[10]

Three years before Food Network was bought out, Scripps chief executive Ken Lowe held up a newspaper to his board. He said the front page represented CNN, the sports section symbolized ESPN, and the home-and-garden section could be owned by Scripps.[11] When Scripps purchased Food Network, Lowe's vision took a step toward being fulfilled. The network lost $13 million in its first year under Scripps, but it became profitable by 2000.

The success can be credited to a change in brand concept. What grew up as a network where food equaled cooking morphed into a concept where food meant lifestyle, opening the floodgates for consumers who love to eat even if their idea of cooking is spaghetti with Ragu. Food Network evolved to describe itself as, "A unique lifestyle network and Web site that strives to be way more than cooking." According to senior VP of programming, Bob Tuschman, one of the station's strengths is that its appeal transcends demographics.[12] Food Network executives work under the premise that everybody likes to eat—whether by cooking or going out to restaurants, by eating alone or in big groups, or by tailgating or hosting dinner parties.

Framing its brand concept through the lens of experiences rather than demographics has helped the network increase engagement across the board. For instance, after Guy Fieri won "Next Food Network Star" in 2006, the network's median viewer age dipped from between 51 and 52 to 48.[13] With a rock-and-roll attitude and a youthful demeanor that successfully straddles the line of edgy, Fieri embodies a subtle but safe departure from the brand's instructional heritage, ensuring that Food Network stays true to its brand while bringing in new viewers through his diner food-focused content.

As Food Network started to better understand its potential consumers, it tweaked the experience delivered to consumers. First, it spiced up the Utilitarian experience by creating programming around engaging hosts such as Rachael Ray and Emeril Lagasse under the implicit intention of delivering an Anchor Camaraderie experience. "We decided to shift our emphasis from people who like to cook to people who love to eat," Gruen said.[14] "We needed to make the shows more personality-driven." The network then tweaked the delivery, using consumer insight and cultural inferences to shape delivery and add experiences. By 2005, its tagline read, "Way More Than Cooking," which pushed the experiences away from utilitarianism once and for all.

A MENU OF EXPERIENCES

The key to strategically presenting experiences is to determine what potential viewers want in the network and then shaping contact points around that ideology by using culturally relevant differentiators to distinguish the brand from others. (This is the central point made by Bobby Calder in Chapter 2.) Food Network has done this well, discovering a collection of experiences that together have led to significant success. It's important to note that not every show or extension must capture each of the concept's experiences. Successful media brands such as Food Network use segmentation to deliver relevant experiences to different groups.

The utilitarian experience. As noted, Food Network launched with a concept in which the primary experience was to teach its audience how to make exquisite dishes. A typical show had an expert chef giving unadorned directions, emphasizing the food's quality rather than the chef's personality. According to Calder and Malthouse, this is a Utilitarian experience.[15]

The Food Network's success snowballed as it moved toward providing richer experiences, but that's not to say it doesn't integrate Utilitarian experiences into programming today. The deep relationship many original consumers have with the Food Network centers on instruction. The brand doesn't have to stress this experience, but for legitimacy's and heritage's sake it's important not to completely move past providing instruction.

What makes Food Network so successful is its strategy of using cultural understanding to guide its Utilitarian experience. Food Network knows that its audience seeks quick, easy-to-make dishes rather than the elaborate recipes the network ran in its infancy. With that in mind, it tweaked its touch points to make instruction accessible to everyday people. Nearly every show on the network operates under a philosophy of easy cooking for everyday people. Trademark shows include *Everyday Italian*, *5 Ingredient Fix*, and *30 Minute Meals*.

Food Network has also started to use cultural references to create utilitarian content relevant to today's economic downturn. The self-explainable *Ten Dollar Dinners*, for instance, premiered in August 2009 after host Melissa d'Arabian won "The Next Food Network Star" contest with affordable recipes.

Although utilitarian shows are vital to Food Network's heritage and deliver on one brand promise, there's a strategic way to convey that experience and an appropriate time to deliver it. That's why programming differs drastically during the day and in prime time. Instructional programming dominates the daytime hours, as the network aims to capture stay-at-home moms. During prime time, several other experiences are used to reach and engage the consumer base.

The anchor camaraderie experience. The biggest change in Food Network's brand concept over the years has been placing tremendous importance on talent. This first manifested itself in on-air talent, but it's now a huge part of every Food Network contact point.

Emeril Live, hosted by the brand's first major personality, Emeril Lagasse, was Food Network's marquee show for 11 years, starting in 1997. An instructional program at its core, *Emeril Live* differentiated Food Network from its old self by being taped in front of a live audience with the gregarious host and a house band. Lagasse became a David Letterman with a toque and a spoon.

Today, personalities serve as the network's primary ingredient—so much so that Scrippsnetworks.com describes it as "a unique network and Web site that strives to surprise and engage its viewers with likeable hosts, personalities, and the variety of things they do with food." "We are a personality-based network," Tuschman said.[16] "When people think of the Food Network, they think of a particular talent." The rationale behind this tweak increased the entertainment value and engagement through a secondary but vital and classic Anchor Camaraderie experience.

Food Network now places as much—if not more—emphasis on personalities than cooking skills when hiring talent. If a chef can't keep the audience entertained while slicing and dicing, then he or she can't become Food Network talent, no matter how *magnifique* his or her cooking skills may be. In his blog during *The Next Food Network Star*, brand icon Bobby Flay credited Melissa d'Arabian's win to her personality.

> In the end, Melissa's personality "popped" more for me than Jeffrey's did. When I referred to him as the "Zen master," I worried that at times his "steady as he goes" demeanor could feel slightly flat and predictable in comparison to Melissa.

Food Network ensures that the Anchor Camaraderie experience seeps into each of its contact points. This experience works in concert with Utilitarian experiences to guarantee that the network never feels like school even if consumers indeed learn something. During instructional cooking shows, hosts talk to the camera as if they're speaking with a friend. They use interactive diction such as "you" and in some cases tape from studios designed to look like homes, giving off the impression that viewers are welcomed into the hosts' lives.

Food Network strategically employs this experience through its other media platforms. On Food Network's online store, shoppers can browse by host. Then in the middle of foodnetwork.com's home page, a "Who's Cooking" module allows viewers to visit personality-specific vertical sites where they can watch videos, search for their recipes, scan through photo galleries, or learn more about their favorite host. Most TV stations prioritize talent, but giving each personality an online vertical shows how serious Food Network takes this experience.

Comfort experience. Symbolic of Food Network's cultural understanding, the brand has added an important experience that, although not specifically discussed in this book, became especially relevant during much of the past decade. This Comfort experience started to surface after September 11, 2001 when consumer insight revealed a desire to escape from reality in a secure manner—to be able to feel good. "We had to change our focus," said Susan Stockton, Food Network's senior VP of culinary production.[17] "People wrote in and said they loved watching, but more as armchair cooking. The recipes were fabulous but complicated. They really wanted to know how to make a great meatloaf or perfect brisket." The network tweaked its menu to reflect the cultural shift, relying on its diverse talent pool to help viewers create easy-to-make comfort food. Now much of the programming touches on this category, which probably has gained renewed experiential relevance during the economic recession.

The Comfort experience is loosely related to the Timeout experience (Chapter 11) but is differentiated by its goal of making consumers feel good. Most shows are filmed in non-threatening sets, with muted décor and everyday cooking utensils. Other than in *Iron Chef America*, you won't see much chrome. And shows like *Giada at Home* and *Down Home with the Neelys* are filmed on sets that appear to be the hosts' actual home.

Then there are the actual hosts. While Food Network emphasizes personality, it makes sure its talent appeals to a wide array of people. No host is too in your face; rather, they're likable in non-threatening ways. Rachael Ray, perhaps the network's breakout star, is attractive in a young-motherly way. She appeals to men but dresses conservatively and acts in a way that doesn't threaten women. Giada De Laurentiis, the closest thing the brand has to a bombshell, nevertheless dresses rather conservatively while drawing in teenage boys with her natural good looks.

By using formats familiar to potential consumers, the content is presented in a manner that audiences find comfortable. To supplement its prime-time schedule in lieu of the stand-and-stir shows, Food Network builds off our nation's obsession with competitions to attract male viewers. This is especially evident in prime-time shows such as *Iron Chef America*, which pits chefs against one another and features Alton Brown delivering play-by-play commentary as if it's a football game.

Makes me smarter experience. The final experience tied into Food Network's brand concept is the Makes Me Smarter experience (Chapter 3). Closely related to the Utilitarian experience, the Makes Me Smarter experience is geared to educate about food in an easy manner. It delivers utility to consumers in a more subtle way than stand-and-stir experiences.

In the case of Food Network, the key differentiator between Utilitarian and Makes Me Smarter experiences comes in the delivery. When delivering the Utilitarian experience, Food Network uses a step-by-step process in which viewers can follow along to explicit direction. In well executed Makes Me Smarter experiences, the nuggets seem to appear organically. The consumer is more concerned with being entertained than with getting explicit directions, even though the subconscious motivation may be to know what to order at fancy restaurants.[18] In *Iron Chef America*, for instance, viewers learn new ways to consume the often-exotic secret ingredient through an entertaining delivery. Then at the end of each episode, judges casually explain how to taste and talk about the exquisite food the contestants made.

In *Food Detectives*, Ted Allen and his team conduct experiments to find the truth behind well-known food questions such as, "Does turkey really make you sleep" or "Is double-dipping really unsanitary." And *Unwrapped* host Marc Summers unveils secrets behind the ingredients in such everyday food as candy.

CONTACT POINTS AND MEDIA EXTENSIONS

One of the keys to Food Network's past success and future sustainability is the media neutrality of its four primary experiences. That is, these experiences can be carried over to platforms other than the cable network. Beyond the obvious media (Web site, TV, and magazine), Food Network has successfully provided brand-relevant experiences on several other platforms.

According to Bobby Calder's "Integrated Marketing Paradigm," the brand concept is part of a continuous cycle in which a group of experiences combines to accentuate the concept. The experiences are in turn created by several contact points, which are any moments in which the consumer experiences the brand in a way that clarifies or distills the concept. Effective contact points lead to the consumer's heightened perception in accordance with the brand concept.

By looking at what Food Network hasn't taken on, you get a sense of the importance the network places on its four primary experiences. When longtime Food Network personality Mario Batali's newest show, *Spain...On the Road Again*, premiered in 2008, it ran on PBS rather than Food Network. The series featured Batali touring around Spain with *New York Times* food columnist Mark Bittman, Spanish actress Claudia Bassols, and American actress Gwyneth Paltrow, consuming local cuisine. The show's goal was to go back to exploring food on an educational basis. "My shtick was information. And the Food Network, quite honestly, was tired of me and couldn't find a way to use my information," Batali said.[19]

The slow-paced, low-production show starred scenery and food rather than the personalities. The manner in which the hosts traveled (driving through Spain in a cramped car) and ate (typically fancy fare) represented the antithesis of a comfortable experience. There were also few step-by-step recipes. The only Food Network experience somewhat captured by the show was the Makes Me Smarter experience. Because it didn't encapsulate other Food Network experiences, the Food Network strategically passed on Batali's show.

The web site. Foodnetwork.com feeds into Food Network experiences with a strong emphasis on their Utilitarian, Anchor Camaraderie, and Comfort aspects. The homepage includes several above-the-fold modules dedicated to recipes. Running content pieces include the self-explanatory "Featured Recipe" and the aptly named "What's for Dinner" utilitarian content pieces.

Of course, plenty of cookbook Web sites thrive on the Internet; the key for foodnetwork.com's success involves differentiating its recipes to feed into the brand promise. To accomplish that, the site as of this writing makes it easy to find simple recipes with its "Quick Meals" module and locate affordable options with its "Budget-Friendly Cooking" section. There's even a permanent listing for "Quick & Easy" in the navigation bar. Competitor Web sites foodandwine.com and allrecipes.com place far less emphasis on budget constraints and ease of recipes. Foodandwine.com tailors to more sophisticated foodies with navigation links to "wine & cocktails." Allrecipes.com is a portal for recipes that are mostly organized by food type, whether it's the main ingredient (chicken), time of the year (holidays), or cooking type (grilling).

Rather than running a portal of user-generated recipes, foodnetwork.com focuses on personalities by featuring a database of the best recipes from each of its hosts. Users can also go to pages for any of their favorite chefs and link to any of their shows, videos, recipes, or short bios.

The print magazine. The magazine's early success can be traced to how well the brand's experiences translate to the print platform.

Each magazine experience gets delivered in a meaningful, yet different, way than on TV or the Internet. In the August–September 2009 issue, for example, the middle 70 pages were dedicated to utilitarian recipes that would be tough to convey on TV, including Makes Me Smarter experiences such as calories per servings, serving sizes, and the time it takes to make each recipe. The magazine differentiates itself from competitors such as *Food & Wine* and *bon appétit* by framing the recipe sections around easy and affordable options while bulwarking the Anchor Camaraderie experience by presenting recipes through the network's talent.

The front of the magazine speaks to the Makes Me Smarter experience with its "In the Know" department. With elements such as "25 Things Chefs Never Tell You" or features on the country's weirdest food laws, this entire department helps readers learn something in a light manner, perhaps mobilizing the Entertainment and Diversion experiences (Chapter 12).

The very act of expressing these experiences via a magazine also speaks to the Comfort experience in and of itself. Despite current stresses, magazines are historically a safe, secure way to find news and an alternative for consumers who aren't comfortable with getting their news on the computer.

Books. By framing cookbooks around personalities rather than food types, Food Network provides a product that effectively meshes together Utilitarian and Anchor Camaraderie experiences. Then by focusing on comfort foods, these books add the Comfort experience for good measure.

T.G.I. Friday's. Food Network partnered with T.G.I. Friday's for *Ultimate Recipe Showdown*, a Fieri-hosted program where cooks from across the country competed to earn the chance to have his/her recipe featured at T.G.I. Friday's restaurants nationwide. A Middle America staple, T.G.I. Friday's was recognized by the American Brands Council in 2006 as one of the country's strong brands. Although it typically features a bar, the 600-location chain is considered a family-friendly restaurant.[20] From burgers to pasta to steak to ribs to fried seafood, the menu at T.G.I. Friday's is full of traditional comfort food as well, served in an atmosphere that makes everybody feel at home. Food Network's first foray into hawking actual food was designed to intensify the Comfort experience it strives to deliver.

Food Network game: *Cook or be cooked*. During the 2009 holiday season, Food Network released a Nintendo Wii video game, *Cook or Be Cooked*.[21] With the goal of simulating authentic cooking situations, Food Network's game features 30 recipes for players to virtually prepare through step-by-step directions. Once your meal wraps up, Food Network personalities evaluate it and provide one-on-one feedback. By having users actually interact with the network's personalities, the game could give the brand its most powerful Anchor Camaraderie experience.

Kohl's. In perhaps the brand extension furthest from its core, Food Network partnered with Kohl's in 2007 to release a line of kitchen items. The choice of partner allowed the network's experiences to align with the brand concept and bring about a sense of comfort—Kohl's isn't as controversial as Wal-Mart or as expensive as Nordstrom, but it's large enough to

be easy to find and affordable enough to not be out of reach. Food
Network's penchant to attach its personalities to products fits this partnership. Bobby Flay, for instance, attached his name to grilling and kitchen
products whose Southwestern colors and style fit his personality. Kohl's
Web site features a Flay bio and videos full of tips from Flay, ensuring he's
not just a non-involved name. And while you're looking for Food
Network-branded plates or cutlery, you'll find modest, classic designs in
lieu of ultra-modern chic products.

ENGAGEMENT

Food Network's strategic approach to managing its contact points has created a brand that engages its consumers well. According to the 2008 Beta
Research Brand Identity Study, Food Network ranked number one among
52 basic cable companies for women 18 and older in terms of being "One of
my favorite channels" and number one among adults 18 and up when it
came to "Has hosts and on-air personalities I like." It tied for number one
among adults in terms of "Pay attention to commercials airing on the network" and, most important, tied for first among adults for "More likely to
buy products advertised on my network."[22]

Such engagement typically supports a medium conducive to effective
advertising. A 2007 study led by Malthouse and Calder found that stronger
experiences were associated with higher ad effectiveness for 36 of 39 measured magazine experiences and 38 of 44 measured newspaper experiences.

Food Network uses the concept of engagement to sell ad space. In
January 2009, Food Network saw a 44 percent spike in online ad revenue
from food marketers from selling congruent advertising and presenting digital content in tune with its audiences' needs.[23] The success was indicative of
a larger trend, not to mention another example of the network's consumer
insight. Between July 2007 and January 2009, FoodNetwork.com grew by
more than 3 million unique users, to 11.3 million, according to ComScore.
And according to senior vice president of ad sales, Jon Steinlauf, Food
Network's online properties account for between 7 and 8 percent of its
annual revenue, a percentage that trumps most of its cable counterparts.

Engagement works best when selling congruent advertising. Kraft has
been one of the network's largest partners for more than a decade, basing its
marketing spending on the idea of engagement. As early as 1998, Kraft partnered with Food Network for a series of customized content that tried to
capture already engaged viewers.[24] *Kraft Food Bites* featured vignettes where
Food Network hosts offered clever cooking tips in which Kraft products
organically served as key ingredients. "If you can parallel the brand's essence

with a meal solution, you've heightened the attentiveness of your audience," said Gary Gruneberg, then-director of media buying at Kraft Foods.

Kraft products remain sprinkled throughout the network to this day, taking advantage of its high engagement. This engagement and a diverse audience base also attract plenty of non-food ad partners. In the magazine's August–September issue, the opening spread had an advertisement for Intel, the following spread had an ad for Buick, and the back cover had a Clinique ad.

THE FUTURE

As the magazine demonstrates, Food Network is healthy. That's not to say it won't face challenges. One key to help brands such as Food Network remain successful and relevant is to stay ahead of the cultural spectrum. Much of Food Network's success can be credited to its universal experiences. That is, people have and will always (at least in the foreseeable future) equate food with social settings.

But the Comfort experience and many differentiators could change with the culture. As previously noted, Food Network really started to stress comfort after September 11, 2001, because it spoke to a psychological need of consumers. Since then, the U.S. has faced two wars and a recession, and tumultuous times have historically led to consumers seeking comfort and stability. But eventually the wars will end and the economy will turn around—and consumers may lose interest in being comforted through food and instead may seek out fancier food in chic settings. In that case, Food Network would risk losing much of its market share if it didn't tweak its core experiences. Or what if the culture starts to revolt at the country's hectic lifestyle? What if family time again becomes a priority? Then quick-and-easy recipes may lose their appeal, and Food Network may lose ground.

The point is that while it's important to try to stay culturally relevant, even success to date doesn't preclude Food Network from having to be open to changing and/or continuously managing its experiences.

NOTES

1. Ovide, S. (2009, July 10). Ad pages in consumer magazines fall 30%. *The Wall Street Journal*. Retrieved from online.wsj.com/article/SB124726569778525439.html

2. Flamm, M. (2009, July 22). *Food Network Magazine* is cooking. Retrieved from http://www.crainsnewyork.com/article/20090722/FREE/907229971

3. Bell, L. (2009, July 23). *Food Network* expands borders, rate base, and campaign. Retrieved from http://www.dmnews.com/food-network-expands-borders-rate-base-and-campaign/article/140542/

4. Moses, L. (2009, January 19). Magazine ad/edit balance falls off. Retrieved from adweek.com.

5. Flamm, M. (2009, July 22). *Food Network Magazine* is cooking. Retrieved from http://www.crainsnewyork.com/article/20090722/FREE/907229971

6. Berr, J. (2009, July 28). Yummo! Food Network soars as restaurants flounder. Retrieved from http://www.dailyfinance.com/story/media/media-world-yummo-food-network-soars-as-restaurants-flounder/19100672/

7. ScrippsNetworksInteractive.com

8. Lafayette, J. (2009, February 15). Fieri has recipe for luring younger viewers to Food Network. *TV Week*. Retrieved from http://www.scrippsnetworks.com/newsitem.aspx?id=276

9. Calder, B., & Malthouse, E. (2008). Media engagement and advertising effectiveness. In *Kellogg on Advertising & Media* (pp. 3–5). Hoboken, NJ: John Wiley & Sons.

10. Pollan, M. (2009, July 29). Out of the kitchen, onto the couch. *The New York Times*. Retrieved from http://www.nytimes.com/2009/08/02/magazine/02cooking-t.html

11. Beard, A. (2003, October 8). Growth from homes and gardening. *Financial Times.* Retrieved from ft.com

12. Alper, N. (2007, Fall). Recipe for success: The Food Network phenomenon. *Celebrated Living.* Retrieved from http://www.celebratedliving.com/tabid/3097/tabidext/3247/default.aspx

13. Lafayette, J. (2009, February 15). Fieri has recipe for luring younger viewers to Food Network. *TV Week*. Retrieved from http://www.scrippsnetworks.com/newsitem.aspx?id=276

14. Essex, A. (1998, November 13). Recipe for success. *Entertainment Weekly.* Retrieved from ew.com

15. Calder, B., & Malthouse, E. (2008). Media engagement and advertising effectiveness. In *Kellogg on Advertising & Media* (pp. 11–12). Hoboken, NJ: John Wiley & Sons.

16. Alper, N. (2007, Fall). Recipe for success: The Food Network phenomenon. *Celebrated Living.* Retrieved from http://www.celebratedliving.com/tabid/3097/tabidext/3247/default.aspx

17. Alper, N. (2007, Fall). Recipe for success: The Food Network phenomenon. *Celebrated Living.* Retrieved from http://www.celebratedliving.com/tabid/3097/tabidext/3247/default.aspx

18. Pollan, M. (2009, July 29). Out of the kitchen, onto the couch. *The New York Times*. Retrieved from http://www.nytimes.com/2009/08/02/magazine/02cooking-t.html

19. Heilemann, J. (2008, Sept. 21). Living large. *New York Magazine.* Retrieved from http://nymag.com/arts/tv/profiles/50476/

20. Retrieved from www.tgifridays.com

21. DiMola, F. (2009, June 8). Food Network: Cook or be cooked. *Nintendo Power.* Retrieved from http://www.nintendoworldreport.com/impressionsArt.cfm?artid=18829

22. No byline. (2008, April 30). Scripps Networks proves the passion. Beta Research, Business Wire. Retrieved from http://newsroom.scrippsnetworks.com /images/1003/bwstory.pdf

23. Hampp, A. (2009, March 2). Food Network seeing huge growth from web offerings. *Advertising Age.* Retrieved from http://adage.com/results?endeca=1& return=endeca&search_offset=0&search_order_by=score&x=0&y=0&scarch_p hrase=food+network+seeing+huge+growth

24. (1998, April 13). Kraft Campaigns.

16

EXPERIENCE CASE STUDIES

Examples From Medill's Innovation Study Projects

David L. Nelson

At the Medill School, "consulting classes" taught with industry partners have worked with many media companies to develop strategies to increase audience awareness. The goal is to get the partner engaged in reaching new markets by using research to create focused, user-friendly, and desired new products. Graduate students and their professors target underserved or non-served audience segments and then recommend content and distribution approaches to meet their needs.

Sometimes the Medill teams' suggestions are simply alterations to the existing operation; other times they are brand extensions through new products allied to existing ones. On occasion, separation of the new product from the existing brand is recommended to connect with, engage, and provide target audiences with experiences heretofore not available—at least not through our industry partners. Medill's graduate magazine program, which has won so many awards that it has attracted an almost cult-like following among those who want to work in that field, counts *Reader's Digest*, *Ebony*, and Bonnier Corporation among its past and present clients. Capstone courses in broadcast documentary journalism have placed Medill on major networks and at PBS stations in major cities. And digital media innovation projects directly link Northwestern technology and journalism students in creating concepts that industry adopts to adapt to virtual and mobile opportunities. In 2004, students created *GoSkokie*, a Web site that served this Chicago suburb with content contributed from residents, government agencies, and local institutions. It won notable recognition in the Knight-Batten Awards for Innovative Journalism. Then there was *News Mixer*, a finalist for the Gannett Foundation Award for Technological Innovation in the Service of Digital Journalism, in which students in 2008 built experiences around Facebook Connect for a variety of innovative community structures.

This tradition of Medill working with the real world actually dates back well into the 20th century, when Professor George H. "Ted" Gallup joined the faculty and taught a course titled "Readers' Interest," in which journalism students explored how their creative work would engage or interest the consumer. The course description was good in 1931 and would work well today.[1] It explored experiences that readers engaged in and then analyzed what content could best provide information or solutions to help improve the quality of their daily lives. Decades after Ted Gallup taught here, it's worth reviewing some of the more recent Medill innovation projects—ones I had a direct hand in running—as case studies of implementing experiences. So, with the accuracy of a Monday morning quarterback, we'll look back and see why some of them worked well—or, if you will, made first downs or an occasional touchdown—while others appeared to be not much more than a hand-off. And then, as always happens with innovation, there were some false starts and maybe even a fumble from which we can learn.

NOT HEARING SIGNALS

The core finding seems really quite simple: Many journalists—at any age and in any position—have perception problems understanding the specific lives of the people for whom they wish to write, communicate with, or just plain serve. For example, while conducting a focus group of young residents near Milwaukee, Wisconsin, in 2003, the Medill team seemed stunned to learn that many of the younger female respondents—younger than the graduate students—had children or had been married more than once. The students, in their mid-20s, could not get a grip on the reality facing them when interacting with that focus group. It was quite a task for them to first understand what these younger parents needed and then to create a product with that information.

Actually, the recommendation resulted in two products—one directed to the active youth audience seeking entertainment and (not surprisingly) each other and the second directed to young parents seeking a way to simplify their complicated lives. The Medill team's prototypes, *Milwaukee24* and Milwaukee24.com, were launched under the MKE brand, essentially providing distinct experiential opportunities for each of these two audiences in the 18- to 34-year-old market segment. They were differentiated by the experiences they sought, whether fun or family ties through active involvement in their communities, both social and geographic. By way of example, one third of the target audience said they would attend a sporting event monthly. Four of five said they were actively looking for better jobs on the Web—but not necessarily on the partner's site. And almost 100 percent of the respondents expressed an interest in using online features for movies and show times[2]—this before the advent of Netflix downloads!

Not all of those forward-looking ideas were adopted. In fact, interestingly, in several of the more recent Medill community innovation projects, we encountered a reluctance on the part of some who managed the media—in some cases, even those who invited us in—to take the steps necessary to change the product, alter the organization, or act on simple recommendations that, based on realistic budgets, would have increased revenue as well as market reach. The old cliché—change is difficult to embrace—well, we saw that up close on more than one occasion.

SCORE!

But let's begin with a touchdown. Schurz Communications is based in Mishawaka, Indiana, where Joe Montana lived when he led the Fighting Irish of Notre Dame. Schurz' senior vice president, Charles V. Pittman, was a legendary Penn State football great, and the organization knows something about growing, changing, and winning. It is a diversified, privately owned, nationwide communications company that got its start in South Bend, Indiana, in newspapers five generations ago and since has expanded from Alaska and California to Maryland with an array of broadcasting, cable, and print products. One of its jewels is based in Bloomington, Indiana—home of Indiana University—a town not necessarily known for winning football teams, but other than that, a beautiful Midwestern community with many attractions.

Pittman and others, including Mayer Maloney (the Schurz chief executive in Bloomington), wanted to know whether media in a south-central Indiana region experiencing some intriguing demographic changes were providing residents with all the information they needed to engage in healthy lifestyles. In short, Medill was commissioned by Schurz Communications to develop a strategy that would do four things for the *Hoosier Times* newspapers:

- Increase readership;
- Address the health and fitness needs of residents, some of whom research indicated did not read the available Schurz products;
- Strengthen community bonds;
- Tap into revenue sources not captured by the Schurz products.

Students conducted original research on the three communities that Schurz reached: Bloomington, Martinsville, and Bedford. There was a significant variance in demographics, but psychographic similarities did emerge. These were close-knit, active, and friendly people. They shared a concern about health and fitness. And they were not satisfied with existing local information about these topics. Maloney, our active partner, had thought that there might be an underserved audience segment based on the feeling that baby boomers were moving to the area because of its medical, cultural, and retirement or pre-retirement quality-of-life offerings. Our research proved him correct. Working with databases from the university and government, a recent market research study from the newspaper, and its own qualitative research drawn from interviewing 300 area residents, the Medill team came up with two key conclusions:

- The target audience valued its community and an active lifestyle;
- Although an older group, it indicated a willingness and the necessary skill to log online to gather and share information—via a user-friendly format.

Thus was launched myINstride.com[3] and, a few months later, its companion print magazine, *INstride*. The content provided success stories. It inspired readers to lose weight, quit smoking, run, get together, and have fun (Inspiration, Chapter 6). It showed them not only where to run but also whom to run with and how to have fun while doing it (Utilitarian, Chapter 5). Other experiences also were mobilized; *myINstride.com* included photo-sharing spots for audience activities (Community-Connection and Co-Producing, Chapters 9 and 8, respectively).

We learned that the baby boomers of south central Indiana were concerned about health and fitness and often could not find relevant, local health information. They also wanted to get the news and get to know one another and live a long, rewarding life. To a certain extent, a micro-community was created for those who previously had no place to get together. They could not locate these experiences other than by word of mouth or happenstance until *INstride* came alive. It was a new experience for them.

And advertisers noticed this. Fifteen businesses that had never placed an ad with the existing Schurz products in the area decided that this was the right way to reach these potential customers. And the right time. We conducted field research in the summer of 2008, and they were buying ads when it launched in the spring of 2009.

"The students recommended marketing *INstride* as a healthy lifestyle publication that can stand alone and be visible in the community," said publisher Maloney, adding that the publication made money from Day One. By experiencing what the audience experienced, Medill students made some specific marketing suggestions. Maloney reflected on them: "*INstride* sponsored the local YMCA's Spring Run...and we thought this was a perfect match for what we wanted to do with the magazine. At the event we handed out the water bottles created by the Medill students with the *INstride* stickers on them."[4]

FIRST DOWN AND STILL ON THE FIELD

Not far from South Bend, about an hour's drive north of the football stadium, Medill had connected with *The Holland Sentinel*. This Michigan newspaper had new life breathed into it when Morris Communications purchased it in the 1990s. But it also had limited opportunities for growth— what with Lake Michigan to the west and Booth Newspapers, owned by Newhouse, bordering the northeast and southeast. Some of the audience opportunities that did exist lay between Holland and Grand Rapids, in traditional Dutch farming communities that had given way to sophisticated agri-business, manufacturing, and collar-community-like status. One of these communities was Zeeland, Michigan, about 10 minutes away from Holland and 20 to 30 from Grand Rapids. This is a rich town with traditional family values and an audience that advertisers would want to reach. Oh, and the younger generation was not reading newspapers that much. The question: Where would they go to get what they needed for hyper-local information, community get-togethers, religious news, local sports news, and so on?

Publisher Pete Esser, also a big Notre Dame football fan, did not want to lose ground to the *Grand Rapids Press*. In 2007, he engaged Medill— aided by an aggressive and excellent marketing staff at Morris headquarters in Georgia—to dig deep into what made the emerging Zeeland audience tick. What experiences mattered to them? What could Esser provide either through existing *Sentinel* products or new channels to engage this market? And, of course, how could we strengthen community bonds and tap into new revenue sources not captured by existing publications?

Again, we learned a lot. The Medill team looked at available market research and took several trips to interview community leaders, parents, students, and senior citizens. The result was an original survey to determine residents' interests, shopping habits, Web use, and perceptions about the community. In all, some 200 surveys were completed and analyzed in an area of approximately 20,000 residents. Recapping key research findings:

- Residents described Zeeland as friendly, conservative, religious, small, quiet, safe, but growing. They were positive about their community.

- Although they had strong local interest in schools, sports, religion, local government, and people, they did most of their shopping in Grand Rapids or Holland, not in Zeeland.
- Their local interests included active community participation in school concerts, sports events, church dinners, and youth-related recreational programs.
- They used the Internet and local newspapers but expressed dissatisfaction with Zeeland coverage—this negative response also came from local businesses and advertisers.
- More than half of the residents who responded were less than 35 years of age.
- Average annual household income was $66,000.

"The lessons learned and the interaction between staff and students was uplifting, motivating, and in the end resulted in us better serving readers in this neighboring community. As for the Northwestern students, they were professional, inquisitive and very engaged—a joy to be around," said publisher Esser.[5]

The Medill report connected marketing concepts of engagement with experiences that the Zeeland resident would realize through the new media products it recommended:

> The interests, concerns, and personalities of Zeeland played a big role in shaping the tone, structure, and content of our proposed products. Zeeland is changing, but it is still a conservative community with traditional values, so our design strategy was to be innovative but not intimidating. Zeeland is also an extremely friendly area with a small-town feel, so we aimed to create products that would complement and enhance their sense of community. Engaging residents with one another became the backbone of our product ideas.[6]

This appealed to both Zeeland residents and the advertisers seeking to reach them.

In short, over several seasons now, myZeeland.com and its companion print product have delivered the experiences to its target audience—certainly a first-down play—and even with a handoff it's still moving down the field. The handoff? Morris sold the operation to publicly traded GateHouse Media, and it decided to keep the Zeeland product in the game.

YOU CAN'T WIN 'EM ALL

A more recent endeavor with another Midwestern communications company did not result in a first down or even a kick-off. Perhaps the game may be played later, but at this time there seems to be no action on the field. Medill graduate students undertook a major research effort in a complicated and blurred media landscape of approximately 500,000 persons. About 20 percent of them—again, Medill focused here on those between the ages of 21 and 34—indicated a need for information they could not find. For the most part, they were "Googling" and not using site-specific media. As elsewhere, newspaper circulation was in a downward spiral, and the organization's Web sites were being obscured, if not clobbered, by competition.

Using original market research along with census data and designated market area advertising information provided by Borrell Associates, the Medill team created personas, built a Web-based portal prototype, and conducted focus groups to measure the potential effect the intended audience would experience with the new product. Some of their comments follow. But first, some of the market research highlights:

- Respondents expressed strong feelings about family values and said their community was friendly;
- Respondents also said their community was boring and that they could not find activities for families or individuals—and that there was a general lack of awareness about how to find this information.

Medill graduate students conducted content analyses of all local media and concluded that, indeed, there were many activities to choose from but no central place to learn about what to do, where to go, how to get there, what it would cost—or whether it even was worth the effort. The Medill team actually went to events and asked participants to evaluate or review their experience, and the residents' opinions (rather than those of the Medill students) became a central content component of the Web project we designed for the client.

Focus group participants provided these reactions after viewing the prototype:

- "Sometimes I wish there was more culture, but then I realize there is," said one 24-year-old female, expressing frustration at not finding what she wanted when she wanted it.
- "We have sources like whatzup...and local newspapers/sites, but nothing that really compiles everything together," according to a person in the target demo.

- "It would be nice to categorize events by age," said one 33-year-old male. "As a parent, I'd like to see what I can do with my children, versus what I might want to do with my wife."
- Finally, reacting to what the prototype provided and what she could not find elsewhere, a 24-year-old female had this to say: "I wish there was an events calendar for everything going on in the city with festivals and movies in the parks. You have to try to find everything on individual Web sites. We're always looking for things to do that are different and it would be fun to have them all listed in one place."[7]

So the appropriate Web site—and the one the Medill team recommended—would contain not only comprehensive information about where to go but comments from those who went there. The possibility of upsetting an advertiser or two loomed, but the transparency that could come from open and honest reviews seemed to provide the target audience with what it wanted. Or, more to the point, what it would have wanted had this project gone forward. It did not—due to an indifferent board of directors that took a pass on the project. We might call this a false start—not yet a fumble.

POST-GAME REPORT

Medill students involved in these innovation projects can be puzzled when nothing happened with their proposals. (Of course, when something good happens, they put it on their resumes.) But sometimes it's easy to explain why nothing happens:

- A company gets sold and the new owner has different ideas;
- The publisher moves on and the replacement has different ideas; the local economy drops more than the national average, and the publisher battens down the hatches, saying this is no time to experiment;
- Advertisers simply don't buy into the concept—even if audience is there.

Other times, it's pretty much summed up in two words: bad management. Most media enterprises at any level have had plenty of this. In media, opportunities for radical change have been available for decades. In 1976, internationally known Northwestern marketing professor Philip Kotler recommended several steps newspapers could and should take in an article I wrote for the *ASNE Bulletin*[8]—all keyed to helping managers better understand how their newspaper was perceived by different groups within the community. Most took no note. Profits were good. Competition was slight. Unless there was a crisis, why change?

Some 33 years later, Sammy Papert III, the final owner of the Belden Associates newspaper research firm, lamented the timidity or inability of the newspaper industry to be "BOLD" and lambasted publishers for not even following their own advice in terms of making their business the "local information connection utility." A year after shutting down Belden, he asked how many newspapers had "faithfully followed" the prescription for the local utility concept. His answer: "That's right, exactly ZERO!"[9] This chapter's conclusion is that most managers could not adapt to necessary changes because they did not or could not experience the same things that their customers experienced. Myopic management ignored marketing research until that data was dusty or of no use. The market—indeed, the world—had moved on.

When John Lavine launched his "2020 vision" of curricular change at Medill shortly after taking over as dean in 2006, he acknowledged that sweeping changes to any institution would break some things—or, as he would say, "a few bottles on the assembly line."[10] I knew what he meant, literally, having grown up in a Swedish family that owned a Chicago-based factory. It needed major renewal and repositioning to survive. The old Swedes wouldn't change; they would not shift from metal to plastic. The consumer, however, wanted lighter and less expensive lawn mowers. A "few bottles" were broken on the assembly line—as were a few egos. And a few were let go; perhaps now with enough time on their hands to mow their own lawns and experience what the customer wanted.

Again, an understanding of audience and how it experiences and acts on information is nothing new at Medill. In his 1931 course description, young Ted Gallup wrote: "Students are given the opportunity to assist newspaper and magazine editors in the solution of actual problems."[11]

And so it is today and we hope tomorrow. Know the reader, viewer, or visitor. Engage the audience. Experience what they experience and then give them more. That's the Medill way.

NOTES

1. *Northwestern University Registry of Courses*. (1931). Evanston, IL: Northwestern University Archives.
2. Innovation project. (2003, June). *2010: Reaching the next generation*. Evanston, IL: Medill School, Northwestern University.
3. Retrieved from http://www.myINstride.com
4. Maloney, M. (2010, January 4). Email exchange.
5. Esser, P. (2010, January 10). Email exchange.

6. Innovation project. (2007, June). *Connecting Zeeland: Strengthening community through hyperlocal news.* Evanston, IL: Medill School, Northwestern University.
7. Innovation project. (Date and identification withheld).
8. The marketing of an editor. (1976, April). *The Bulletin of the American Society of Newspaper Editors.*
9. Papert III, S. (2009, December). *On the Horizon* [newsletter].
10. Lavine, Dean J. (2007, December). Private conversation at annual herring breakfast.
11. *Northwestern University Registry of Courses.* (1931). Evanston, IL: Northwestern University Archives.

APPENDIX

This appendix provides a more comprehensive, annotated list of the experiences identified by the Medill studies. As discussed in the Introduction (Chapter 1), we excluded original experiences from this book if they (1) described the product more than the relationship between the product and consumer, (2) focused on disengagement or advertising content, or (3) could be derived from experiences covered here.

At the same time, we feel that the detail in this expanded list of experiences could still be useful to a journalist. For example, the It Helps Me Keep Track of Celebrities experience is focused on a specific type of content and can be viewed as a specific form of the overarching Makes Me Smarter experience, perhaps with elements of the Visual experience mixed in. Although we have elected not to devote entire chapters to such specific topics, the specific items (sub-experiences) under the Celebrity experience could be useful to a journalist working in this area.

From a research perspective, the multi-item scales in this appendix have been shown to have good psychometric properties. We have been able to show that the statements below "hold together" as a scale in multiple studies using different data-collection methods and across many publications within a medium. The experiences marked as "exploratory" below have at least grouped together in an exploratory factor analysis. The others have passed stricter psychometric tests by having good reliability (e.g., coefficient alpha greater than 0.7) and producing acceptable fits in confirmatory factor models with at least several other experiences. See the research articles cited in Chapter 1 for details.

An organization may wish to add or substitute statements that are more specific to its media product. Care should be taken to find items (sub-experiences) that relate to the motivational experience called for by the concept. Ideally, the reliability and validity of these items should be confirmed for the brand being measured.[1] Either a marketing research department or vendor could perform such tests.

ENGAGEMENT EXPERIENCES

Ad Receptivity

- I look at most of the ads.
- I like the ads just as much as the articles.
- I click on ads from this site more often than most other sites I visit.
- This site has ads about things I actually care about.
- It makes me want to go shopping.
- I use ads to know what is on sale.
- I value the coupons in the newspaper.

Anchor Camaraderie (Chapter 10)

- I enjoy watching the people doing the news talk with each other.
- I feel like I get to know the anchors on the news programs I watch.
- The anchors and reporters on the programs I watch are qualified professionals.
- I look forward to reading certain writers in this magazine/newspaper.
- I feel like I get to know the anchors/people writing the articles.

Background (exploratory)

- I like to have TV news on in the background while I'm doing other things.
- I can read this newspaper/magazine and watch TV at the same time.
- I visit this site when I'm on the phone or waiting on something.

The experience of having media "on" in the background is especially common with TV and radio. This is the ultimate form of "passive" media consumption.

Civic (Chapter 4)

- Reading this newspaper/watching the news makes me feel like a better citizen.
- I count on this newspaper/station to investigate wrongdoing.
- Reading/watching makes me more a part of my community.
- Our society would be much weaker without newspapers/TV news.
- I think people who do not read this newspaper or one like it are really at a disadvantage in life.

Community-Connection (Chapter 9)

- A big reason I like this site is what I get from other users.
- I'm as interested in input from other users as I am in the regular content on this site.
- Overall, the visitors to this site are pretty knowledgeable about the topics it covers.
- This site does a good job of getting its visitors to contribute or provide feedback.
- I'd like to meet other people who regularly visit this site.

Co-Producing (Chapter 8)

- I contribute to the conversation.
- This site does a good job of getting its visitors to contribute or to provide feedback.
- I do quite a bit of socializing on this site.
- I often feel guilty about the amount of time I spend on this site socializing on this site.
- I should probably cut back on the amount of time I spend socializing on this site.

Easy for Me (exploratory)

- I can get what I want on this site without having to go through a lot of uninteresting stuff.
- This site is very clean and straightforward.
- If I don't have a lot of time, this magazine/newspaper is perfect.

This is closely related to the Makes Me Smarter experience.

Entertainment and Diversion (Chapter 12)

- It often makes me laugh.
- This Web site always has something that surprises me.

- It is definitely entertaining.
- Once I start surfing around this site, it's hard to leave.
- I like stories about the weird things that can happen.

Feel Good (Introduction/Chapter 1)

- Reading this magazine makes me feel good about myself.
- Overall, it leaves me with a good feeling.
- I am a better person for using this site.
- When reading/watching this magazine/program, I am worry-free.

Guides Me to Other Media (exploratory)

- This site often leads me to other good sites.
- I enjoy other media more because of this site.

Newspaper readers have a version of this experience when they look at TV and movie listings. This could be viewed as a special type of Utilitarian experience.

Habitual (A Regular Part of My Day)

- It's part of my routine.
- I use it as a part of getting my news for the day.
- I usually read this newspaper at the same time each day.
- This is one of the sites I always go to anytime I am surfing the Web.
- It helps me to get my day started in the morning.

A more specific habit is reading with breakfast, lunch, or snacks. Habitual experiences usually have high correlations with usage, and this experience is conceptually similar to behavior itself. We think of habits as a consequence of the experiences discussed in this book, although associating the consumption of a media product with regular events such as breaks and meals is a good strategy.

High-Quality Content

- It is very professional.
- The articles really are in-depth.
- You learn things first by reading this newspaper/magazine.
- They do a good job covering things; they don't miss anything.
- The newspaper offers a variety of different perspectives.
- This newspaper does a good job with follow-up stories.

This experience is closely related to Makes Me Smarter, Trust and Credibility, and Poor-Quality Content, with large cross-loadings in a factor analysis and items that switch between factors depending on the data set.

Identity (Chapter 7)

- I like to have it around so that others might read it.
- I show some things in this magazine to others so that they will understand.
- Reading/watching is a little like belonging to a group.
- I like for other people to know that I read/watch it.

Inspiration (Chapter 6)

- It makes me feel like I can do important things in my life.
- Reading it makes me want to match what others have done.
- It inspires me in my own life.
- Reading this magazine makes me feel good about myself.

It Helps Me Keep Track of Celebrities (exploratory)

- I'm very interested in the stories about celebrities.
- I like to check out who is on the cover.
- You see how normal some well-known people can be.

This can be viewed as a special form of the Makes Me Smarter experience.

It Helps Me Look Good; It's Sensual, Even Sexy (exploratory)

- I learn how to improve my appearance.
- There are things in it I find very sexy.
- There is a sensual aspect to the magazine.
- You could get an erotic dream or daydream from reading.

This experience is closely related to the Utilitarian, Visual, and Identity experiences.

It Reinforces My Faith (exploratory)

- It reinforces my religious faith.
- I think of the magazine as faith-based.

This is probably a special form of Identity and perhaps Makes Me Smarter.

It Shows Diversity (exploratory)

- This newspaper/magazine includes people of color.

This is probably a special form of the Identity and Visual experiences.

Killing Time (exploratory)

- It's mainly good for when I don't have anything else to do.
- I use/watch/read it mainly when I'm bored.

This experience is a more negative version of Timeout.

Makes Me Smarter (Chapter 3)

- It addresses issues or topics of special concern to me.
- It updates me on things I try to keep up with.
- It's important I remember later what I have read/looked at.
- Even if I disagree with information in this magazine/newspaper/television programming/site, I feel I have learned something valuable.
- I look at it as educational. I am gaining knowledge.

People I Know (exploratory)

- I always read the obituaries and weddings.
- This newspaper has stories about people I know.
- I always read about crime in my community.

This is a special form of the Makes Me Smarter, Civic, and perhaps Social.

Portability (exploratory)

- I routinely carry the magazine/newspaper with me.

Positive Emotional (Introduction/Chapter 1)

- The magazine/show definitely affects me emotionally.
- Some articles/episodes touch me deep down.
- It helps me to see that there are good people in the world.
- It features people who make you proud.

Save and Reference (exploratory)

- I save back issues for a period of time.
- I sometimes go back to old issues to find things.
- I tear out articles to keep/I often save articles on this site to keep and go back to.

Talk About and Share (Chapter 14)

- Reading this Web site gives me something to talk about.
- I bring up things I have read in this newspaper in conversations with many other people.

- I use things I have heard on this TV program in discussions or arguments with people I know.
- A big reason I read it is to make myself more interesting to others.
- I show things in the magazine to people in my family.
- Watching the news makes me a more interesting person.

Another aspect of this is emailing articles to other people.

Timeout (Chapter 11 and the Introduction/Chapter 1)

- I lose myself in the pleasure of reading/looking at this magazine/newspaper/television programming/site.
- It is a quiet time.
- I like to kick back and wind down with it.
- It's an escape.
- The magazine/newspaper/television programming/site takes my mind off other things that are going on.
- I feel less stress after reading it.
- It is my reward for doing other things.
- I like to go to this site when eating or taking a break.

Trust and Credibility

- I trust it to tell the truth.
- It does not sensationalize things.
- It is unbiased in its reporting.
- I don't have to worry about accuracy with this newspaper.
- I would trust this site with any information I give it.

See note after High-Quality Content.

Utilitarian (Chapter 5)

- I learn about things to do or places to go in this newspaper.
- This Web site gives good tips and advice.
- It shows me how to do things the right way.
- I get good ideas from this magazine.
- I learn how to improve myself from this TV program.
- It helps me make up my mind and make decisions.
- This magazine provides a lot of how-to information.

Visual (Chapter 13)

- I look at the pictures in it and think "Wow."
- Most often I look at the pictures/videos before anything else.
- I like to look at the pictures/videos even if I don't read the story.

- I sometimes show a picture in it to someone else.
- I like to look at the pictures for a while.
- I love the photography on this show.
- The photography is one of the main reasons that I watch this show.

DISENGAGEMENT EXPERIENCES

Ad Interference

- I am annoyed because too many of the ads on this site have too much movement.
- Sometimes the ads are overdone or even weird.
- I don't like that the ads are trying to sell me things.
- I don't like the number of pop-up ads on this site.
- I make a special effort to skip over or avoid looking at the ads.
- The number of ads makes it harder to read the stories.
- I hate the inserts they put in it.
- All too often the ads are dull or boring.

Cynicism (exploratory)

- Too much of what they do is done mainly to try to get more people to watch.
- Occasionally this newspaper tries to shock you.

Lack of Local Focus

- This newspaper/news program does not have a local flavor. It could be from anywhere.
- It does not have a lot of really local news.
- You could move this newspaper to another city and it wouldn't make a difference.

Negativity (exploratory)

- There is so much sad and scary news that it is hard to watch.
- Too much time is spent on negative things.
- Gossip is a big part of this newspaper/magazine.
- Not enough effort is made to cover the good things that happen.
- They are always trying to catch people or tear them down.
- Some of the stories make me feel bad.

Overload (Introduction/Chapter 1)

- Reading this newspaper makes me feel like I'm drowning in the flood of news that comes out each day.

- It tries to cover too much.
- Too many of the articles are too long.
- It has too many special sections.
- I wish this newspaper had fewer pages.

Political Bias (exploratory)

- I wish this site had more conservative views.
- They always take the same slant on issues.
- This program/newspaper gives only one side of the story.
- I'm resigned to the fact that newspapers aren't going to present a balanced view.

This experience can be engaging or disengaging depending on the respondent.

Poor or Annoying Design (exploratory)

- The page numbers are hard to use.
- It is hard to follow the articles because they are continued on too many pages.
- I find it difficult to fold and unfold.
- This newspaper takes up too much space when I am reading it.

Poor-Quality Content (exploratory)

- I worry about the accuracy of the stories.
- The writing style is boring.
- I feel my time has been wasted after reading/watching it.
- Sometimes the writing looks like no one has edited it.
- Much of it is uninteresting.

See comment after High-Quality Content.

Poor Service (exploratory)

- Sometimes it comes too late to be relevant.
- Often the paper arrives in poor condition.

Racial Bias (exploratory)

- This newspaper perpetuates racial or ethnic stereotypes.
- This newspaper is basically about white America.
- I worry that other people reading this paper will get the wrong impression of minority groups.
- This paper is sometimes unfair in its stories about minorities.

Sameness (exploratory)

- Sometimes I feel it is the same from issue to issue.
- The different news programs I watch are all very similar in the way they do the news.
- The different news programs all have the same stories.

Shallowness (exploratory)

- The local news that I watch covers accidents and crimes way too much.
- It can be pretty shallow.
- Some people would think this magazine/newspaper is dumb.

Skim and Scan

- For most stories, I just read the headlines or the first paragraph or so.
- I try to skim the articles as quickly as I can.
- Many of the articles I start but don't finish.
- I only read it for a few of the sections.
- I only read the articles that I especially want to read.
- When watching TV news, I try to see what stories are coming up so I can catch the ones I want to see and avoid the ones I don't.

NOTE

1. See, for example, Hatcher, L. (1994). *A step-by-step approach to using the SAS System for factor analysis and structural equation modeling.* Cary, NC: SAS Institute.

ABOUT THE CONTRIBUTORS

Abe Peck, co-editor of *Medill on Media Engagement,* is a professor emeritus in service at Medill, where he has served as chair of journalism and cross-media storytelling, head of the magazine program, associate dean, holder of two named chairs, director of the National Arts Journalism Program, and most recently director of business to business communication. He wrote *Uncovering the Sixties: The Life and Times of the Underground Press,* edited *Dancing Madness* while an editor at *Rolling Stone,* and has contributed to other books. He also reported/edited at the *Chicago Daily News,* the *Chicago Sun-Times,* and *Outside.* He consults worldwide on magazines across platforms, including for the Media Management Center, where he is a senior director and worked on the magazine experience study. His Web site is http://www.peckconsultants.com/main/

Edward C. Malthouse, PhD, co-editor of *Medill on Media Engagement,* is the Theodore R. and Annie Laurie Sills Professor of Integrated Marketing Communications at Medill/Northwestern University and the co-editor of the *Journal of Interactive Marketing.* A primary researcher for the experience studies conducted by the Media Management Center, he has written numerous scholarly articles on topics in media marketing, customer relationship management, and computational statistics that have appeared in marketing and engineering journals. He has won many teaching awards at Medill and is a regular visiting professor at universities in Europe, China, and Japan.

Beth Bennett is a senior lecturer at Medill focusing on video storytelling. She is producer of the documentary "Under the Ice," which is about sturgeon spearing in Wisconsin. The short documentary was released in 2009 and is on the film festival circuit. She is an award-winning television news reporter and producer who spent the first decade of her career in local television news. She worked as a reporter in Green Bay, Milwaukee, and Chicago before moving on to teaching and longer-form work.

Bobby J. Calder was one of the lead researchers in the experience studies conducted for the Media Management Center. He is Charles H. Kellstadt Distinguished Professor (and department chair) of Marketing and Professor of Psychology at the Kellogg School of Management and Professor of Journalism at Medill. He works primarily in the areas of marketing, strategy, media, marketing research, and the psychology of consumer behavior. He has consulted to companies from Aetna to Coca-Cola, and to Hearst, The Tribune Company, and Time Warner. His most recent books are *Kellogg on Advertising and Media* and *Kellogg on Integrated Marketing*. His research has appeared in publications such as the *Journal of Marketing Research* and the *Journal of Consumer Research*. He previously taught at Wharton/Pennsylvania and the University of Illinois and consulted to Booz Allen Hamilton.

Steven S. Duke is an associate professor at Medill and managing director of training for the Media Management Center and the Readership Institute, where he consults and leads executive education seminars for media professionals worldwide. Prior to joining Northwestern, he was a journalist for 26 years at newspapers and magazines, including the *Chicago Sun-Times*, *Chicago Daily News*, *Sacramento Bee*, *Cincinnati Enquirer*, and *Digital Chicago*.

Jeremy Gilbert is an assistant professor at Medill, teaching interactive storytelling and human-centered design. He has directed award-winning, student-based digital projects, helped revamp Medill's interactive curriculum, and is researching the future of mobile journalism. Before coming to Medill, he led The Poynter Institute's Web site redesign and worked as a design director, redesigning a pair of award-winning Florida newspapers.

Rich Gordon is associate professor and director of digital innovation at Medill, where he launched and directed the school's master's program in new media journalism. Before joining Medill, he was the first new media director for the Miami Herald Publishing Co., responsible for editorial and business operations. He served as a reporter and editor for the *Herald*, *The Palm Beach Post*, and the *Richmond Times-Dispatch*.

Ashlee Humphreys, PhD, is an assistant professor of Integrated Marketing Communications at Medill. Her research uses a sociological perspective to examine core topics in marketing management and consumer behavior. Her current research interests include the role of institutions in markets, processes of co-production, and the development of online communities through social media platforms. She received her PhD in Marketing from the Kellogg School of Management at Northwestern University.

Josh Karp is an adjunct lecturer at Medill and the author of two books, *A Futile and Stupid Gesture: How Doug Kenney and National Lampoon Changed Comedy Forever* and *Straight Down the Middle: Shivas Irons, Bagger Vance and How I Learned To Stop Worrying and Love My Golf Swing*. His Web site is www.joshkarpbooks.com.

Matt Mansfield is an associate professor at and co-director of Medill's Washington Program and Medill News Service. He is the former deputy managing editor of the *San Jose Mercury News*, where he earned a reputation as one of the leading visual journalists in the United States and edited the news organization's influential Silicon Valley business and technology coverage. He is a former president of the international Society for News Design and is a member of the programming committee for the Online News Association's annual conference.

Rachel Davis Mersey, PhD, is an assistant professor at Medill. Her research publications include articles on journalism and communities in *Newspaper Research Journal* and *Journalism Practice*. She has professional journalism experience as a features reporter at *The Arizona Republic*. She holds a PhD in mass communication from the University of North Carolina at Chapel Hill.

David L. Nelson is director of Medill's Community Media Innovation Projects. He has been director of the School's undergraduate and graduate programs, chair of the newspaper department, and associate dean. He is author of the book *The Root of Suburban Is Urban* and previously was editor of *The Evanston Review* and suburban editor of *The Miami Herald*. Nelson serves on the boards of several media companies and has received five teaching awards from Northwestern University, where he has served as chairman of the General Faculty Committee and secretary of the University Senate.

Ellen Shearer is the William F. Thomas Professor at Medill and co-director of Medill's Washington Program and Medill News Service. She also is co-director of the school's new National Security Journalism initiative. She has served as assistant dean and head of the Newspaper Department at Medill. She is co-author of the book *Nonvoters: America's No-Shows*, has written chapters in five other books, and is a regular contributor to *The American Editor* magazine. She is vice president of the Washington Press Club Foundation.

Ben Sylvan is digital editor-in-chief for ESPN RISE, a sports and lifestyle brand targeted to high school athletes. He oversees the editorial strategy of the Web site and mobile platform. He also has experience in newspapers, magazines, and wire services. Sylvan, the recipient of the Stan Tannenbaum Memorial Award for scholastic achievement and promise in marketing communications, earned his master's degree in Integrated Marketing Communications from Medill in 2009.

Charles Whitaker is an assistant professor and co-director of the Magazine Innovation Project at Medill, where he holds the Helen Gurley Brown Magazine Research Chair. His teaching and research areas of expertise include magazine writing, editing, and publishing. Prior to joining Medill, he was a senior editor at *Ebony* magazine, a staff writer and features editor at the *Louisville Times*, and an education and municipal reporter at *The Miami Herald*.

Patti Wolter is an assistant professor and co-director of the Magazine Innovation Project at Medill. Her teaching and research areas of expertise include magazine writing, editing, and publishing; health and science journalism; and fact-checking. Prior to joining Medill, she was managing editor and acting editor in chief at *Mother Jones* and senior features editor in charge of investigative women's health issues at *Self*. She continues to work in the profession as both an editorial consultant and a freelance writer on health, lifestyle, and nutrition issues.

Owen Youngman is the Knight Professor of Digital Media Strategy at Medill. His 37-year career at the *Chicago Tribune* focused on product development in print (*RedEye*) and online (chicagotribune.com, metromix.com), change leadership, and strategy. His blog about offline and online journalism, "The Next Miracle," can be found at owenyoungman.com, the Web site he launched in 1994.

AUTHOR INDEX

SUBJECT INDEX

Note: All experiences are listed under "Experience(s)," in alphabetical order.
Mentions of Medill authors are not indexed.

CPSIA information can be obtained at www.ICGtesting.com
Printed in the USA
LVOW13s1312160114

369685LV00002B/17/P